248.4

JACK CAVANAUGH

Gift from Dave Horton,
Bethany House

Christmas 2000

- the arts define us, pp. 114-116.
  - good quote re: the flaw of the modern church. p. 116

- "the more aware you are of God, the more involved
  you will be in working for him." —Richard Baxter, p. 137.

Into *the* Depths *of* God

Where Eyes See the Invisible,
Ears Hear the Inaudible, and
Minds Conceive the Inconceivable

CALVIN MILLER

BETHANY HOUSE PUBLISHERS
Minneapolis, Minnesota 55438

Published by Bethany House Publishers
A Ministry of Bethany Fellowship International
11400 Hampshire Avenue South
Bloomington, Minnesota 55438
www.bethanyhouse.com

Printed in the United States of America by
Bethany Press International, Bloomington, Minnesota

Library of Congress Cataloging-in-Publication Data

Miller, Calvin.
    Into the depths of God / by Calvin Miller.
       p. cm.
    Includes bibliographical references.
    ISBN 0–7642–2172–8
    1. Spiritual life—Christianity. I. Title.
BV4501.2 .M47255   2000   CIP
248.4—dc21   00–008429

To Barbara, companion, lover, friend,
who for more than forty years
has committed herself to my well-being
and who has inspired me to be the best
believer I can be.

CALVIN MILLER is a poet, a pastor, a theologian, a painter, and one of Christianity's best loved writers with over thirty published books. His writing spans a wide spectrum of genres, from the bestselling SINGER TRILOGY to *The Unchained Soul* to the heartrending novella *Snow*.

Miller presently serves as professor of Preaching and Pastoral Ministries at Beeson Divinity School in Alabama, where he and his wife, Barbara, make their home.

Acknowledgments

It seems to me that I know so little about how to pursue the riches that lie at the depths of godliness. Yet many have instructed me in the pursuit that I describe. Sometimes they were writers and thinkers. Sometimes they were lay mentors who were on the same pilgrimage as I. Many of them have been students of mine. They came to graduate school to prepare themselves for a life in ministry and to be taught by professors like me. Then suddenly they were the teachers, who in quiet moments of prayer were instructing me in the ardor of the worshiping life. There were various peers—professors, fellow pastors, and lay ministers—who joined me in my hunger to serve the pleasure of Christ, and traveled through the same spiritual disciplines on our way to him.

Chief among those to whom I owe so much is Deron Spoo. I have often wondered why God gives a special hunger for himself to some, while others seem not to own it. Deron is a friend full of joy and a hunger for the depths of God, and this joy is his and touches all those he knows. I look forward to the time when he will write of his own affair with Christ. In the meantime, his unyielding love for Christ well serves both of us.

I would be remiss not to pay homage to Steve Laube, my editor and friend, who has a strong love for the Lord and one that is very informed. I rely on him for insights into this subject, but I depend on him completely to enable me to know when my writing is intelligible and when it is not. I have a bad habit of assuming others understand concepts with which they are not acquainted. He always bids me return to solid footing and explain myself.

Greg Johnson, my agent, calls me at least once a week to be sure that I'm working, and when I assure him that I am, he promises not to bother me for another week or so. Greg has been a genuine friend, who is eager that people—for reasons that he understands better than I—come into contact with my thinking. Without him, I would never find the motivation I need to feel my ideas important.

David Shepherd also keeps me thinking and working. His mind rarely sleeps and is ever waking my own to the wonder of Scripture.

Finally, I have a circle of friends and fellow teachers—Bill Tolar, Wallace Williams, Fisher Humphries, Bob Smith, Jerry Batson, Denise

George—who motivate me from moment to moment in life. One's achievements and the quality of one's friends vary proportionately. We are all the product of those whose lives instruct us formally and informally. We are all debtors to those whose friendships purchase our security and reputation.

Contents

Introduction: A Hunger for Inwardness 11

The Disciplined Life

1. Breaking the Sensual Thrall 21
2. Breaking the Thrall of Materialism 35
3. Breaking the Tyranny of the Urgent 45

The Listening Life

4. Aesthetics: Enjoying the Beauty of God 61
5. Christ: The Desire of the Heart 79
6. Expression: The Place of Praise 91
7. Centering: Avoiding Sterile Fascination With God 101
8. Mysticism: Keeping in Touch With the Holy Spirit 117

The Informed Life

9. Into the Depths by Finding Our Calling 133
10. The Discipline That Ends in Godly Character 147
11. Arriving at Self-Understanding 161

The Confessional Life

12. Confession and the Glory of Our Neediness 177
13. Confession and Guilt-Free Discipleship 189
14. Confessional Principles for Personal Growth 203
15. Dwelling in Foreverness 213

Epilogue: Into the Depths 223
Study Questions 231
Notes 241

The eye cannot see, nor the tongue tell,
nor can the heart imagine how many paths
and methods I have, solely for love
to lead them back to grace so that
my truth may be realized in them.[1]

—CATHERINE OF SIENA

Man's soul is not absolutely bound
by space and matter.
It can also see events through
darkness and at very great distances,
as if they were happening nearby.
It is we who do not give power and momentum
to this capability in our souls,
and we which squelch it beneath the bonds
of either the carnal fleshiness of our bodies
or our confused thoughts and scattered ideas.
Yet when we focus our attention on the inner self,
divert our concentration from everything external,
and refine our mind, then the soul finds
its truest fulfillment and exercises its highest powers,
which is quite natural.[2]

—THE WAY OF A PILGRIM

Would that our conversation were more heavenly.
Would that we were more taken with the person,
the work and the beauty
of our incarnate Lord.
Through meditation, the beauty of the King
flashes on us with resplendence.[3]

—CHARLES HADDON SPURGEON

"Deep" is not a place we visit in our search for God, it's what happens to us when we find him.

What startling differences there are among men. We are sometimes tempted to attribute their special powers and success to their circumstances, times, parents, and teachers. But there is a deeper and more satisfactory explanation. Adopting the words of the forerunner, men have nothing that they have not received from heaven, by the direct appointment and decree of God.

This is a golden sentence, indeed!—"A man can receive nothing except it be given him from heaven." Do you have great success in your life work? Do crowds gather around your steps and throng your auditorium? Do not attribute them to yourself. They are all the gifts of God's grace. You have nothing that you have not received. Be thankful but never vain, because He who gave may take. Great talents given imply great responsibility in the day of reckoning.[4]

—**F. B. Meyer**

A Hunger for Inwardness

I met one of my best friends on the day she learned that she had less than six months to live. No life should be lived without one such friend. For only when the edges of life are clearly marked, does friendship celebrate all its gifts with understanding. Our friendship knew no single day of ease or levity. It contained no midnight card parties, ski excursions, or holiday cruises.

Her name was Anne, and while—by her own confession—her last months were far from morose, she spent her days "sorting." With Anne's short life-span, we had time to contemplate and enjoy only the absolute essentials of our relationship. The dial of the clock's finality moved with hands so swift that things cheap and temporary held no fascination.

Anne was physically beautiful. She had spent a great deal of her life maximizing that beauty with cosmetics. Her skin was ivory and warm. But things dermal and outward lose their importance when things visceral and inward go wrong. Down where creams and oils cannot penetrate, the body must sometimes reckon with strong judgments. Then the deep issues of life hold final sway over all things surface.

Most of us dress our Christian faith in an ill-fitting discipleship that, like a cheap suit, leaves us uncomfortable most of our lives. Among our friends at church we struggle to keep our reputation for godliness bannered forth. We would like to appear to be like Jesus without the discipline of really being like him. Reading several dozen fill-in-the-blanks self-help manuals, we talk ourselves into a spiritual reputation we have never really earned. We continue to live on the surface, only talking of the deeper life. I delivered the eulogy at Anne's funeral, and I was overwhelmed by a need to tell more of her walk with Christ than it was possible to tell. At the center of all she had become, her affair with Christ defied communication. So it is with all things deep.

But in Paul's first letter to the Corinthians, our bogus inwardness is laid bare for all to observe: "No eye has seen, no ear has heard, no mind has conceived what God has prepared for those who love him" (1 Corinthians 2:9b), says the apostle.

Paul is speaking of eternity and all that is futuristic. Here he gives us the final glimpse of what we shall own when we open our eyes to take our first glimpse of heaven. Yet it is not only heaven of which he speaks. There is also something here-and-now about this verse. It does no violence to read it, "No eye *can* see, no ear *can* hear, no mind *can* conceive all that God has prepared for those who love him." Inwardness is a way to have heaven— at least some of it—now! The course we follow into inwardness is a course too overwhelmingly real to be measured by our senses alone. Eyes, ears, and fingers have their limitations. They are instruments too neural—too tiny—to measure the immensity of being that God has in mind for us. It is futile to make a purely sensual run at God, for it inevitably collides with his fullness. It is like trying to measure the cubic volume of the Pacific Ocean with a thimble and a teacup.

Yet how gloriously sensate is Paul's description of our inwardness! Those who enjoy it have eyes that see the invisible, ears that hear the inaudible, and minds that conceive the inconceivable. True spirituality is not extrasensory, it is *ultrasensory*. Where the chamber of our heart ultimately empties itself of self, a new kind of being is born—one that thrills at his presence. There in our inmost being we discover that our hearts are not chambers but doorways. We have but to climb to the portal of the heart, lay our hand on the latch, and enter into our hidden rendezvous with God. When we've closed the door on our side of reality, we can open it on God's.

To play with God's depth is to be overwhelmed with his vastness. I remember once flying over the state of Montana with a Japanese businessman from urban Tokyo. "Does anybody live in all this empty space?" he asked.

"Not many," I replied. On we flew.

"Nobody?" he asked.

I nodded. We flew some more.

"So huge, so beautiful, so vast," he said.

I knew what he was trying to say. I knew those words: so huge, so beautiful, so vast. It is what I feel each time I encounter God. I lie down to sleep, but do not pray "the Lord my soul to keep." Instead, I stalk a greater immensity in a near nightly ritual of euphoria. His blessings swarm about me in a wonderful lightness of being. It is an odd insomnia sponsored by sheer joy. My mind at first begins splashing through some tiny rivulet of

God's grace. Gradually the stream grows . . . and *Gloria in excelsis!* I am in an ocean too wide to measure, too deep to fathom. I am deliriously adrift on the sea of his endless being. Yet I always step out into this ocean from the tiny beachhead of my heart. I am amazed that in the center of my shallow tidal soul I have such immediate access to the vast oceans of his presence.

The heart is a plain door, yet its airy frame opens on majestic vistas of reality. It would seem that the opposite is true. Are not the vaulting thunderheads above the craggy mountains a better place to seek him than the earthy doorways of our soul? No, for natural vastness inspires, but it rarely results in an intimate togetherness with God. The rapture we feel standing before the Grand Canyon is more likely to erupt in a shout than in a conversation. The soaring galaxies are more prone to cause us to take our eyes from heaven and ask, "Father, are you there?" The best answers never come from beyond us. Why? Because God best declares himself from within us.

God becomes visible to those who look for him in the right place. Therefore, no eye—no literal eye—can see him! No ear can hear him! No mind can conceive him! He hides his vastness only in the deepest dimensions of our inner existence.

The world around us is the world of "outer" relationships. In such outer places we make friends, achieve success—get on in the world! In this busy, worried world we have appointments, face disappointments, and force our ego-driven souls to stab at achieving power. On the surface of our lives, things frenzied and dyspeptic dominate us. But in our hearts it is quite another matter.

First Corinthians 2:10 contains one little word that lunges at us with challenge: "But God has revealed it to us by his Spirit. The Spirit searches all things, even the *deep* things of God."

The apostle uses the word *bathos* for "deep" here. This is the symbol that I want to keep central in this book.

Deep is the dwelling place of God. *Deep* is the character of the ocean. Hold the metaphor for a moment and savor its lesson ahead of time. For deep is where the noisy, trashy surface of the ocean gets quiet and serene. No sound breaks the awesome silence of the ocean's heart. Most Christians, however, spend their lives being whipped tumultuously through the surface circumstances of their days. Their frothy lifestyles mark the surface nature of their lives. Yet those who plumb the deep things of God discover true peace for the first time.

Deep is the gift of discipline.

Bathos is a word I really discovered at the Great Barrier Reef. Like all visitors to the Reef, I was at first overwhelmed by the odd sensation of standing up—only ankle deep—seventy or ninety miles out in the middle of the ocean. It was for me the odd sensation that Peter must have felt when he walked on the Sea of Galilee.

But once my "ankle-deep wonder" had passed, I remembered why I had made the trip. I was with my wife and son. My son had come to scuba dive while my wife and I snorkeled. Snorkeling is a pastime more than a sport. For while my son plunged deeply beneath clear waters to bury himself in the wonder of the mysterious ocean depths, my wife and I, wearing masks, only floated on the surface facedown.

In some ways what we were all seeing looked the same. But my wife and I literally sunburned our backs in our surface study of the reef, while our son plumbed its wonders.

There were other differences in the day. Our son had spent many years learning to go deep. Deep requires years of practice. Deep cannot be achieved instantly upon the first dive. The equalizing of pressure in the head and facial sinuses must be developed gradually, for going deep can be dangerous, even fatal.

What amazes me most is what we reported upon returning from the Great Barrier Reef. Ask me if I've been there, and I will hastily answer yes. So will my son. However, the truth is that the content of our experience was greatly different. We will both spend the rest of our lives talking about that experience and our enthusiasm will always be exuberant. But only our son really knew the Reef; only he understood the issue of depth.

Abraham Maslow conceptualized the pyramid of priorities. Only a few people, he said, ever become self-actualized. Only a few know who they are and live life to the fullest extent. Only a few live adjusted lives at the peak of his pyramid. In fact, Maslow said the whole world is comprised of non-peakers talking to non-peakers about peak experiences. In some ways it seems to me that much of Christianity is a conversation of snorkelers talking to each other of scuba experiences. If mere conversation or study groups were the path to depth experience, the church would be deep indeed. But it is those who read and pray, not those who philosophize and chatter, who arrive at lives of real power.

The issue is going deep. Deep reveals the reality of God. Yet the snorkelers can use the language of divers, for the metaphors pass close. But they are not the same. It is odd that this state of reality lies so near us. It is utterly accessible, yet only a few ever know it or pass its gates with any regularity. Prayer is the gleaming doorway to the depths.

> *Why do we shun the grand doors of entrance unto God?*
> *Busyness is the best answer. Though sometimes we may*
> *doubt that prayer really does any good. Sometimes we're*

angry with God in our hearts, and our refusal to pray is our
way of saying, "I'll fix Him. I won't pray." How much
wiser we would be to shuck our temper tantrums and
head directly into the depths.[5]

In the depths of real inwardness lies the treasure. There is little use bragging where we think we are in Christ. Hungering for a Christ-conformity is the treasure.

It is perhaps the oddest of paradoxes that "how-to" lectures on the subject of inwardness are at risk of speaking beyond experience. Real spiritual divers are so in love with the depths that they don't spend much of their lives trying to make oceanography real in a world where birdbaths define the smaller passions.

The word *bathos* gives its Greek form to the word "bathysphere." A bathysphere is a steel-walled diving bell in which oceanographers, armed against the crushing pressure of the sea, may safely descend and study the depths. Not only is the ocean depth quiet and still, it hides a wondrous mystery. Consider the bathysphere scientists who descend into the heart of the ocean. There is a passionate curiosity in such souls. They must unravel mysteries! Or, if they cannot unravel them, they must bask in them until utter transcendence washes them with the only reality that can satisfy them. Hushed by the watery vastness, they learn a splendor they can never communicate to snorkelers. The inscrutable glories of the deep cannot be described to those hooked on the safety of shallowness.

But do such seekers enter the silent deep world to solve or to experience the mystery? In 1 Corinthians 2:7, and twenty other times in the New Testament, Paul speaks of the mystery of God. We do not go deep to study God, we go deep to taste his reality. In such experience we cannot define God, for he is not definable. But we do, ultimately, define ourselves. In the depths we meet our smallness, our powerlessness, our need. On the positive side, we discover the folly of trying to find our satisfaction in surface relationships. We learn to our credit that God hides neither his greatness nor our self-understanding in three hurried minutes of Bible reading a day. We suddenly know that the immensity of God never comes wrapped in contrived public prayers, where many—either consciously or unconsciously—are prone to approve themselves to their merely human auditors.

The nobility of much surface intercession runs aground here. Much of our intercession, like our spiritual lives, is but evidence of our addiction to self-infatuation. We are stopped short of the deep hunger to know him by our contentment to play in the shallows of our little "askings." Unlike the scuba masters, we have a fear of the depths. Or worse, an apathy toward the depths. We can see that the tide pools hold no deep adventure. We can even feel the lure of the dark and haunting indigo of the ocean's soul. Still, we balk at real inward adventure. Our shallow spirituality holds nothing profound, but it is safe.

"For who among men knows the thoughts of a man except the man's spirit within him? In the same way no one knows the thoughts of God except the Spirit of God. We have not received the spirit of this world but the Spirit who is from God, that we may understand what God has freely given us" (1 Corinthians 2:11–12). Let our ordinary senses bring us to discovery. Let them confess their shortcomings. Let the ear be shamed by rich silence. Let the eye discover what can't be seen. Let the mind be challenged by the inscrutable wall of the mystery of godliness. Let us see his significance by turning from our insignificance. Our smallness then becomes our glory! Nay, rather his glory. We have tasted the deep and our interest in the shallows is gone forever. Now we are in pursuit of the living God.

It is a beautiful pursuit! How immediate it is! Spirituality is not some distant thing for which we have to struggle all our lives. It's quite the opposite, actually. It presumes that deeper living is possible because God is near. Not only is he near, he longs to empower us in a deeper way and lure us ever deeper into the splendor of our affair with him.

But to receive the fullness of Christ, you must empty yourself of your own fullness. It is as the professor who was serving a student a cup of tea. He filled the teacup, then kept on pouring until the tea spilled over the rim of the cup. Finally the student said, "Sir, you're overfilling my cup!" The professor answered, "Well, if you would just empty it, I would fill it with better stuff than this."

We just keep filling our lives with the same old appetite for spiritual expression, rarely stretching ourselves or expanding our horizons. But the way of the depths is better. When we reach for God in love, and God reaches back, he meets us deep in the center of our existence, where "no eye has seen, no ear has heard, no mind has conceived what God has prepared for those who love him."

Come then, let us enter into the depths.

The Disciplined Life

O Lord God, how comfortable we are.
How exquisitely complacent.
How deliciously at ease.
We, your church, loll drowsily amid our privileges.
We treat our spiritual treasures cheaply,
as if possessing them in abundance
were a natural state of affairs,
always to be expected.[1]

—RAYMOND C. ORTLUND JR.

On a dark night, kindled in love with yearnings
—O happy chance!—
I went forth without being observed,
my house being now at rest.
(Briefly then, the soul means by this stanza
that it went forth—being led by God—
for love of him alone, enkindled in love of Him,
upon a dark night, which is the privation and purgation
of all its sensual desires,
with respect to all outward things of the world,
and to those which were delectable to its flesh,
and likewise with respect to the desires of its will.)

—JOHN OF THE CROSS

To renounce what one has is a minor thing;
to renounce what one is, that is asking a lot.[2]

—GREGORY THE GREAT

Should we not all be flexible before we know God's will? Should we not all be immovable after we understand what he wants done?

He has put us like a statue in its niche.

When there is added to this simple staying some feeling that we belong completely to God, and that he is our all, we must indeed give thanks to his goodness. If a statue that had been placed in some niche in some room could speak, and was asked, "Why are you there?" it would say,

"Because my master has put me here."

"Why don't you move?"

"Because he wants me to remain immovable."

"What use are you there; what do you gain by doing so?"

"It is not for my profit that I am here; it is to serve and obey the will of my master."

"But you do not see him."

"No, but he sees me, and takes pleasure in seeing me where he has put me."

"Would you not like to have movement so that you could go nearer to him?"

"Certainly not, except when he might command me."

"Don't you want anything else, then?"

"No, for I am where my master has placed me, and his good pleasure is the unique contentment of my being."[3]

—FRANCIS DE SALES

CHAPTER ONE

Breaking the Sensual Thrall

Appetite is a life sign. Healthy people get hungry. Our appetites can at last define us. Christians are to be people who hunger and thirst for righteousness (Matthew 5:6). In other words, Christians are to be defined as people who are hungry for God. They are hungry to please Christ. Martyrs are not necessarily those who are hungry to die. They are merely souls with an excessive appetite to please Christ. They would rather please him by having to die than disappoint him by selling out on key issues of obedience.

Most of us don't hunger to this extent. We are perhaps a trifle hungry for Christ, but we more often pursue the ordinary Maslovian values: shelter, food, safety, power, and sexual fulfillment.[4] These are all perfectly normal human appetites, but they can become truly dangerous when we lose our mastery over them and allow them to take over our lives.

There is but one check that provides the balance to all appetites. It's that word we'd rather not agree to, or at least push as far to the side as we can—"self-denial." But without self-denial, every eater is a glutton, every earner is a larcenist, every lover is a rapist. So at the outset of our call to follow Jesus is his entreaty—stern and yet beautiful—"If any man will come after me, let him deny himself, and take up his cross daily, and follow me" (Luke 9:23 KJV).

BAM! There it is! All fun gone, every second helping done away with. Every grasping desire supplanted with charity. Every sexual fantasy stabbed with moral integrity. Yield to self-denial and marriage endures, for no mates ever cheat. No banker ever embezzles. No addictions ever occur.

So then why don't we do it—why don't we deny ourselves? We fail at self-denial for three reasons. First, our focus is usually on the braking system rather than the steering wheel. Second, we live at too great a distance from the Grand Enabler. Finally, we cannot get heaven's perspective on the real values.

I can hear some objecting to such a well-outlined path to self-denial. And it's a fair objection. Can self-denial really be this simplistic? Can we *one-two-three* our way to moderation and spiritual well-being? Let us walk a bit together and measure the victory.

The victory always lies in our hunger for the spiritual intimacy of our union with Christ. In some sense it is more than a hunger, it is a stalking—pursuing God as a safari tracks the spoor of big game. But it is more than our stalking of God. God is also haunting us with his intangible reality. Like children trembling in an old, dark, empty house, so God's lovers tremble before the reality of silence in his presence. Why do children quake in a large empty house? They fear it is not empty but filled with some portent of terror. So we tremble, knowing his reality is all about us, so real that we feel what we cannot see—the terrifying reality of God. We are not afraid he will destroy us. We are only afraid of what he might require of us.

We are so hungry to know him in his fullness that we cry out like Catherine of Siena: "O depth of love! What heart could keep from breaking at the sight of your greatness descending to the lowliness of our humanity! We are your image, and now by making yourself one with us you have become our image. . . . You, God, became human, and we have been made divine!"[5] This is the glory of spiritual image: the merger of two likenesses.

But best of all, new appetites become our focus. This unceasing craving is for more of Christ—and even more the imitation of Christ. Thérèse of Lisieux wrote of union with Christ as an all-consuming appetite she called the work of love. What a spiritually exotic term this is! She wrote, "Now I wish only for one thing—to love Jesus, even unto folly! Love alone attracts me . . . my only guide is self-abandonment, I have no other compass."[6] She recognized that her work of love was identical to that of the Carmelite St. John of the Cross, who wrote, "I drank deep within the hidden cellar of my beloved. . . . My soul is content to serve him with all its strength. I have finished all other work except the work of love."[7]

Focusing on braking before steering

Consider the brakes and steering wheel metaphor. It would seem odd to a driving examiner as he assessed our driving skills, if we arrived at the vehicle test station with an eighteen-inch brake pedal and a six-inch steering wheel. Yet this is often our spiritual profile. Many people are reluctant to become Christians because they don't feel "their brakes are big enough." They wonder, *Can I slow my appetites down enough to be a good, moral Christian?*

For most outside of Christ, Christianity is an old jalopy, not a sports car. It is generally thought to be no fun and to do very little good for one's image. It seems to those outside the church that brakes are all that really matter to Christians. But these brakes do not only apply morally. They apply culturally as well. In every era of progress, it always seems to be the Christians who are harking back to yesteryear and putting the brakes on the future of all cultural advancement.

Further, personal evangelists are always trying to lure swanky sinners into the faith by asking grim questions like, "If you died right now, do you know for sure you'd go to heaven?" or "Can you stop sinning? How's your braking system?" Such no-joy mystiques make would-be converts doubt that they have brakes enough to be a Christian. These reluctant converts should not be asked "Can you put the brakes on your sin life?" but "Where do you want to go in life?" These then must be told that Christ is there to help them steer into the future God has for them.

> Christians are not to be so much *quitters* as *starters*. They do not endear themselves to God because of all they lay aside at conversion. Rather, it is what they take up that catches heaven's esteem.

Evangelicals for most of their history have had a curious emphasis on the brakes rather than on the steering wheel. They are forever *quitting* this or that. It is with some embarrassment that I must confess that most of my Christian life I've been trying to quit doing those things I felt were a barrier in my devotion to Christ. Indeed, I was decades into my life in Christ before it seriously occurred to me that we do not become vibrant believers because of the things we quit. Christians are not to be so much *quitters* as *starters*. They do not endear themselves to God because of all they lay aside at conversion. Rather, it is what they take up that catches heaven's esteem. It is the newness of life that causes them to bless each new dawn and the possible beginning of a new and closer walk. Spiritual growth occurs by ever starting, starting, starting every day some creative new thing that will sponsor a creative, never boring walk with Christ.

Where then do we get the odd doctrine of *quitting*?

This erroneous view came early in my life because of the perennial revivals that came to our church and community. Brother Flame (and he went by many names) came to us twice a year with two-week revivals. He exhorted the lost to be saved, and, of course, they were. That alone brought joy to the church. The motivation, however, with which he challenged the lost, was neurotic napalm. Fire fell (and a good bit of brimstone) in every sermon, and at least one of the community's worst villains would cry out and come out of his sin, and in time wind up the chief of severe deacons. For all the melodrama of their art, I sometimes miss these flaming country heralds.

But one function of their preachment was always the call to quit. "Quit drinking—give up your godless whisky and come and put it on the altar," was a typical plea. "If God had wanted you to smoke, he'd have put a smokestack on your head," cried one such evangelist in our church. Some went forward and laid their cigarettes on the altar. We all could see that these chimney-heads were cleaning their lungs and perfecting their faith. Hallelujah for the brakes! Some vowed that never again would they be guilty of "having a dancing foot and a praying knee on the same leg." Some gave up cards and quit canasta for the glory of God forever. Some, however, went back to their card-playing to the delight of the demons.

I was young, and I loved Jesus more than might be imagined. I wanted to "quit stuff" like everybody else. But I usually felt guilty that I had so little I could quit. I wanted to know that devoted, neurotic spirituality that comes from quitting drinking or dancing or smoking. Alas, I was thwarted by a major absence of real sin in my life. I was playing life pretty straight for a nine-year-old.

Then my pastor, noticing that I was sinless and pretty smug about it, began to condemn movies. Thank God! At last I had something I could quit. I adored westerns: Hopalong Cassidy, Lash LaRue, and Gene Autry were among my favorite characters. Alas, they were not God's favorites: they were movie stars. God liked Christians but not movie stars. He despised these vile seducers of the heart, I was told. Further, if God and I ever got together, I must confess my worldly affection for them. A pox on Hoppy, Lash, and Gene! This infernal trinity of damnable heroes, I could quit. So I did—I gave up movies.

Now at last I was a first-class Christian. I could hardly wait till Sunday to announce my new asceticism to the church. Only gradually did Sunday come. But when it finally did, my spiritual delirium was at its zenith. At altar time, while our little congregation "just-as-I-ammed," I walked to the front of the church. I visualized myself laying Hoppy, Lash, and Gene on the altar for Jesus. Heaven stood at attention over my glorious new self-denial. The angels wept. The wicked Hollywood demons fled, totally expunged from my life. I was free. Now when my pastor said, "Do you want to be in a godless movie house when Jesus comes again?" I could cry, "No, for I have separated myself from the world and put behind me the unclean thing."

I was from time to time puzzled about the supposed depth of degradation in the '40s western. But I accepted the judgment of those evangelists, knowing that I was neither as old nor wise as they. I knew their walk with Jesus allowed them to measure the unseen corruption I did not immediately see. So when the revival was over, without the godless Hollywood cowboys, I was living the deeper life as I understood it. My unsanctified friends tried to lure me back to sin, saying, "Want to go and see *Riders of the Purple Sage*?" I at first answered, "No, thank you, I've quit all that!"

Still, the cinema sin was all-alluring. I couldn't hold out! I usually went back to the movies soon after the revival closed. I fell from my large professions as often as I clung. But on and on they went, till I lapsed and went back to my old ways. My strong intentions were as dry as the old crusted wads of spearmint gum stuck to the undersides of those heathen theater seats. I couldn't really enjoy the movies, because, after all, Jesus might come again, and there I would be, "riding the purple sage" into the abyss— where all unfaithful backsliders perished because they didn't keep their revival commitments. Alas, I had fallen, and there was nothing to be done except wait for the next revival—then maybe I could purge my soul and quit once again before I lapsed once again, before I quit once again.

So it was years before I realized that I rarely focused on Jesus, but rather on all the things I needed to quit. I was guilty of the I-wish-sin-wasn't-so-much-fun complex. Many, if not most, Christians spend their lives thinking, *I really wanted to follow Jesus, but I wanted to have fun too.* It was not possible, they said. So I was led to believe that Jesus and fun were antithetical. The recent *What Would Jesus Do?* bracelets can feed this same neurosis. Would Jesus have gone to see Hoppy, Lash, and Gene? Maybe in 1999, but not in 1948. The oddity of our new WWJD propositions almost always caused me to say no. But in reality it was always hard for me—particularly as a young person—to see Jesus in my world. With all my mental powers, it was hard for me to imagine Jesus in Enid, Oklahoma, walking around the courthouse in his long white robe. However would he have managed not to get sandburs in his sandals? And never could I imagine his glow-in-the-dark halo in the dimly lit movie murk of the Mecca Theater watching Hoppy, Lash, and Gene.

I was trapped by the imagery of it. In my late teens I learned to waterski. It was from the skiers that I finally got an answer to "Would I want to be in an Enid theater when Jesus came again?" I did love to ski—it was fun. Would Jesus water-ski? Of course not. Jesus never had any fun. He loved prayer meetings. Then the old revival loomed out ahead of the towrope. Jesus was driving my motorboat and wagging his finger back across the foam. *"Do you want to be on these skis when I come again?"* he seemed to say.

I knew it must be wrong; it was so much fun! What would Jesus do? He would pray and pass out revival fliers, wouldn't he? Even if he were not averse to good times, his halo and sandals would mandate that he behave himself, remaining stern and self-directed, and, of course, deeply Baptist. Jesus? Water-ski? Of course not—his long white robe would drag in the water.

Then for the first time I focused not on what Christ might do (for indeed he seemed to have fun in the Bible, what with always going to parties) but what he sanctified. In other words, there might actually be a difference between what Jesus would actually do and what he sanctified.

He was a carpenter who blessed those who fished, though he himself seemed to have no preference for fishing. Who can say whether or not he would have skied or, for that matter, gone to the movies? If the moral content of anything we do does not ignore holiness, then the presence of Christ in our lives may indeed sanctify it.

But the key thing that I learned in this area was that I needed to quit *quitting*. Quitting involves a cathexis that is focused on what or what not to quit. Those who focus on Christ rarely have to quit anything, because their desire for union with Christ prohibits them from starting anything they might later want to quit.

The sin of living too distant from the Great Enabler

Indulgences that at last ensnare us in their mesh of addiction are at first quite weak in the spell they cast over us. People don't always begin to drink because they wish to be drunk; they often get drunk as a habit of empty living. But this is not merely true of drunkenness, it is true of all our addictions.

Gluttony destroys as does unbridled envy or unchecked lust. But the seven deadly sins rarely root themselves in a busy, purposeful life. All of them grow best in the soil of human emptiness.

Emptiness is the central neurosis that sires so many smaller addictions. I have known several ministers who compromised themselves with illicit affairs. Without exception, all confessed it was not the appetite for the illicit that first lured them toward a fallen witness. They felt the church had abandoned them and left them alone, depleted in spirit with no one to talk to. Their adulteries sprung from their own weak spiritual rapport with Christ. Their infidelities grew as their neediness warred against their emptiness.

Emptiness leaves us wanton till we fill it with whatever secondary appetite might seem to stop our hungers of soul. One of the loneliest Christians I have ever known was an executive for a large company. He commanded an entire galaxy of enterprises, but he confessed that on the leather-chair side of his great glassy desk he found himself alone. His wife was busy raising their four children, and gradually between his late hours and her fatigue their relationship died. He began drinking to ease himself off to sleep, and finally a dependency developed. When I suggested that he could be an alcoholic, he protested. Gradually, though, he consented and began a detoxification program, which along with Alcoholics Anonymous delivered him forever—one day at a time.

I wouldn't have brought the whole thing up except that he was a clear example of a man who was a Christian before he became an alcoholic. His emptiness preceded his addictions. In him, once again I could see the truth in Jung's proverb: "The absence of Inwardness is the central neurosis of our time." The absence of inwardness is the lost freedom we trade for addictions. Pascal was right. There is a God-shaped vacuum in our lives that only God can fill. Here I must ask the question: Are you already a Christian in whose life there is a vacuum yet unfilled? Even Christians can have such vacuums. How did they come to own such emptiness? Through the simple neglect of their God relationship.

When God fills our inner vacuum with his Holy Spirit, life works. When God does not fill the vacuum, a host of consuming appetites swarm through our better intentions. Brilliant people who should be masters of their appetites are at last managed by some dread fiend that was at first unwelcome in their lives. Then the fiend was made welcome. Then his presence was customary. Then he became habitual. At last, the addiction and not the Christian was master.

Consider how many neuroses flood into the lives of various addicts.

Gilbert Grape's mother allowed her gluttony to destroy her inside a house whose floor joists would barely support her. Upton Sinclair's *Cup of Fury* deals with the addiction to alcohol, as does *The Lost Weekend*, or *Ironweed*, or any number of titles. Books and films and national politics hold tales of sexual addictions. An unbridled lust for power is the theme of *Primary Colors, Wag the Dog*, any of the *Godfather* films, and virtually half the novels and films released.

Sex itself is a common inhabitant of our inner lives. It can come so regularly into our minds that it takes the place of the thought and time we ought to give to God. Frederick Buechner has referred to sex as "the ape that gibbers in our loins." He calls it the great secret we hold within ourselves to the point it produces an unhealthy spiritual pathology. "I suppose sex is the secret that to one degree or another all of us keep from each other . . . the great open secret that, whatever else we are, we are bodies and that as bodies we need to touch and be touched. . . . Once they sinned, Adam and Eve tried to hide their nakedness from each other and from God, and to one degree or another, we all have been hiding it ever since for the reason, I suppose, that we know that our sexuality is yet another good gift from God which as sinners we can nonetheless use to dehumanize both each other and ourselves."[8]

The most popular films and novels are tales of our losses to our appetites. But the saddest commentary on contemporary Christianity lies also at this point. Many Christians from publishing house to publishing house and from church to church are owned by a spirit of ungodly competition. Megachurches wear an altruistic (and sometimes evangelistic) face while all the time waging their zealous, jealous wars of Madison Avenue growth tactics. While many theologians and thinkers have tried to call them back from this stance, the race to be the biggest and best and most famous goes on. Under other names pressed with pretended sanctity these vying Christians rarely lay aside their sanctified brinkmanship.

It all adds up to a kind of powerlessness, which always results from living too far from the Grand Enabler. When we will not provide a place for the direction of the indwelling Christ, all that is left is the frenzied agenda of our hassled discipleship. The sad thing about all this is that true discipleship can never be frenzied, for it emulates its Master and turns from the turbulent to embrace a steady devotion and a silent adoration.

Failing to get heaven's perspective on the real values

There is only one real question for the believer: How does God view my discipleship?

During the years of the Clinton presidential scandal, I developed a dull weariness with public opinion. News and talk shows presented gossipy editorials of viewpoint and irresolution. Church leaders and theologians also opined and theorized. But rarely did anyone set forth the presence of divine viewpoint. I believe those who remained the quietest did so because they had seen with the eyes of God and measured our national sin with the plumb line of God's expectations.

No culture is quite so blind as those who will not see. No Christian is quite so dead as one whose vitality has been sapped by being out of touch with God. Institutions (and most were established to do noble and sacrificial service in obedience to God as they understood him) degenerate at last into little more than ladders of egoistic advancement. Denominations, once founded for the altruism of missions, end up little more than religious clubs protecting their vested interests. Catherine of Siena wrote that the church leaders of her day lived shackled to luxury. They were ignorant of Latin and so could not perform a sensible mass. They were barons of power with nothing but empty lives and weak preaching to define their competitive, non-compassionate lives. Their service to God was hurried and pretended.[9]

Perhaps the weightiest of all personal vision is to see with the eyes of God. To know what God wants of a nation, but to have zero ability to make that happen, inevitably leads to brokenness.

The first step toward healing always lies in the admission of our illness. Israel, in moments of decline, did not consider her ways wicked, so healing was not possible. Oswald Chambers felt that we ought to feel the pain of our sins if we were to convince ourselves we took our sin seriously. "The entrance into the Kingdom is through the panging pains of repentance crashing into a man's respectable goodness; then the Holy Ghost, who produces these agonies, begins the formation of the Son of God in the life."[10]

The unceasing Niagara of opinion polls during the Clinton presidential scandal caused few to ask, "Does God have an opinion on this?" If he does, maybe we should alter our opinion to match his. Perhaps it is the greatest of hypocrisies to swear presidents into office with their hand on the Bible, when those presidents never again open that Bible to pursue God's moral objectives.

Among all Christians there is not much noble living, but here and there arises a man or woman whose discipleship begins the day by asking, "Lord, what will thou have me to do?" Such a question prescribes a way of living for that day and such a way of living describes a way of life. Dietrich Bonhoeffer, near the end of his life, realized that his life held no firm definition except that which God gave it. He wrote exquisitely:

> I bore the days of misfortune equably, smilingly, proudly,
> like one accustomed to win. Am I then really that which other men
> tell of? Or am I only what I know of myself? Restless and longing
> and sick. Whoever we are, we are God's.[11]

How are we to treasure God's final ownership of our lives? I must confess that my own life is ever torn by my desire to be a writer of significance and my desire to be nothing more than a soul who wants to discover God's agenda for my life—one minute at a time. Ambition rises in most every heart. It fuels our careers, of course, but it is too intrinsically selfish to be a reliable guide. Only heaven's view will guide us to joyous, error-free obedience. And only godly living will enable us to see our lives as they should be lived, desiring for God's world all it should become.

In the crowded city of Tokyo, there is wide agreement (actually a city ordinance) that no one can erect a skyscraper, or any other building, that shuts off anyone else's view of the sun. The Japanese feel that for some time during every day, everyone has a right to see the sun. Long ago God gave me the conviction that I must try to help people end their emptiness. It seemed to me that everyone has a right "to see the Son." Then all purely human appetites would lose their power. Let us move toward the appetite *gallant*. We shall have him in our heart of hearts. We will then need no Christian jewelry to tell the world of our cravings. They will see beyond our jewelry into our lives.

Conclusion

The difference between what God wants for us and what we ultimately become rests in how we break the thrall of those appetites that chain us to selfish lifestyles and selfish life goals. The steps to freedom are simple but always demanding. First, our focus needs to be on hungering after what God wants rather than merely trying to quit what he doesn't want. Second, we must agree to live close to the Great Enabler. Finally, we must live in abundant inwardness until we can see the kind of world God wants to exist and endeavor to become the kind of Christian God wants us to be.

Oswald Chambers felt that most of us do not intentionally renounce God's vision for our life. We lose the vision through neglect. When we are born again we seem to catch sight of the significance of our worth to both God and ourselves. We become disobedient to that vision when we begin to live as though it cannot be obtained.[12] We rarely deny the vision or argue with God's dream for us. "We lose the vision by spiritual leakage," says Chambers.[13] This is too bad, for we can never know spiritual happiness until we accept God's vision for our lives.

When we accept God's vision for our lives, we pray. But it may be that we expect too much instant revelation from our prayers. We want to pray for a fiery chariot in the morning and be riding to church in it by nightfall. We rarely pray for fire and open our eyes to find a box of matches in our hand.

> *Thunderclaps and lightning flashes are very unlikely. It is well to start small and quietly. No need to tell one's friends and acquaintances. No need to plan heroic fasts or all-night vigils . . . prayer is neither to impress other people nor to impress God. It's not to be taken on with a mentality of success. The goal, in prayer, is to give oneself away.*[14]

Can the issue be so simply resolved? Yes. Living the God-life is all that ever can satisfy us. Of course, those who see what it is and know what God wants must weep from time to time. But weeping over the waywardness of those he created is the nature of our living, loving God. Loving was why he sent his Son. Calvary is not a very complex solution to human sin, but it cost God all he had. And Calvary was God's crying place. To change a world is to spend everything and then to wait and weep.

Come, in my labor find a resting place
And in my sorrows lay your head,
Or rather take my life and blood
And buy yourself a better bed—
Or take my breath and take my death
And buy yourself a better rest.[1]

—THOMAS MERTON

Use what you have.
The five barley loaves and two small fishes
will increase as they are distributed.
Do not envy one more successful than yourself,
or you will be convicted of murmuring against
the appointment of our Lord.[2]

—F. B. MEYER

Am I allowing my natural life to be slowly transfigured
By the indwelling life of the Son of God?
God's ultimate purpose is that His Son
might be manifested in my mortal flesh.[3]

—OSWALD CHAMBERS

How shall we break free of this world except by thinking of the next?

Was it not through prayer that St. Paul, St. Augustine, St. Thomas Aquinas, St. John of the Cross, St. Theresa, and so many other friends of God found that wonderful knowledge that has enraptured the greatest intellects? Archimedes said, "Give me a fulcrum and with a lever I will move the world." What he could not get, the saints have been given. The Almighty has given them a fulcrum: Himself, Himself alone. For a lever they have that prayer that burns with the fire of love. Thus they have moved the world, and it is with this lever that those still battling in the world move it and will go on moving it till the end of time.[4]

—THÉRÈSE OF LISIEUX

CHAPTER TWO

Breaking the Thrall of Materialism

The Desert Fathers went into the desert to be "freed of their plenty." Having plenty isn't an abominable state, but to be controlled by it is. God wants his people to live free from the "green addiction." He doesn't want people to be miserable because of greed. Quite the opposite. The most miserable people are those who are possessed by materialism. The etymology of the word "miserable" is formed of the same stem as "miser." *Miser-y* is really *misery*.

Catherine of Siena was convinced that hardship was a better friend of materialism than wealth. The wealthy often consider their income and the keeping of it with less fervor than do the needy. The needy (perhaps because they have to scrimp more to attain it) often dote on their little treasures more than the wealthy cherish their larger ones.

She cautioned her prosperous friends to live united to God's will. She also stressed that there is goodness in material possessions, for God wishes us to live in the joy of his gifts. But she also cautioned us that we must not love these gifts in such a way that, instead of our possessing them, they begin to possess us.

In Luke 18 Jesus meets a rich young ruler. The man had great wealth, but the mere having of it was not his sin. It was the clinging to it.

Barnabas also had great wealth (Acts 4:36–37), but he sold his estate and brought the money and laid it at the apostles' feet. What did Barnabas do that the rich young ruler couldn't do? He set himself free from a great addiction. The young ruler was a slave of the passion called *having*. Nor had he trained himself in the art of detachment. The ancient monks interpreted detachment as "not allowing either worldly values or self-centeredness to distract us from what is most essential in our relationship with God and with each other."[5]

Having and the sin of materialism

Annie Dillard wrote a short poem that states the foolishness of trying to keep Jesus and mere dollars in the same safety deposit box:

We keep our paper money shut
in a box, for fear of fire.
Once, we opened the box
and Christ the lamb stepped out
and left his track of flame
across the floor.[6]

"Having" is not the first sin of materialists. The sin that precedes it is the sin of *regarding what we have as our own*. Most new Christians begin their life of having by not seeing their goods of any consequence, and so are quite willing to give God the glory for giving them what they have. But sooner or later some of them forget the source of their material blessings. To those who forget, "having" is not what God makes possible but what they feel they have achieved and thus have a right to.

In two recent round-the-world mission junkets, I have had the opportunity to try out that materialist bumper-sticker epigram: *He who has the most toys wins*. Wins what? Some sort of Dow-Jones esteem, perhaps, but little more. The happiest people I met were often in places like Calcutta, where there was no possibility of wealth. There are few rich young rulers in Calcutta. The only reasonable goal in that teeming mass of humanity is to be alive the next morning.

I traveled in villages and cities where the inhabitants can't imagine a credit card. Any idea of a shopping trip is not possible. "Shop till you drop" is a condemning slogan devised by those whose larders are already full and whose large garages are the manifest bunkers of unnecessary vehicles.

In Calcutta, a lot of other materialist bumper stickers also disappeared: *I owe, I owe—so off to work I go* was missing, as was *My child and my checks go to the university*. Strangely absent were questions like "How many square feet . . ." or "What's your second car . . ." We were told again and again not to compliment any object in the homes we visited because the Christians who lived there were apt to give it to us.

The editors of LEADERSHIP magazine suggested nine rather drastic steps wealthy Westerners would have to take to truly identify with the developing world:

> First, take out the furniture: leave a few old blankets, a kitchen table, maybe a wooden chair. You've never had a bed, remember?
>
> Second, throw out your clothes. Each person in the family may keep the oldest suit or dress, a shirt or blouse. The head of the family has the only pair of shoes.
>
> Third, all kitchen appliances have vanished. Keep a box of matches, a small bag of flour, some sugar and salt, a handful of onions, a dish of dried beans. Rescue the moldy potatoes from the garbage can: those are tonight's meal.
>
> Fourth, dismantle the bathroom, shut off the running water, take out the wiring and the lights and everything that runs by electricity.
>
> Fifth, take away the house and move the family into the tool shed.
>
> Sixth, no more postman, fireman, government services. The two-classroom school is three miles away, but only two of your seven children attend anyway, and they walk.
>
> Seventh, throw out your bankbooks, stock certificates, pension plans, insurance policies. You now have a cash hoard of $5.
>
> Eighth, get out and start cultivating your three acres. Try hard to raise $300 in cash crops because your landlord wants one-third and your moneylender 10 percent.
>
> Ninth, find some way for your children to bring in a little extra money so you have something to eat most days. But it won't be enough to keep bodies healthy—so lop off 25 to 30 years of life.[7]

Materialism is the worldview of those who keep their eyes focused on "getting ahead" in the world at hand. Christ championed a higher focus. Jesus encourages us in Matthew 6:33 to treasure the kingdom of God and his righteousness, and the values of the world at hand will be exposed for what they are. Materialism sponsors a lot of bogus values. What God wants us to treasure is inward and spiritual. Only as we get the God's-eye view of things can we escape becoming forever trapped in minor material hungers and surface values.

Grace is the antidote to materialism. Grace is never a show-off that calls attention to itself. The overwhelming wonder of all God has done for us and given to us washes us with quiet gratitude. A rhythm then comes in with his visitations of spiritual plenty. His grace comes and goes, furnishing us with everything beautiful in life. Suddenly we awake to the wonder, and feel ashamed that we have lived so long never thanking him for his abundance.

Materialism often takes over at the same rate at which our spirituality decays. I have noticed that as people grow older, the sparkle they once had in their eyes begins to die. Sometimes their zeal also dies and they start hoarding cash for the "golden years." They quit trusting God and start stashing goods. Gone are the easy-giving days of first faith.

Remember first faith?

Francis de Sales had sipped the elixir of first faith, and refused to ever let it become secondhand: "Alas! Every day we ask him that his will may be done; and when it comes to the doing we have so much difficulty. We offer ourselves to God so often; we say to him at every step, 'Lord, I am yours. Here is my heart!' "[8] This was what we said to become Christians. This is what we must still say to demonstrate our faith.

> When we trade our spiritual treasures for mere trifles, the grand dream we had for serving God seeps away through the glitzy pores of our greed.

When Jesus Christ comes into our lives with soul-force, something is born in us that says, *I can make a difference. I can reach my world. I can live for him as I sacrifice myself for him.* But our former greed stays with us and we are never out of danger. At any moment we can return to our old values and become a goggle-eyed shopper leaning against the sports car of our choice. When we trade our spiritual treasures for mere trifles, the grand dream we had for serving God seeps away through the glitzy pores of our greed.

The substance of inwardness

We must break the habit of treasuring our treasures and develop the habit of treasuring the abundance of God's grace. We must cherish what François Fénelon called the "state of bare faith." Bare faith treasures God, for all other values are seen to be only nakedness and poverty.

> *When you feel yourself to be in dryness, obscurity, poverty, and almost powerlessness of soul, remain humble under the hand of God in a state of bare faith, recognize your own misery, turn yourself toward the all-powerful Lord, and never doubt his assistance. . . . All greed flees in favor of endurance.*[9]

Paul says that our inner life is a reaching after such endurance—after Christ.

In 1 Corinthians 6:12, the apostle reminds us that while all things may be permitted, some things aren't good for us. Those things that steal my vision for God are not good for me. I will not be brought under the power of any of them. Consider materialism as chief of these addicting powers.

Under the power of what? Remember this list: "Do not be deceived: Neither the sexually immoral nor idolaters nor adulterers nor male prostitutes nor homosexual offenders nor thieves nor the greedy nor drunkards nor slanderers nor swindlers will inherit the kingdom of God" (1 Corinthians 6:9b–10). But what is the origin of these motley states? How does an adulterer become an adulterer? How does a drunkard become a drunkard? How does an immoral man become immoral? He becomes so by losing his mastery over his appetites.

If we had all the spiritual maturity we need we would be able to see this. God never denies us what we want in an attempt to be mean to us. He withholds what we don't need so that what he wants will become possible for us. And what does he want? Our conformity to the image of his Son. So let us never be guilty of thinking that our cravings for material things will ever produce Christlikeness in our lives. It cannot be, for Christ himself repudiated the emptiness of the material world. When he died on the cross absolutely bereft of all goods, he told us just how far we would have to go to be as unselfish and non-materialistic as he was.

The best time to deal with a temptation of any sort—materialism notwithstanding—is to meet the allurement up front. To hold anything in our hearts that is contrary to the single-minded call is to split our attention between Jesus and whatever else is calling for first place in our allegiance.

One of the bedfellows of materialism is *busyness*, or *busyanity* as it has been called. It is a kind of sanctified hassle by which Christians vie for importance by comparing their agenda and the speed at which they serve the various programs of the religious community. The idea is that *the more one does for Jesus* the more the angels must be impressed. So we brag that we're here on Tuesday and there on Wednesday. We belong to half a dozen clubs or run day and night to church as though there's some kind of inherent life in sanctified speed. Fast living and fast spending keep company. A heavy appointment calendar and the sheer egoism that comes from heavy spending are close companions.

Materialism and busyness can lead us to claim that we are living the "good life." Paul, after reminding us that we are the temple of God says, "You are not your own; you were bought at a price. Therefore honor God with your body" (1 Corinthians 6:19b–20). Now when God purchased us, he took us out of that way of life. He changed both our moral preferences and the way we feel about getting and having and hurrying for the sake of acquiring a bogus reputation for sincere living.

Thérèse of Lisieux said that the key to answering all of our appetites, material or otherwise, was to imitate Christ. She had a linnet that she kept in a cage, having had the bird since it was a fledgling. She also had a canary that was given to constant singing. The quieter linnet, in time, began to try to imitate the canary. It was not easy, but he kept at it. "It was charming to watch the efforts of the little thing," she wrote. "It obviously found it hard to make its own voice harmonize with the vibrant notes of its master, but to my great surprise its song did in time become exactly like the canary's."[10]

To fail to imitate Christ is to grieve the Holy Spirit (Ephesians 4:30). How exactly do we do it? The key to understanding this is to remember that "grieve" is a love word. When we do not live up to the thing that God saves us to do, it's not that God gets mad at us and becomes bent on some path of getting even. Instead, God hurts for us.

I cannot remember getting much new furniture in our house in Oklahoma when we were growing up, but I do remember when we got two brand-new chairs. My mother probably spent every last dime she had to buy them. It was not as though we didn't need them, but we rarely had money for furniture. Most of our family spending was done for more basic things. I remember at first thinking how obscene those new chairs looked. They were polished and beautiful, ruling as maple thrones over the rest of our furniture. At some point, they wound up on the front porch of our house (when you have three rooms and nine kids, you spend a lot of time on the front porch).

Across the street came one of my little friends. He had something brand-new too—a pocketknife! I can remember that as we talked, he took his brand-new pocketknife and carved on those brand-new chairs. I never thought to stop him; he seemed more creative than evil to me. But I do remember that when my mother came out on the porch, I saw a condemning flash of fire on her face. There was open hostility and anger. But those who really know their mothers and fathers can look past the hostility and see that behind it there is deep hurt. Something beautiful was spoiled. It made me want to cry.

When Paul says, "Do not grieve the Holy Spirit of God," he is really saying, "As a Christian it is impossible for you to make God mad, but it is possible to hurt the heart of God." To keep this from happening, the indwelling Christ lives within us. We are bought. We were purchased that day when Jesus hung on a tree. It was an expensive ordeal. It cost thorns! It cost blood! It cost the whole crucifixion of Jesus Christ! Yet he hung there—purchasing, buying, spending, writing "paid in full" across all our neediness!

I think I know the pain that Jesus must have felt when he looked out, having done no wrong, and cried, "Father, forgive them!" Then he cried, "It is finished!" Not "*I* am finished," but "*It* is finished! I have paid the purchase price," called the Christ unto our souls. "You are bought with a price. Therefore glorify God in your body."

Since we are bought with a price, maybe we should forgo the fruitless pursuit of our own shallow getting and spending. Perhaps Christ's ownership of us will be altogether more important than our ownership of any mere material thing.

But best of all, his ownership establishes a rich sense of inwardness— a wholeness of life and attitude that makes our access to God immediate. Embracing this ownership is a giant step in our attempt to cease loving things, and it enhances our love of God.

In a sense, it is also a step in breaking the material thrall. This is done by hiding heaven's treasures—not our own—in the inward life. By such a simple act, a massive displacement takes place. The appetite for having is replaced by the appetite for being. The heart given to Christ is not a toy-shopper. He sets us free to love him, and loving him displaces the adoration of mere material things. We have been purchased by his dear blood. How petty must be whatever trifles our paltry coins might buy. For us it can never be "he who has the most toys wins" but he who has been purchased by the blood of Christ wins and will continue to win throughout the ages.

Times change and so to keep up with them
we must modify our methods.[1]

—MADELEINE SOPHIE BARAT

Happy are they who give themselves to God!
They are delivered from their passions,
from the judgments of others,
from their malice,
from the tyranny of their sayings,
from their cold and wretched mocking,
from the misfortunes which the world distributes to wealth,
from the unfaithfulness and inconstancy of friends,
from the wiles and snares of the enemy,
from our own weakness,
from the misfortunes and brevity of life,
from the horrors of a profane death,
from cruel remorse attached to wicked pleasures,
and in the end,
from the eternal condemnation of God.[2]

—FRANÇOIS FÉNELON

Lord, I am yours;
I do yield myself up entirely to you,
and I believe that you accept me.
I leave myself with you.
Work in me all the good pleasure of your will,
and I will only lie still in your hands and trust you.[3]

—HANNAH WHITALL SMITH

It is amazing that we take our individual schedules so seriously that we never wonder if God has anything else for us to do.

It has been observed that if the 50,000 years of man's existence were divided into lifetimes of approximately 62 years each, there have been about 800 such lifetimes. Of these 800, fully 650 were spent in caves. Only during the last 70 lifetimes, has it been possible to communicate effectively from one lifetime to another—as writing made it possible to do. Only during the last 6 lifetimes did masses of men ever see a printed word. Only during the last 4 has it been possible to measure time with any precision. Only in the last 2 has anyone anywhere used an electric motor. And the overwhelming majority of all the material goods we use in everyday life have been developed within the present 800th lifetime.[4]

—ALVIN TOFFLER

CHAPTER THREE

Breaking the Tyranny of the Urgent

One of the first machines was the clock. First driven by water, later by spring and pendulum, and finally by quartz and dials, it remains a controlling machine whose tick-tock power leaves us neurotic. Clocks were created to make us the stewards of our time but sometimes end up making us nervous.

Of all the gifts God gives us, surely the most precious is the gift of time.

Seconds, minutes, years are all life-parts, assembled and ready for our use in his service. The sand of our lives is running through the hourglass—fast, steady, precious. It is so precious that when we give it back to God, it sets the angels at their alleluias. Yet we cannot give our entire lives to God at one time and have it done with for all time. We must surrender second by second.

Making holy the days of our lives

Therefore, the primary question for the indwelling Christ is not "What wilt thou have me to do in life?" but "What wilt thou have me do *today*?" The clock belongs to Christ, and each tick summons us to surrender every second to the glory of his name. The rhyme on the dial of the grandfather clock states the diminishing nature of our ongoing sacrifice of time: "Lo, I stand by thee upright, to give thee counsel day and night. For every tock that I do give cuts short the time thou hast to live."

Jesus knew his earthly life had its limits. "Mine hour is not yet come"

(John 2:4 KJV), he said. "The hour is coming, and now is" (John 5:25 KJV), he said on one occasion, and on another, "Behold, the hour is at hand, and the Son of man is betrayed" (Matthew 26:45 KJV). He criticized the Pharisees because they could not "discern the . . . times" (Matthew 16:3 KJV).

The apostle Paul also seemed to be aware that his time upon the earth was brief. He said, "But when the fulness of the time was come, God sent forth his Son, made of a woman, made under the law, to redeem them that were under the law, that we might receive the adoption of sons" (Galatians 4:4–5 KJV). Toward the end of Paul's life, he wrote, "For I am now ready to be offered, and the time of my departure is at hand" (2 Timothy 4:6 KJV). The apostle understood that only those who obey in the moment can link their obedient moments into a significant lifetime. The point is not to merely live a long time (oat bran and a regimen of herbs will help see to that). The point is that we are to offer our days as a sacrifice of silver on an altar of gold.

Time may be either the friend or the enemy of our surrender to Christ. The Chinese sage summed up our clockish biographies in three words: hurry, worry, bury. How often this trinity of words describes our surface churchmanship. Church is so often the busiest of all madness. We run from meeting to service and back again. Exhausted by our frantic externalness, we collapse in bed at night, and for what? Does our hurried religiosity cause us to lift up our eyes to our King? Have we looked upon our small performance with spurious pride? Have we sighed over our small prayers and been satisfied? All the while we know—deep in our hearts—there must be some deeper, more meaningful way to live for Christ.

When we sum up our large professions and our little faith, we know we need to confess our spastic obedience to time. "Lord Jesus, forgive us our hurry. Help us to remember that across from *hurry, worry, bury* stands a loftier trio of words: cling, linger, and savor." We need to pray, "Lord, our spiritual dysfunction is an indication that we are splashing about on the shallow surface of our religiosity to avoid diving into your depths."

What mature believer does not delight in seeing new converts talk with Christ? As we get older, we sometimes hurry past the ardor we knew as younger Christians. Hurried Christians beget hurried disciples. Hurried disciples become a hurried church—a hassled fellowship of disciples who serve the clock and call it God. But this subnormal Christianity has become so normal we don't see anything abnormal about it. In fact, we've come to believe that the most sincere Christians are supposed to be shallow neurotics. Yet the church holds only one possibility of relevance: Time itself must be surrendered to the pursuit of the depths of God. God does not wear a watch. His unthinkable glory is learned only in our time-consuming communion with him. But once we learn it, we are delivered.

Delivered?

Yes, from our horrible addiction to hurry.

The child of one of my friends said that one Sunday they were singing in the worship services of the church the chorus, "I exalt Thee!" Only the child was singing, "I exhaust Thee!" If God were not all-powerful, he would likely be exhausted by the pace of our neurotic adoration. We cannot possibly flatter the Almighty by hurrying into his presence, flinging a song and a prayer at him, and hurrying out of church back into our hassled lifestyles. God is never flattered by our sanctified exhaustion.

Like the frantic rabbit in *Alice in Wonderland*, we seem ever convinced that we're always late for this or that.

> We cannot possibly flatter the Almighty by hurrying into his presence, flinging a song and a prayer at him, and hurrying out of church back into our hassled lifestyles. God is never flattered by our sanctified exhaustion.

I've always wondered if that white bunny was not an evangelical rabbit with a watch and a Day-Timer. Churches are hassled hutches of busy bunnies, publishing their agendas by date on the assumption that those who really want to experience God must "calendar him in." The tyrant is urgency. We can see our spiritual apathy, but we are convinced that even our apathy should arrive on time.

We must slow down and get quiet in our worship. Why are we frightened of silence in evangelical churches? When worship gets quiet, evangelicals get fidgety. Thomas Merton suggested that people who don't like each other have trouble being quiet together.[5] The Quakers long ago learned the power of corporate silence. Evangelicals need to learn that to be quiet before God is to see him.

But God does not meet with us in the silence so that he can produce something in our lives. There is nothing to produce. These silences do not exist to create product but to bless us with authenticity.

How much time do these prayer rendezvous take? Time is not the object. We do not punch a time clock in our fellowship with God. We meet and wait and measure nothing.

Identifying time zones

Let us examine two Greek concepts of time: *chronos* and *kairos*. *Chronos* (from which we get words like "chronology" and "chronometer") is clock time: minutes, decades, centuries—past, present, and future or *is-ness, was-ness,* and *will be. Kairos,* on the other hand, is time as substance. It is nonsequential and indivisible. Such time is merely *is-ness.* It is God's category of time just as *chronos* is the human category.

Most of us spend our lives serving *chronos;* we run from it and yet surrender to it. Clocks dictate our pace and wall us in with agendas and deadlines. Tick by tock we serve the clock.

At the basis of entering into the depths is God's entreaty to change time zones—to move from *chronos* to *kairos.* In *chronos* the second hand drives life forward, but in *kairos,* time doesn't move. *Kairos,* like God himself, is not static. It ever moves; still it is ageless. *Kairos* never looks back and wishes it had achieved more; with *kairos* there is no back. Therefore, there is no drivenness in *kairos,* which would make us want to do more planning or strive to achieve more.

Kairos is the "is" of being, the "I am" of all existence. As Jesus pointed out to the Pharisees, God did not say to Moses at the burning bush, "I *was* the God of Abraham, the God of Isaac, and the God of Jacob," but "I *am* the God of Abraham, the God of Isaac, and the God of Jacob" (Mark 12:26, emphasis added). God is all present tense. To say he has been or he may be, is to strip all godhood from him and make him a prisoner of mere measured time.

Changing time zones. How is it to be done? Paul says it this way: "Be very careful, then, how you live—not as unwise but as wise, making the most of every opportunity, because the days are evil" (Ephesians 5:15–16). Time belongs to God: "Now listen, you who say, 'Today or tomorrow we will go to this or that city, spend a year there, carry on business and make money.' Why, you do not even know what will happen tomorrow. What is your life? You are a mist that appears for a little while and then vanishes. Instead, you ought to say, 'If it is the Lord's will, we will live and do this or that.' As it is, you boast and brag. All such boasting is evil" (James 4:13–16).

Mythologically *Chronos* was the name of a short Greek god whose legs were muscular and whose heels were winged. He moved fast. He was bald and slick at the back of his head, but scalp-locked in the front. The implication was that if you could grab him as he came toward you, you could take hold of him and make him respond to your wish. But if you waited till he was past you, it was too late, for he was smooth-headed in the back and could not be grabbed once he had passed.

Chronos is like water flowing through a pipe. The pipe could be cut into three parts and water would be equally present in all three. *Kairos,* by contrast, is a grand ocean, and oceans are immeasurable. There, a single drop of rain might fall into the grand sea of measureless time and be absorbed.

In the Christian view of time, our earthly lives are like time in the pipe. Once our frail lives are over, we too join the sea of God's immensity. Our ultimate joining of *kairos* does not mean we will lose our own separateness. We will retain our identity all through eternity, but we will no longer need to chop time into parts. Until that time—the grand *kairos* to which our present *chronos* is headed—we will always be in the hands of God. Even Jesus, during his earthly sojourn, admitted that he did not know the time (*chronos*) of his second coming. William R. White is a masterful storyteller who has a quaint tale that reminds us of the hiddenness of *kairos* time.

> *There once was a king who ruled his small country with justice and love. Unknown to his subjects, the king would put on a disguise in the evenings and roam the streets of the towns in order to understand life from the perspective of the people.*
>
> *One night as he walked in disguise, the king was drawn to a simple cottage. The doors and windows of the house were thrown wide open, and inside a rather robust man was eating and singing with great volume. Knocking on the door, the king inquired, "Is a guest welcome here?"*
>
> *"A guest is a gift from God!" the man shouted. "Please, enter and eat with me."*
>
> *The king sat down and began to eat the very simple but substantial food that rested on the table. The two men talked freely, immediately feeling a bond between them. Finally the king asked, "What is your trade, my friend?"*
>
> *"I am a cobbler," came the enthusiastic reply. "Each day I take my tool kit and wander about town fixing people's shoes. They give me some pennies, and I put them in my pocket. When the day is over, I spend it all to buy my evening meal."*
>
> *"You spend all of your money each day?" the king asked incredulously. "Don't you save for the future? What about tomorrow?"*
>
> *"Tomorrow is in the hands of God, my friend," laughed the cobbler. "He will provide, and I will praise him day by day."*
>
> *Before the king left that evening, he asked if he might return the next night. "You are always welcome, my friend," the cobbler replied warmly.*
>
> *On the way home the king developed a plan to test the simple cobbler. The next morning he issued a proclamation prohibiting the repair of shoes without a permit. When he returned the next evening he found the cobbler eating and drinking and making merry. "What have you done today, dear friend?" the king asked, hiding his surprise.*

"When I heard that our gracious king had issued a proclamation prohibiting the repair of shoes without a permit, I went to the well, drew water, and carried it to the homes of people. They gave me some pennies, I put them in my pocket, and went out and spent it all on this food," the cobbler sang. "Come, eat, there is plenty for all."

"You spent it all?" the king asked. "What if you cannot draw water tomorrow? Then what will you do?"

"Tomorrow is in the hands of God!" the cobbler shouted. "He will provide, and I, his simple servant, will praise him day by day."

The next morning the king decided to test his new friend again. He sent his heralds throughout the land announcing that it was illegal for one person to draw water for another. That evening when he returned to visit the cobbler, he found him eating and drinking and enjoying life as before. "I worried about you this morning when I heard the king's proclamation. What did you do?"

"When I heard our good king's new edict, I went out to chop wood. When I had a bundle, I brought it to town and sold it. People gave me some pennies, I put them in my pocket, and when the workday was over, I spent it all on this food. Let us eat."

"You worry me," the king said. "What if you cannot chop wood tomorrow?"

"Tomorrow, good friend, is in the hands of God. He will provide."

Early the next morning the king's heralds announced that all woodchoppers should report immediately to the palace for service in the king's army. The cobbler-turned woodcutter obediently reported and was trained all day. When evening came, he was given no wages but he was allowed to take his sword home. On the way home, he stopped at a pawnshop where he sold the blade. Then he bought his food, as usual. Returning to his house, he took a piece of wood and carved a wooden blade, attached it to the sword's hilt, and placed it in his sheath.

When the king arrived that evening, the cobbler told him the entire story. "What happens tomorrow if there is a sword inspection?" the king asked.

"Tomorrow is in the hands of God," answered the cobbler calmly. "He will provide."

In the morning the officer in charge of the palace guard took the cobbler by the arm. "You are to act as executioner today. This man has been sentenced to death. Cut off his head."

"I am a gentle man," the cobbler protested. "I have never hurt another man in my life."

"You will do as you are commanded!" The officer shouted.

As they walked to the place of execution, the cobbler's mind was exploding. As the prisoner knelt before him, the cobbler took the hilt of his sword in one hand, raised his other palm to the heavens, and prayed in a loud voice. "Almighty God, you alone can judge the innocent and the guilty. If this prisoner is guilty let my sword be sharp and my arms be strong. If, however, he is innocent, let this sword be made of wood."

Dramatically, the cobbler pulled his sword from the sheath. The people were amazed to see that the sword was made of wood.

The king, who had watched the events from a distance, ran to his friend and revealed his true identity. "From this day forward you will come and live with me. You will eat from my table. I will be the host and you will be the guest. What do you say about that?"

The cobbler smiled from ear to ear. "What I say is, the Lord has provided, and you and I together will praise him day by day."[6]

Changing time zones

To change from *chronos* to *kairos* time is to discover that prayer is not a pry bar given to us to open the future. All watches must be checked at the gates of the throne room. None who wish to commune with God can ever see him while they insist that he tell them exactly where their lives are going. God is to be met and listened to, not sat down and talked to. God alone says when he is through talking and the time of our communion is over.

To run in and out of the presence of royalty or to try to set the limits on our conversation is to forget who we are and to whom we are talking. God is the King. We are fortunate to have an appointment with God. We must lay down all our appointment books; they are not significant in the King's presence.

Throughout history, those who wrote about prayer were not largely people of intercession. They rarely went to God to get him to do things for them. Rather, they were enthralled by a hunger for relationship. They seemed to understand that intercession begs a "to-do" list. Those who serve such lists actually make notes of the time when they asked God for something, and then leave a column in their prayer ledgers to record the date God gives them the answer. It is an odd kind of bookkeeping on the faithfulness of God. It can foster the notion that when the checklist is through, our prayer responsibilities are through. Or that in order to pray longer, our lists will have to get longer.

The purpose of praying devices, such as rosaries, is probably an attempt to extend time in prayer. Most new converts in a zealous attempt to spend more time in prayer have tried to rise early in the morning to pray, only to find their unfocused minds wandering in and out of the throne room. Those with intercessory prayer lists probably do better with the struggle. However, these can become a kind of rosary with a "give me, God" focus that also serves to keep the mind from wandering.

Satan has no desire to see anyone develop an abiding prayer life, so he will always be there, like the sandman in Gethsemane, making sure that none of us stays awake to watch one hour with Christ (Matthew 26:40). I remember those initial attempts. I rose very early, because it is generally agreed that no real prayer warrior ever prayed at two in the afternoon. I wanted so much to be faithful in my praying, so I set the alarm early enough to impress St. Francis. Then I got up and made a long intercessory list—pages and pages. Yet after I had finished asking God for reams of things, very little time had passed. Then I began to pray for everyone I knew by name, in what seemed a pious recitation of the county telephone directory. Still I had prayed only a few minutes. Then as I tried to begin the process all over again, I found myself falling asleep.

This drowsiness that destroyed my prayer intention overcame me largely because I conceived of my prayers as my doing all the talking. If I wasn't talking, I wasn't praying, or so I thought. Fénelon instructed me, "Our conversation with God resembles that with a friend. At first there are a thousand things to be told, and just as many to be asked. After a time, however, these diminish, while the pleasure of being together does not."[7] Once I discovered the pleasure of his presence, I learned that prayer is not a human monologue offered in somber tone with upturned eyes. Prayer is being with God.

The basis of real praying is longing after relationship. Real relationships never keep their eye on the clock.

John Wesley often attributed his power in preaching to prayer that lost itself in such heavy adoration that it never watched the clock. At Fetter Lane on December 31, 1738, John and Charles Wesley, along with George Whitefield, sat up most of the night praying. Wesley wrote of it in his journal: "About 3 o'clock in the morning as we were continuing in prayer, the power of God came mightily upon us so that many cried out for exceeding joy and fell to the ground. As soon as we had recovered a little from the awe and amazement at the presence of his majesty, we broke out with one voice, 'We praise Thee, oh God! We acknowledge Thee to be the Lord!' "[8] Wesley knew that praise of that sort was rapture out of control. It was a kind of rapture that forbids us to keep our eye on the clock because we are lost in the wonder of an all-consuming adoration.

So how do we change from *chronos* to *kairos*? How do we change time zones? Obviously the answer does not lie in the grit of our intention. We cannot grind our teeth to show we are serious. That would be the equivalent of an unoccupied young suitor grinding his teeth till he managed to secure a date. Then, after he had a date, grinding his teeth to be sure it lasted from seven to ten o'clock. It is not possible to strain at *chronos* till we arrive at the unending, unmeasured joy of *kairos*.

In changing time zones, we fall in love with God. Then we fall in love with the wonder of our togetherness with him. Can we force this to happen? No! It happens on its own under the gentle urgings of our need for God. It has its own language—the language of praise. I am not speaking here about a special prayer language or the gift of an unknown tongue. I am speaking of good, intelligible adoration. Praise is the language of spiritual lovers. In the joy of such togetherness, the clock disappears, and our relationship transcends clocks. Then time doesn't matter. Only God.

It is difficult for time-conscious American suburbanites to imagine great worship services in other parts of the world. It is not unusual for these services to go on hour after hour. People who come to Christ in order to know him, grow ever deeper. None complain that prayers and altar times are too long. God is on the earth! The church is alive in his presence! No one wants the glory of his presence to end.

The stewardship of our days

We have been given 86,400 ticks of the second hand each day. And only 8,760 strikes of the hour hand each year. Having been entrusted with this precious commodity called time, we must realize that, once spent, the treasury cannot be replenished. Thus our stewardship of the clock must be defined by four truths.

1. *We are clearly not the owner of our days*. James reminds us that our lives are fleeting. "What is your life? You are a mist that appears for a little while and then vanishes" (James 4:14). Evangelicals have a hymn that never lets the church forget the passing of years is an issue of stewardship: "When the trumpet of the Lord shall sound and time shall be no more. . . ." In other words, whatever work God has given us to do, we are always working against a deadline. We recognize that Jesus is coming again, and at that moment every pendulum will cease to swing and all mainsprings will break. A grand new infinity will amputate the hands of all clocks. Their numbered dials will melt and flow down like Salvador Dali's "Clockscape." Then time, that tyrant that has hurried us through all our lives, will no longer be our

master. Then we will meet Jesus, whose very life taught us that mere dead-lines are a small reason ever to have lived.

2. *We are to be faithful in our management of all those gifts and goods God has given us* (1 Corinthians 4:2). In terms of natural talents, such as communication or music or administration, these natural and spiritual gifts should be used in the church (Ephesians 4:8–12). The material gifts, such as salary, income, and inheritances, are to be spent in such a way that our use of all our money will indicate that we understand that our material possessions were never our own. On the other hand, neither were our days. God gives them to us to be spent like currency drawn from the wallet of our lives.

I have never known anyone who wanted to waste life, but I have known only a few who could make decisions and stick to them until they held the destiny and dream of God.

3. *The ultimate purpose of Christians is to glorify God* (1 Corinthians 6:19–20). The tiniest of gods are to be found in the mirrors of egotists. Yet this little "mirror of the me" is where most of the world's masses worship. They may occasionally peer past the edges of the mirror to see that there is a worthier vastness beyond it. But most continue to adore the little image of themselves, always asking at every turn, "What's in this for me?"

But praise—authentic adoration—smashes such little altars and bids these micro-idolaters to get real. Praising Christ calls out, "Come past yourself and see the heavens opened and hear the seraphim crying, 'Holy, Holy, Holy.' Smash your little mirrors, for past your slavery to the clock lies the vastness of his glory. There you will see the Lord, high and lifted up—there you will praise him and be forever free of your ego."

Augustine said that to glorify God was the very reason we were given life and being. Our management of our days tends to move in two direc-tions. We either use our time to magnify God or to exalt ourselves. Since our days are owned by God, our stewardship must consider every second precious.

Using time without regard to God is indeed to lose it. Whether we run to please the clock or we merely live as captives to its hassled demands, we have failed to understand that hurriedness is no substitute for calcu-lated usefulness.

4. *We are the trustees of our glorious individuality* (1 Timothy 6:20). No two of us are alike in this universe, and we have each been given unique kinds of gifts. There is something given us to do that no one else can do quite like we can. DNA is God's chromosomal stamp that speaks to the individuality of our lives. This glorious and God-imparted uniqueness should put zeal into our stewardship of life. But our self-esteem must never be a springboard into arrogance. On the other hand, we must use the years

so that our management of time may end in eternity with the compliment of Christ, "Well done, good and faithful servant!" (Matthew 25:21).

A final word about the tyranny of the urgent: Most of us live our lives serving some form of Christian institution. This may be a church, a college, a hospital, or a school. In these places, our lives will be mandated by those who impose on us deadlines, forms, corporate agendas—in short, clockly restraints. But the believer who wants an in-depth affair with Christ must not allow time clocks and ledger sheets to destroy that wonderful holy leisure by which we make friends with God. To be a godly disciple means that we transcend the clock, because to be with God mandates that we give our life to become one who waits on God for the sheer pleasure of his company.

The Listening Life

Outside the open window
The morning air is all awash with angels.[1]
—RICHARD WILBUR

One is nearer God's heart in a garden
than anywhere else on earth.[2]
—DOROTHY GURNEY

Western theology, particularly since the Reformation,
has emphasized propositions,
a particular way of knowing truth,
that discounts imagination in favor of reason.[3]
—CHERYL FORBES

While the caged bird sings,
is she caged?
When art flourishes in prison,
was the artist ever in that prison?

Who am I? This or the Other?

Am I one person today and tomorrow another?
Am I both at once, a hypocrite before others,
And before myself a contemptible, woebegone
     weakling?
Or is something within me still, like a beaten army
Fleeing in disorder from victory already achieved?

Who am I? They mock me, these lonely questions
     of mine.
Whoever I am, Thou knowest, O God, I am thine!⁴

—**DIETRICH BONHOEFFER**

CHAPTER FOUR

Aesthetics: Enjoying the Beauty of God

Few have the ability to enjoy the beauty of God. It is not always found in the lives of artists. It is more likely to reside in simple believers whose souls are arrested by the overwhelming awe of a sunrise. A poor Methodist woman wrote in the eighteenth century:

> I do not know when I have had happier times in my soul than when I have been sitting at work with nothing before me but a candle and a white cloth, and hearing no sound but the sound of my own breath, with God in my soul and heaven in my eye. I rejoice in being exactly what I am—a creature capable of loving God and who, as long as God lives, must be happy. I get up and look for a while out of the window and gaze at the moon and stars, the work of an almighty hand. I think of the grandeur of the universe, and then sit down, and think myself one of the happiest beings in it.[5]

God lives freest in those whose eyes are snagged by his artistry.

Christ lies at the center of artistry and devotion. Creativity is one way we respond to the center. There art becomes a form of praise. Cathedrals are the very throne of such praise. Every stained-glass window is some artist's adoration of God set in translucent splendor. Every hymn is a testament that some poet was so in love with Christ that he or she refused to speak of him in mere prose.

Artists spend their art esteeming all that is central in their souls. Christian artists too should exist to glorify the focus of their adoration. Therefore, while all artists praise the wonder of being, Christian artists praise the glory of Christ as well. Oil flows on canvas; marble splits its quarried soul; ink flows on stanzas; and Christ is exalted. It is a pity that evangelicals haven't paid much attention to art, when art has always been the soul of the church. Even worse than ignoring art, some evangelicals have become junk dealers, substituting art for trinkets of our "sloganeered faith." Kathleen Norris laments,

> One finds in Christian gift shops T-shirts depicting Jesus as one of the guys: in a baseball uniform, beneath the slogan, "Jesus is my designated hitter"; holding a guitar, with the words, "Jesus is my Rock and I'm on a Roll." A pastor of my acquaintance recently challenged his congregation to "Be an ad for their Heavenly Dad!" I have never heard him quote anything else that might approach poetry.[6]

The Westminster Confession declares, "The chief duty of man is to glorify God and enjoy him forever." There are many ways to glorify God, yet "Jesus junk" bears no glory and indeed is but the tinseled foolishness of evangelicals who have never seen the Lord high and lifted up. The arts are an important way to glorify God. Still, the church—particularly the evangelical church—has traditionally been a little schizoid over whether or not the arts are a sanctified way to go about praising God. On January 1, 1519, on the eve of the Swiss Reformation, Huldrych Zwingli became the "people's priest" at Grossmünster church in Zurich. Incensed over what he considered to be the "pagan icons" of the church, he swept through the building, ripping down the paintings and casting the religious statues to the floor, shattering them. He purged the church of "images, organs, decorative priestly vestments, and other such hodgepodge of human ordinances."[7] Twelve years later, in 1531, he was slain in a war for religious liberty. By then, however, he had widely established Reformation sentiments against religious art—at least artful idolatry. But a great need in the center of the human soul has rendered his argument unavailing.

Hidden in all that it means to be human is a desire to draw, paint, and sculpt what most represents one's values, what is most precious. Zwingli's dash through the cathedral ended oddly. There stands in Zurich a well-sculpted statue of the old statue-

> God lives freest in those whose eyes are snagged by his artistry.

smasher, Bible in one hand and a sword in the other. If he were alive today, this statue of himself would be too big for him to push over. All of this introduces the problem that has raged for centuries, first among the Reformers and later among evangelicals.

Evangelical sermons and sanctuaries have been void of both art and interest. Our chatty religious spewings have become an idolatry of froth. Our many words produce a dullness of soul, a dead litany of boredom. Artists pass the rattle and wonder that we never tire ourselves with God talk. Thomas Merton said that to say God is love is like saying, "Eat Wheaties"—it holds little interest.[8] Art would solve some of the problem, but art seems to evangelicals to be beside the point.

As evangelicals read the Bible, they agree with Zwingli. "Thou shalt not make unto thee any graven image" (Exodus 20:4 KJV). Did not Aaron set up a golden calf and lead Israel unto sin? Even the brazen serpent of Numbers 21, by 2 Kings 18:4 has become "Nehushtan," an object to worship. Joshua called on Israel to put away the gods of Mesopotamia and Egypt. Habakkuk pointed out that the idols were dumb before their artisans (2:19). What exactly is his point? Idols are dumb and they are powerless as gods. Not every statue, though, is an idol; an idol is not art. Art is the *definition* of our praise—an idol is the *recipient* of it.

I like to paint. I also love Christ. When first I beheld a print of Salvador Dali's "Christ of St. John of the Cross," I was overwhelmed by its majestic message. When I later learned that Dali was an atheist (a fact that most evangelicals don't seem to acknowledge), I was morose. He had painted the painting to deny Christ's divinity, and I had bought the print to celebrate it. What did Dali celebrate? His philosophy only. But I did not worship the picture. I simply allowed the excellence of the canvas to stand for my definition of all that Christ did on the cross.

Art is praise—high praise—and comes in all degrees of excellence. When Jesus touched Handel, he wrote "The Messiah." When he touched Fanny Crosby, she wrote "Blessed Assurance." When he touched a certain country-western star, she wrote "I'm Just a Jesus Cowgirl in the Holy Ghost Corral." Which of these is most valuable? Let us bypass all rating systems. In each case, Jesus was praised by a specific artist in a way that, to that individual, was worship.

Jesus saves. We define his glory. Art is born. Art doesn't become idolatry until our praise of God dies and all that is left is our praise for the art form. Idols are born when artists quit worshiping God and begin singing *te deums* to their own genius. Idols are always ego gods. Artists who will not offer God their self-denial begin to worship only their creative genius. Idols are personal portraits of self-interest. They exist to assure worshipers they can have their way.

But can an artist really live a life of self-denial and paint, write, or sculpt? Don't these activities exist to gratify the painter, writer, and sculptor? Would any poet write a poem for God alone, never willing that anyone else see it? Of course not!

The arts grow from ego—individual selves—and are not content to create works that no one else would ever see. All artists want their art to be public celebrations of their love affair with life. But the Christian artist wants more—he or she wants Jesus to be honored by what is painted, written, or sculpted. The Christian artist lives by an aesthetic focus on those values that are transcendent and enduring. And where people exalt art together, community is born. Indeed, where they exalt Christian art together, the church itself is at worship, and the kingdom of God is born.

> Art doesn't become idolatry until our praise of God dies and all that is left is our praise for the art form.

Why then do most evangelicals and Protestants seem to have such an antipathy toward art? Because art for them seems trivial business in the face of all the almighty things that God commissioned the church to do. The church, after all, exists to call the world to salvation. Why should we take the time to paint, to sculpt, to write, to sing, to play, or to act when the world is in danger of hellfire? I once gave a floral painting to a friend who said, "Did you know that during the time you spent creating this, many people died and went to hell?" I wished I had given the canvas to someone else.

Christ may be carved as a statue that never becomes an idol. The individual who stops to contemplate the statue makes of that statue either art or idol. If the statue turns the worshiper beyond himself, then it is art. If the sttue stops the worshiper, demanding total focus, it is an idol.

The difference may lie in how the worshiper sees God. Idols may intrigue us, and even become objects of idolatry, but they do not cause idolatry; they do not change the worshiper. I have a grandson who came to us as a ten-year-old from Thailand, where he was raised as a Buddhist. We have tried gently to bring him to Christ. One day after a Sunday school lesson, he said to his mother, "Mom, you know why I like Jesus more than Buddha?"

His mother (my daughter), befuddled by the question, answered, "No, why?"

"Well," he said, "Jesus said to the sea, 'Peace, be still,' and it obeyed him. But Buddha . . . well, he don't do nothing but just sit there." In his own way he had paraphrased Habakkuk 2:19: Idols are indeed dumb before their makers.

I object to the artist Doré, who once told one of his students (who was painting a picture of Christ), "You don't love Him or you would have painted Him better."

We who love him paint him as well as our paltry talents permit. We always wish we could paint him better. But we must paint him, we must praise him. We are too much in love with him not to be creative. So we create. If we have not the excellence to do it well, he will understand. We have done it as well as we could, and could we do it better we would at once, for our love for him demands our finest effort.

Children are forever drawing pictures during my sermons. This once haunted me because I felt they were drawing out of boredom. I thought that if I could preach better they would draw less. Still, they often gave me their pictures at the back door following services. One such child drew a picture of me in the pulpit with Jesus hovering over me in midair. Was it good enough for the Louvre? Not the point! She achieved a worldview of Christ as she wanted him to be and I needed him to be.

I rarely ever start to preach but what I see her art, defining my life as I would like it to be. If she loved him, would she have painted him better? I think she did love him and could not possibly have painted him any better. So the angels sang, Christ was praised. Art had spoken with glory!

Art is how we make God beautiful, and his beauty is one of the reasons we worship him. The gospel must always deal with the sinful desperation of humankind. But we must never allow the desperation to destroy our adoration of the God of beauty.

While walking through the Rijksmuseum in Amsterdam, I felt dwarfed by the large Rembrandt canvases. I was awed even more by the story the curator told about the fate of these huge canvases during World War II. When the Dutch realized they were about to be conquered by the Third Reich, they took the unwieldy canvases off their immense stretcher bars and rolled them up like carpets. They sealed them in with wax and began to move such splendid paintings as "Night Watch" and "Dutch Masters" all over Holland in a huge art underground. The canvases were passed from culvert to granary to silo to mill to warehouse, all in an attempt to keep high Dutch culture out of the hands of the Germans.

As my guide at the museum told me this story, I began to realize how unfriendly political crisis is to art. Painting and sculpting rarely flourish in actual times of war. We may paint our war heroes later, but the actual battles preclude art.

Desperation threatens to render culture artless.

But if this is true in a political sense, it is even truer in a spiritual sense. The desperation at the center of Christianity sometimes keeps us from enjoying God. Theology is desperate stuff. The very word "Savior" means "deliverer"—and our preachment is as serious as our Savior's last words: "Go ye into all the world, and preach the gospel to every creature" (Mark 16:15 KJV). Desperation is rarely friendly with the arts.

Nevertheless, the bleakness of our lost condition—once we are redeemed—fades quickly into passionate, joyful exaltation. Now is our discontent swallowed up in bliss so rapturous we must call in the poets and painters to help us praise God. He has acted on our behalf to save us. So Miriam, on the far side of the Red Sea, must sing and play the tambourine, and Paul, in the midst of instructing the Bohemian Corinthians, must stop and sing 1 Corinthians 13.

Only through the influence of the Holy Spirit was Paul able to write such a beautiful, compulsive hymn—the result of an outrageous adoration. How did Mary of Nazareth sing the Magnificat? She never meant to, I suspect. She was overwhelmed with the vast requirements of God. Then the Spirit moved. And the extravagance of her adoration poured forth. Poetry far beyond her young years welled up from deep within her. So it was for John the apostle, writing and recording the doxologies of the Apocalypse. Heaven was all about him. Overwhelming ecstasy took charge, and the Spirit sang the nobility of his coming: "Worthy is the Lamb to receive glory!" Poetry most excellent! Art transcending!

Art presupposes praise and the exaltation of God's beauty as the work of human imagination. But not all evangelicals agree that imagination is good. Some see it as sin. Still, the words "image" and "imagination" come from the same root word, and Genesis insists that we are made in the image of God, the *imago dei*, humankind—as God imagined us to be. Surely imagination is one evidence that we are made in his image. Indeed, we are his art.

Cheryl Forbes says, "No matter what the relationship, imagination is the crucial ingredient for success or failure. Marriage relationships either thrive or die because of imagination, as do relationships between parent and child, co-workers, employer and employees."[9] One wonders why imagination is so little esteemed among evangelicals. Our sense of desperation may keep some of the world from going to hell, but our lack of interest in the arts has certainly made going to heaven less interesting. The arts seem to move around us unnoticed. Except for an explosion of doomsday novels, art's chief geniuses are nearly all secular.

Why? Not because Christians lack the necessary genius. Rather, we have failed to see art as the high channel of praise it really is.

Count Leo Tolstoy was converted after his best fiction was written. Sonya, his wife, lamented the fact that he took his conversion so seriously. He gave himself to publishing religious tracts and quasi-political pieces (in the interest of seeing the poor of Russia treated more equitably). With fervor he set his serfs free. He gave away his wealth because of his newfound love for Christ. He became a cobbler and made his own boots and lived among the poor as a poor man. When he died in 1910, some said Russia had two czars, including one who had risen to the heights of national esteem by living a sacrificial life.

It would seem a beautiful story. But his great years as a novelist were all lived before his conversion. He produced little that was worthy of art after that. And still, when we remember him we do not remember his religious years but his artistic years. It is sad that we must divide his years as an artist from those he spent as a Christian. But then Christians have nearly always esteemed the writing of a tract, even a poorly written one, as time better spent than it would have been writing a great novel.

Christianity has rarely lived at peace with the arts. It is felt among Christians that things pretty lose their place when challenged by things urgent. It is time to face the facts. Art and faith both have a common focus: life. Both artists and preachers are trying to get to the bottom of what life is about and how it is to be lived.

Let art happen! Grace is now! God is now! Praise is now! Art is now!

Well, then, can we not justify the writing of very bad Christian novels as evidence that even bad artists are doing their best? Of course. Their error of extolling bad art lies in the fact that it stops the interest of the beholder at the entry levels of excellence. The same thing happens when a country-western star writes "Drop Kick Me, Jesus, Through the Goalposts of Life." The song may be the best the artist can do, but it may stop the listener forever short of Handel. Ideally, art should help us grow in our hunger for excellence, not stop it at naïve levels of appreciation. Jesus must be praised with the most delicate of poems, the most exalted anthems, the greatest marble forms. Handel yearned not only to praise Christ but to do so from the highest pinnacle of human genius.

It was not on Sunday in church, but on Saturday at the Mecca Theater that I first wondered why Christians had it in for *Snow White* and *The Wizard of Oz*. Why, I wondered, couldn't Christians enjoy *Snow White*? As I earlier pointed out, they also condemned the way I felt about Hopalong Cassidy, Lash LaRue, and Gene Autry. Yet these movies performed in my life what the arts were supposed to perform: an escape from life in Enid, Oklahoma, and the whole of Garfield County, which our pastor said was about to "feel the rod of God." He also said people must quit smoking and dipping snuff or the Apocalypse would come and Jesus would be trampling out the grapes of wrath on the flat, clear prairies around the church. Vanity would be judged first. So, no art! No jewelry! No cosmetics! No gilded crosses on our austere Quakerish buildings.

The worst sin was that there was no greatness of ideas in our church. Our church was small, very small, but just the right size for our worldview. Never in that small church was I made aware of the size of the world in 1946. We never talked much in our little church about the horrors of Auschwitz, Poland, only the damnable "sins of snuffers" in Garfield County. Garfield County in the '40s was nearly sinless, it seems to me, in contrast to Berlin, where the Evil Empire in its lust for power murdered millions of people.

Our church was trapped in such spiritual naïveté, we never spoke of the holocaust. I confess to our shame that it was not deemed important in a world where far too many people still smoked and went to movies. Why would so many people die in faraway Germany and Poland? Who could say? But we secretly believed that some of the Nazis must have dipped some snuff to have angered God the way they did.

We had a little picture of Jesus in our church. He was very handsome, and stretched out in purple, praying on a rock in Gethsemane. I didn't know exactly why he was praying. It seemed to me he was praying for lost souls in Garfield County. There was so much sin in our county—lots of smoking and card-playing.

The little picture was not really dangerous art. Jesus wasn't calling for world reform or anything like that. He was just praying, like we should do, that revival might come to Garfield County. Then people would burn their playing cards and stop buying Skoal.

Art among evangelicals still seems most immature. It somehow lacks grandeur. In the midst of our all-consuming happiness, art seems irrelevant. We are a happy lot. Made giddy by guitars, we sing and sway to Power-Point choruses. We speak of heaven sometimes, but not hell. Without the desperation of eternity, we are too much locked in on what Jesus can do for us in the here and now.

At the Prado, I was stopped by the awe of El Greco's "Trinity." The painting portrays God the Father receiving God the Son back into heaven from the cross, while God the Holy Spirit—like a dove—flutters overhead. The painting is set in heaven, which most artists of that time believed in and celebrated. Today few such images of God flourish. We are too much embroiled in "how-to" Christianity. Talking vegetables tell our children Bible stories on how to be good. Video film series instruct our adults on how to build relationships. Heaven and hell are neither painted nor given much place, having been pressured by all things here-and-now to sit in the corner and twiddle their transcendent thumbs until called for.

The great art that might liberate us is somehow missing. Most evangelicals are forced to admit that if you really want to see great Christian art and architecture you must visit the cathedrals, for great art is neither a focus nor concern among our churches. It is less important than sports ladders and casserole functions. People with small aesthetic sensibilities cannot inspire the most transcendent worship. It is sometimes hard to tell in church if we have real joy or merely a case of high-percussion giggles. Our Christianity lacks a mature beauty. It has no art that will harmonize with our whirlwind of high-calorie praise. We are giddy with glitz, hungry for greatness.

But why should we stop and consider art at all?

For two reasons: First, art locates us in the human condition. Second, art is the way in which artists—and Christians—define themselves.

Art is how we locate ourselves in the human condition

The most popular form of art among evangelicals may be the story. As a child, I liked the stories of my Grandma Kent, whose first name was Sadie and whose middle name was Nebraska. "Why Nebraska?" I once asked her.

"Because I was born in a covered wagon in Nebraska in 1882," she replied. "We were on the way to settle somewhere west when my father turned south to Oklahoma." I loved the simple story. The year 1882 seemed like a long time ago when she told me the story in 1940.

Whenever Grandma would come to northern Oklahoma, I wanted to hear that story again. My grandmother would once more tell me how she happened to become Sadie *Nebraska* Kent. Grandma died in 1951, and my mother and I would often talk about our prairie heritage. Momma, who had been born in Indian territory herself, never tired of telling of our Indian territory heritage. In time I grew up and returned to Nebraska to be a pastor. My own children were born in the state that was part of Grandmother's name. Then they too wanted to hear the stories of our clan, the Millers.

Eugene Peterson says that we tell stories "to locate ourselves in the human condition."[10] I agree! Stories really do locate us in the human condition, and stories bind our families to each other and to the earth. Sadie Nebraska Kent helped me, as a child, to find my place in time.

The first art of primitive nations is usually the sagas of clans. Most early nations were but single families grown large. At the beginning of the tale of Rome is the story of the quarreling twins Romulus and Remus. At the beginning of the tale of the Anasazi Indian culture of southwest North

America is the emergence of life from the spirit-womb of Sipapu. At the beginning of the Hebrew nation is the call of one who may have been a moon worshiper—Abram of Ur, with Sarai his wife. Sometimes these stories by which a people remember their origins are mythical, sometimes they are archetypal. But true or contrived, such stories become the mortar of culture.

Stories, like rolling snowballs, grow with the telling.

It is the accretions that intrigue us. Accretions interweave legend and history so that we cannot tell them apart. Did Davy Crockett really kill a bear when he was only three? Although I have seen vicious, unruly children in Baptist nurseries, I doubt it.

All communities like stories that are told for their community and for whom the various elements of the stories all fit. So while the anthem of the church may appear to be "Tell Me the Old, Old Story," middle-class suburbanites are really singing, "Tell me the old, old, middle-class suburbanite story"!

We must allow the power of our stories to widen rather than narrow our province. Global stories can blow provinces apart. What are we doing by picking a suburban Christ for suburbanites? Or a grenade-throwing Christ for liberation theologians? We are but giving ourselves a particular kind of walled focus. We are reducing the great gospel story by ghetto-izing it. Why do we do this? Because ghettos are comfortable, manageable. We can live securely by keeping our version of our Christ-stories parochial. Making Christ in our image avoids the painful work of being conformed to his. Nothing is so wonderful as naïveté, but it's hard to be as naïve as one would like. Actually it is dishonest to protect our understanding of the world by hiding behind our naïveté.

The story of Christ and the telling of it is the central art of Christianity. It is art universal. It is the art that drives the entire mission enterprise. Christ ultimately hung upon a cross because his stories globalized in a province. Christ is to be praised because he was able to take the not-too-cosmopolitan disciples and say, "Your comfortable Galilee is gone now—you are all stewards of the world. Therefore, go! With all of your limitations,

> It is sometimes hard to tell in church if we have real joy or merely a case of high-percussion giggles. Our Christianity lacks a mature beauty. It has no art that will harmonize with our whirlwind of high-calorie praise. We are giddy with glitz, hungry for greatness.

speaking with a dull Aramaic in the crisp Latin ghettos of *Roma*, tell the global truths—they are the ones that matter." I do like thinking of Peter, the Galilean fisherman who found himself so captive to so great a story that he died two thousand miles from the sea where a common carpenter taught him he was responsible for the world.

Jesus' story interacts with our own and presto! the personal testimony is born. But where these stories intersect, our littleness must be set aside. The art form itself makes us bigger.

The problem is that God almost always asks of us tasks that scare us to death. We want to remain in our province. Jesus has ordered us into all the world. Like those Aramaic disciples, we are thrust into multiculture and into megaculture.

When we are thrown into such a huge puzzle, how do we keep on preaching our simple saving truth in a complex world? Our world seems too large for our tiny Christ to really change. Then Jesus begins to fill our cosmic vacuum, and suddenly he is larger, and we too are larger, and God is altogether able. Then we will paint him in grand strokes, on huge canvases, and hear his glory sung at the Lincoln Center. Still, even the large concert hall is too small to hold the vastness of our praise. Christ too is larger, ever larger. Finally, he becomes so awesome that the best poet fears to lift his little pen to write with ordinary ink the greatness of God.

Such a vast, indescribable God is fodder to the artist's imagination. The Louvre and the Prado are filled with biblical art begging us to see this great, miraculous God. But Paul (in Romans 1:20ff.) points out that those artists who reject God begin to create idols in their own image. Four-footed beasts, creeping things, and mostly their own bodies, laments the apostle. Idols do not come from large hearts and great imaginations. Idols are the work of starved imaginations. These exalt the basest of appetites, never having known the allurement of all that is exalted and holy. Golden calves are the glitzy work of those Aarons who have not traversed the upper slopes of Sinai. Those who have, meet that God who is the only food that can appease their hunger.

The tragedy of the Christian arts in the golden-calf era of church is that we have lost the "global sense" of making God beautiful. And yet there is at the same time a flourishing of peculiar art in this culture of Narcissus. Such art is too immature to challenge the viewer to a beautiful proclamation.

And the church? Can it not paint or compose a lofty anthem to his glory? Perhaps, but it is too much a community center and too little a conservatory. Our current culture of inductive togetherness often glorifies nothing larger than suburban soccer and casserole dinners. The global village of McLuhan is not just for the white, suburban, user-friendly, three-guitar ooze. Further, our art has lost much of its sense of glorious transcendence. In fact, everything is so here-and-now that there and forever is considered irrelevant.

William Carey once took his world map out of his shop where he made shoes. Then he stopped making shoes and acted out his life in a more global way. Carey knew the truth—stories often are nothing more than neo-provincialism we use to protect ourselves. The idea of being salt and light in the development of our insipid art has been traded for a congenial dullness. "Jesus," we must pray, "brush the mediocrity of our praise away. Let us praise you with higher, global art."

Art is the way every Christian defines himself

Ayn Rand once said that art is man defining himself. Once in New Mexico, I backpacked a huge canvas down to a particular mountain waterfall that I had always thought was lovely. It was my intention to paint it. My wife was backpacking with me and had taken a couple of novels along to read while I painted. I began to paint a monochromatic study in blue and had determined to call it "Blue Waterfall." I pictured it in my mind as being very beautiful. The longer I painted, however, the more I despised my work. Finally, I decided that I would not have that horrible picture in my house or in any art show, for that matter. I signed it Kris Kringle and left it leaning against a tree, hoping it would not embarrass Santa Claus. It was a form of litterbugging, I know. It may still be there or some lowbrow may have backpacked it out to civilization, and it may be on some nameless American wall embarrassing guests. I only know that I was not willing for it to stand in any way for my own self-definition.

Are Christians willing to make God beautiful and to let their creative impulses become the art that defines them? Perhaps the art form at which we need to become adept is the telling of the gospel story. Our story is most crucial when it touches heaven with its desire to define God. Billy Budd defines Herman Melville. King Arthur defines primitive England. Miles Standish or Paul Revere are our American stories. Jubilation T. Cornpone is the rallying saga of Dogpatch patriotism. I'm not sure Eva Perón is the defining story of Argentina for Argentines, but every time I hear "Don't Cry for Me, Argentina," I want to cry for Argentina, and since I hardly ever want to cry for Bolivia or Paraguay, I suspect the art of

> Are Christians willing to make God beautiful and to let their creative impulses become the art that defines them?

Andrew Lloyd Webber's story defines the nation for me. Stories and story-tellers define whole areas of our lives.

I must confess that I miss those colorful fire-and-brimstone evangelists of my childhood. I was terrified by their sermons, but at least I was interested in them. And they could hardly be labeled bland or user-friendly. Now the most adrenaline I see in worship has more to do with the announcement of the next super rally. After that, the plodding, nontranscendent sermon begins its low exegetical drone of how to do this or that. I've had it with preachers with Binaca on their breath telling me how to be nice! Oh, Lord. Use us to create an artful gospel.

We are the bland who no longer cry out to make God beautiful. All sense of Apocalypse has disappeared from our user-friendly sermons. Isak Dinesen confessed she liked being awakened with really important news. One morning Kamante, her house help, woke her with the threat, "Msabu, I think you had better get up—I think God is coming." Ms. Dinesen wrote:

> From the door-windows I now saw a strange phenomenon. There was a big grass-fire going on out in the hills, and the grass burning all the way from the hilltop to the plain. . . . I stood for some time and looked at it, with Kamante watching by my side, then I began to explain the thing to him . . . for I thought that he had been terribly frightened. But the explanation did not seem to make much impression. . . . "Well, yes," he said, "it may be so. But I thought that you had better get up, in case it was God coming.[11]

Apocalypse focuses on the best art—God is indeed coming.

Conclusion

I have a lecture called "Christ and Prometheus." In Greek legend Prometheus was the man who stole fire from the gods of Olympus and gave it to humankind. Fire is the very symbol of art, and Prometheus the symbol of the artist. For his punishment, Zeus chained Prometheus to a rock where a huge vulture came each morning and ripped out his liver. His liver grew back during the day only to be ripped out once again the next morning.

What artist has not known the visceral amputation that art demands? Art and faith both know this agony. What servant of Christ does not hunger to give the Lord more and more of the inner will? What poet does not feel the viscera ripped out because of the need to honor Jesus with greater art than the artist can produce? Still, we want to praise him better than we do—with far better art. We want to make all things pertaining to God more beautiful than we have the ability to do.

True praise of any sort is so passionate it leaves us weak when it is over.

We love him too much to stop painting him, and yet we loathe ourselves because our small talents can't make him very real. But on we strive! We must do what we can—all we can—anything less would be blasphemy.

John Donne, after failing to get many important jobs in England, at last decided that homiletics was better than unemployment and took a job preaching. He was, however, quite good at it and became dean of St. Paul's Cathedral in 1621. During his next eight years of ministry, three violent waves of bubonic plague swept through London, the last one killing more than forty thousand souls. In 1623 John Donne thought that he himself had contracted the plague; in fact, his doctors were quite certain that he had. He faced his quarantine with courage, and yet because he rejected the justice of God he felt that God had isolated him with the disease and left him to die.

An invalid in bed, he wondered if the bells he heard rang for his own impending death, which his friends all knew must come. He confessed to a restless night of sleep in which he heard friends and physicians whispering in the next room, and took this as an added surety that he was dying. Again the bells . . . was he dying? Were the bells announcing his death? Or were they for someone else? Thus he wrote the now-famous lines:

> No man is an island, entire of itself: Every man is a piece of the continent, a part of the main. . . . Any man's death diminishes me, because I am involved in mankind; and therefore never send to know for whom the bell tolls, it tolls for thee.[12]

John Donne's sonnet is really not so important as John Donne's story. He did not have the plague and so he went back to preaching, which some would suggest has always run the plague a close second. But art is what really matters; it is the soul of praise. I once set these words in my journal:

> Come let us lift Christ up
> in sculpture and stanza,
> in calligraphy and bronze,
> on canvas and on lithograph,
> in glass and in marble,
> in molten gold or glacial ice,

on banners and pennants,
He is God!
Let us say so—let the works of our hands
lift up this Christ in every church.

May our art say, "Attend our God. He could never be boring. He redeems and gives life. He is forever beautiful."

Those who follow God with faithful reverence and who burn in His love with worthy devotion are not fearfully distracted from the glory of supernal beatitude by any impulse of injustice.[1]

—HILDEGARD OF BINGEN

Because Francis and his companions were called by God and chosen to bear in their hearts and in their works, and to preach with their tongues the Cross of Christ, they seemed—and were—men crucified. . . . Because they preferred to bear shame and insults for the love of Christ over the honors of the world and the respect and praise of men . . . and so they went through the world as pilgrims and strangers, bearing nothing with them save Christ Crucified.[2]

—UGOLINO

A brother asked one of the elders, "There are two brothers, of whom one remains praying in his cell, fasting six days at a time and doing great penance. The other one takes care of the sick. Which one's work is more pleasing to God?" The elder replied, "If that brother who fasts six days at a time hanged himself up by the nose, he could not match the one who takes care of the sick."[3]

—THE DESERT FATHERS

Practice loving worthy things every day, till all you love is worthy of your practice.

Do not ask whether something is enjoyable. Ask if it is worthy of love. Ask if you should depend upon it.

How will you find an answer? Is there an infallible argument or a verse of Scripture that will enlighten you? Can you think of any example or axiom or sacrament that will prepare you to discover these things?

You can tell if something is made of gold. But how can you know if it is worth your love, or if you can depend upon it? Being gold is one thing, but being worthy of love is something else.

Desiring exquisite goods and clothing is like painting firewood. These things are consumables. Clothes keep you warm regardless of their color. Common foods will satisfy your hunger. Desire what is right for you.[4]

—GUIGO I

"God, what have you got against me?"

It was during those days that I began to see that if I looked around me for mere material evidences in this world that God loved me, I would often be disappointed. God's love for us is demonstrated in what he's done for us eternally, not what he does for us in the material moment!

Love and her sister Grace are the greatest of all the attributes of God. God in innumerable ways is always offering his love for us. Why should we ever doubt that we are loved? "When you are sad," said St. Bonaventure, "look at the crucifix and see how much you are loved."[10] He went on to elaborate how Calvary is a demonstration of God's love: "O good Jesus, O sweetest Jesus, it was all simply to show us how much you loved us. You spent yourself on our behalf. The grief, the tears, the spittle, the sneers, the cruelty and insults, the blows, the nails, the blood, all you suffered for us. And I weep."[11]

Francis de Sales called Calvary *the Hill of Lovers*.[12] Yet love that only exists and is content never to learn is at last a bit of gooey sentiment. We are called to love, but we are also called to study and to read so that our adoration can become informed. Again, Bonaventure counsels us: "To grow in the things of the Spirit, love must go hand in hand with learning. At a certain point, one must leave study behind while the heart runs ahead with joy to the gift that is God himself. Speculation is not sufficient with devotion."[13] But then, on the other hand, devotion can never be informed without the discipline of study.

On one occasion the church where I was pastor was burglarized. What assessments should we make of this? The Methodist worship center wasn't burglarized. Did God love Methodists more? How shall I reason away this problem? If I make any application on the material side of logic, do I make the wrong assessments about God's love? The real point of Psalm 37:4 is that we are to trust in the Lord and delight ourselves in the Giver and not his gifts. If you receive from God, and you think only of what God has given you, you have missed the point of God's bounty. If the little things like oxygen and oatmeal remind you of God's goodness and turn your anthems Godward, then the material blessings of God will have a noble purpose.

A young man came to me not too long ago. "I gave my fiancée an engagement ring," he said. "She took the ring, then broke our engagement. Now she won't give it back!"

"Thank God for that!" I said to him.

"How can I thank God? It cost everything I had to get that ring!" he said.

"But look at it this way: thank God she's gone. You don't have to worry anymore. She esteemed the gift more than the giver. Who would want to be married to a person with such misplaced esteem?"

Still, it was hard for him to thank God. When we receive material gifts from God, we must war against our craving for having more and more. But material gifts seen as gifts of God are pitiful allurements that keep us serving him only to get more stuff. The psalmist had it right. It is important to "delight ourselves in the Lord." Material things are not lasting delights. When God doesn't give us what we want when we want it, we should remember that Job laid down one inviolable principle (Job 13:15 KJV): "Though he slay me, yet will I trust in him." Here is a word from a man who had lost everything, who had no family, no money, no house, nothing left! Job had met the "What if?" dragon and lost. "Go on trusting the Lord," says Habakkuk, "even when material things don't seem to be there."

Though the fig tree does not bud
and there are no grapes on the vines,
though the olive crop fails
and the fields produce no food,
though there are no sheep in the pen,
and no cattle in the stalls,
yet I will rejoice in the Lord,
I will be joyful in God my Savior.
   —HABAKKUK 3:17–18

The great lovers of God are those who love Jesus not because of what he's done for them but because he died for them. This is the worthiest sign of God's bounty.

Spirituality is most mature when we arrive at a sense of abundance that is not related to the material. The great sin against God is to live in such a way that others don't see us as wealthy in the spiritual sense. To live a shabby spiritual life makes others see our God as a poor Father. I don't have to have material things to have contentment. Paul wrote from a jail cell, "I have learned, in whatsoever state I am, therewith to be content." Was Paul happy? How could he be otherwise? He was in love with the Giver.

It is a sin to make God look bad! When we do not project that we are living in the midst of great abundance as we follow Christ, we reduce God to poverty! We had a woman in our first church who went around town in the shabbiest clothes possible. Everyone in our town knew she went to our church. They also knew that she was wealthy. She was incredibly stingy as well. When she went to the little country store that was the center of our town, she would ask the grocer if he could break off a small stalk of celery so she wouldn't have to buy the whole bunch. Grudgingly, he did! But everyone in town knew she was a carpetbag Baptist. She made other Baptists envy the Methodists for their self-esteem. Her celery-stalk witness caused the angels to lower their eyes in embarrassment and the Almighty to say, "Tsk, tsk!"

The sin of the Prodigal Son was in his making his father look bad. Anyone who saw him down in the pig trough eating husks of corn with the pigs would surely have believed his father didn't care much for him. They would never have guessed that somewhere on a plaster wall was an expensive portrait of the filthy young swineherd himself. Yet the prodigal was loved by a father who doted on his lost son day and night. The Scriptures say, "He came to himself." He got up and went to his father, who was delighted to have him home.

Learn the glory of the psalm: "Delight yourself in the Lord." Act like it's a great pleasure to know God! Act like your Father is rich! Delight yourself in his abundance. Psalm 37:11 says, "The meek shall inherit the earth; and shall delight themselves in the abundance of peace" (KJV). Abundance is never measured in those things we claim to have.

I have thought much about the thieves who vandalized our church. Do you know what a thief says with his life? It's an admission of poverty: "I am not complete. If only I can steal this, I will be more so!" Contentment does not come from what is grabbed or nabbed. Contentment is not from what you grasp, but from what grasps you. Tatian wrote that we will never know real peace until we quit renouncing our worldly goods and simply renounce the bustle. "Die to the world by renouncing the madness of its stir and bustle. Live for God by throwing off the old man in you through recognition of his nature."[14] If we could only see that our completeness is measured by the Greek word *teleios*. Often in the New Testament *teleios* means God is in the process of "finishing" us. When we stand in his presence, the meek will not only inherit the earth but they will also be clothed in his abundance.

> Contentment is not from what you grasp, but from what grasps you.

The abundance that sponsors joy

In the meantime, knowing what our inheritance is, we ought to decide that we will make our Father look rich. I learned this truth in the oddest of ways. Once when I was very young I took my children to Las Vegas, and we were staying in a little hotel there. The hotel manager had put a roll of nickels on my breakfast tray to stick in his slot machines. So I decided I would try out one of those machines. (I regret the fact that I gambled. Never before, never since, never again. Just that once!) My children by my side, I walked up to a one-armed bandit and put a nickel in it! I pulled the handle down two or three times, and nothing happened. But toward the last of my roll of nickels, the lights went off! The buzzers buzzed! The bells rang! In all this flashing fantasy and ecstasy, nickels belched profusely out of the machine! Wow!

But the greatest thing that happened that day was seeing the faces of my children. In all the lights and the whirring and the buzzing, their faces lit up. There was more money than they could ever imagine. They had certainly never seen so much.

Seeing their delight, I scooped one little pile of nickels together and gave them to Timothy. Then I scooped another pile together and gave them to Melanie.

After leaving Las Vegas, we went on to Glorieta. When we got there, the abundance of my haul suddenly made me nervous. We sat down at a table with a bunch of preachers. One of them happened to ask, "Where have you been on vacation?"

"Las Vegas," I said nonchalantly.

"I certainly hope you didn't play those machines!" one said.

My four-year-old son, Timothy, piped up, "Oh, yeah! Daddy's really good. He got all this money and he gave it to me and Melanie."

Be sure your sins will find you out. But there was something in my son's confession that still marks with joy my one fling at the slot machines. I saw in my son's little face the look of one who had just had "the big payoff." In his young mind he had been enfranchised by some glorious providential abundance.

And I still stand by in wonderment, like a child sometimes, when I see Christ change people's misery to joy! All things seem glorious and God seems good and the Father seems big. Before such joy, the world must stand in awe at the wonder of God. We are to "delight ourselves in the Lord!" What a wondrous calling.

Ignatius of Antioch has laid bare for us the glory of being in love with Jesus. In reality, we have only one calling: to love Jesus. If we are true to that calling, we shall exalt him to the highest place in our adoration. There is only one Physician, cried Ignatius; his name is Jesus. And who is he?

Very flesh, yet Spirit too:
Uncreated, and yet born;
God and man in one agreed,
Very life-in-death indeed.
Fruit of God and Mary's seed;
At once impassible and torn
By pain and suffering here below;
Jesus Christ, whom as our Lord we know.[15]

Jesus is our calling, our life, our all in all. His adoration is the only worthy passion of our lives.

My mother taught me many things. My graduation from high school was a big moment in her life. She had decided that I would have a store-bought suit for the occasion. I was seventeen years old! We didn't have much money, but we went to S & Q Clothiers, which was known to be the most chic, expensive men's store in Garfield County. As we walked in, she said, "Son, pick out a suit."

"Momma, this is too expensive."

"No," she said. "You're graduating from high school! Pick out a suit!"

I picked out one that I liked. It was thirty-seven dollars!

I protested again, "Momma, this is too much!"

"No," she said. "It's your graduation."

I picked out a shirt that needed cuff links, and it was seven dollars. Then I picked out a set of cuff links for three-fifty. When we left the register, my mother had spent almost fifty dollars.

"This is too much!"

"No, this is just right!" she said. "You're graduating from high school."

When I walked across the stage that glorious day, two hearts resonated as one.

A little woman who had scrubbed floors to see her kids celebrated with the best, celebrated the best she knew how in that moment.

As I walked across the stage that day, I was thankful to Mother not because she'd given me a gift but because I was loved by a woman whose character was to be a giver. She was proud of me too. Because I was wearing a suit she'd paid for? No. Because our hearts resonated in delight at the abundance we'd found in each other's love.

"Trust in the Lord and do good. Delight yourself in him, and he will bring it to pass." Make your Father in heaven look good. Live rich in spiritual abundance, and crave peace! Tell all who see their Mercedes as an evidence of God's love that there are chariots of fire. Christ is such a treasure that mere billionaires are to be pitied. Trust in the Lord and make him the desire of your heart, and you shall readily have all you desire.

The soul of man left to its own natural level,
is a potentially lucid crystal left in darkness.
It is perfect in its own nature,
but it lacks something it can only receive from the outside
and above itself.
But when the light shines in it,
it becomes in a manner transformed into light
and seems to lose its nature in the splendor of a higher nature,
the nature of the light that is in it.[1]

—**THOMAS MERTON**

Praise to you, Spirit of Fire!
To you who sound the Timbrel and the Lyre,
Your music sets our minds ablaze!
The strength of our souls
awaits your coming
in the tent of meeting.[2]

—**HILDEGARD OF BINGEN**

We praise thee, O God,
For the son of thy love.
For Jesus who died,
And is now gone above.[3]

—**WILLIAM P. MACKAY**

Stand before the majesty of God. Let its splendor silence you. But when the hush passes, so must your silence. Then it is time for anthems and glad hallelujahs.

I am bending my knee
In the eye of the Father who created me,
In the eye of the Son who purchased me,
In the eye of the Spirit who cleansed me,
In friendship and affection.[4]

A CELTIC TUNE BEFORE PRAYER
AND THE HYMN SUNG AT DAYBREAK

CHAPTER SIX

Expression: The Place of Praise

The presence of God: he picked me up
and swung me like a bell. I saw the trees
on fire, I rang a hundred prayers of praise.[5]

Madeleine L'Engle once said that praise is a cry like a bell. When a bell cries, its bronze voice wakes the world around it to the wonder of God. Yet bells make a single tone, and the volume of their concentration holds no place for any variation or hypocrisy. Praise to Christ only counts when the mind is undistracted. "Do not have Jesus on your lips and the world in your hearts," said Ignatius of Antioch.[6]

There is a lightness of being in our celebration of all things eternal. Praise is the wonderful sponsor of this elevated state of heart. Praise is not a food we provide for God, it is the bread of God that nourishes us—it is the liberation of our souls. How often have we gone to church tired and worn? Perhaps we have even had to talk ourselves into going. But once there, we begin to praise God. We don't feel at all like praising, and it could hardly be called spontaneous. But we participate, and gradually our exaltation begins to wash us with a warm vibrancy—a new will to be.

In spite of all we have said about art, it is at these moments the Christ of high art is passed by in favor of the Christ of things intimate. When I am needy, show me no Rubens or Rembrandts—no golden-robed Christ at home in the halls of the Louvre. Give me a burlapped carpenter who will sit with me until my quiet emptiness is filled by his all-sufficient power.

Then I stand a chance of living my life with meaning. Then will I enjoy being in this world, for I will possess a new zest for life.

And why a new will to be? Because few of us achieve this lightness of being while we are in charge of our world. We come to know the inner Christ more effectively when under duress. Our weaknesses are always a better door for his entry into our lives than our confident control. Throughout time Christians have best achieved this state of being when they were suffering and someone else was in charge. They sang from the flaming stakes of their martyrdoms. Paul and Silas, beaten half-senseless by the authorities of the local courts, praised God from a Philippian jail. When Christians sing under stress, their songs lighten their suffering.

Dietrich Bonhoeffer wrote, "The older the world grows, the more heated becomes the conflict between Christ and Antichrist, and the more thorough the efforts of the world to get rid of Christians."[7]

Jesus is the epicenter of the only reality that has ever mattered. And it is this sense of having touched the great and living Son of God that causes us to celebrate his significant reality. For before we knew Christ, we had neither reality nor significance. When Malcolm Muggeridge "rediscovered Christ," he also found himself unable to break free of the joy of compulsive praise.

Muggeridge realized that Jesus' time in the wilderness was climaxed by the *bath qol*, or the "loud voice," crying, "This is my beloved Son!" The words thrilled Jesus. They were God's *out loud* affirmation—the clear answer to Jesus—as to who he was and why he had come. Speaking of Jesus, Muggeridge said,

> *He made for Capernaum by the Sea of Galilee. I see him a solitary figure, trudging along until the sight of the lake opened up before him; with no luggage, no money, no prospects, no plans; only those magnificent words still ringing in his ears, and a sense of exaltation at the knowledge that he had indeed chosen to give them a new, tremendous reality.*[8]

There is no question of the greatness of Jesus. But our best praise springs from something else. Thanksgiving is the magnificent motive behind it. Vitality in living comes from a vital faith and a vital faith results in celebration. Praise grows from gratitude.

Grateful for all that God has done for us, we feel a subtle stirring in the center of our hearts. Our thanksgiving erupts from those inner feelings of gratitude to God and his Son. Jesus is the focus of it all. Jesus came as the Immanuel God to live in human form, to sample our condition. He came as the Lamb slain before the foundation of the world to taste death for us. He came as the ever-living One to triumph over death so that we too become conquerors in life.

Surely the response of all who love him must be *Hallelujah!* Such praise is the very definition of our need to give him our thanksgiving. Those who will not praise him may bypass the Christ of the inner altar and know only the Christ of theologians. Theologians do us the very great favor of doctrine and definition, but they can never create our worship. Adoration is born when people touch Christ and find they must rhapsodize their gratitude in thanksgiving.

Magnifying his calling as a minister, Francis de Sales wrote, "Live joyful and courageous. . . . For truly if he is with me, I care not where I go. . . . Ah! My God! How I am indebted to this Savior, who loves us, and how would I, once for all, press and glue him to my breast."[9]

Oswald Chambers reminds us that praise is not the only purpose of God, or Jesus would have gone on to heaven from the Mount of Transfiguration.[10] God has a purpose for our lives, and our first obligation is obedience to his will. When we have honored God with our obedience, our concord with the Father will prompt such praise that the glory of it will shatter all our practical propriety.

> Those who will not praise him may bypass the Christ of the inner altar and know only the Christ of theologians.

The Welsh have a word, *gorfoleddu*, which means "ecstatic rejoicing." It refers to exuberance, praise of God for all his creative work.

Lord, be it thine,
Unfaltering praise of mine!
And, O pure prince! Make clear my way
To serve and pray at thy sole shrine!
Lord, be it thine,
Unfaltering praise of mine!
O father of souls that long,
Take this my song and make it thine![11]

Taking our songs and giving them a mind settles our ecstasy with reflection. Ecstasy that thinks is always the best way to praise God.

Still, the agony and ecstasy of our faith are found between our seeking Christ and our finding him. The seeking is the agony of the Christian pilgrimage and the finding is the voice of our spontaneous praise.

The loss of transcendence, the loss of praise

There is a wonderful relationship between ecstasy and transcendence. I have noticed that when worshipers get ecstatic they seem to be looking up and out, past the ceiling of the church. No wonder Catherine of Siena wrote, "Ecstasy is meant to increase our desire for heaven: the power of love in ecstasy causes the body to cry out with all its force for the perfect union of heaven."[12]

Augustine's masterful *Civitas Dei* set Babylon and Jerusalem in juxtaposition. The cities of men and the "City of God" had many differences. Babylon, the secular city, was temporal, and satisfied to be so. But Jerusalem was the transcendent city, and the soul's deepest longings for that city were transcendent.

By the end of the industrial age, the idea of spiritual transcendence had begun to erode. Many theologians believe that the doctrine of hell had begun to disappear by the end of the nineteenth century. But there can be little doubt that it was missing from sermons—even evangelical sermons—by the end of the twentieth. Secularized testimonies dominated popular theology. The truth they carried weakened from one of robust transcendence to a practical "how-to" relevance. Unfortunately, the "how-to" sermon created a "how-to" Christianity that is the last dull step of a church that has lost its voice of praise.

Secular culture is stripping the church of the last otherworldly shreds of a vanishing transcendence. Christianity once championed true reality. That reality caused us to break into a praise that was beyond physical living and therefore gilded with rich purpose. It all ended at one time in heaven or hell. Yet mere here-and-now living seems to have become the church's unworthy pursuit. Eric Hoffer once said that technology was humankind banging on the gates of Eden. It is a braggy technology that always wants to recreate that paradise from which the human race was banned. When the pie gets good enough in the here and now, pie-in-the-sky seems pointless.

> Unfortunately, the "how-to" sermon created a "how-to" Christianity that is the last dull step of a church that has lost its voice of praise.

Rapture needs to reclaim its place in the dull, procedural life of the church. We need to awaken our souls once again. I weary of the repetitive choruses or Christian mantras of our worship that serve to numb our minds rather than to engage them. I weary of sermons that celebrate where we are spiritually rather than enticing us to new vistas of thought and usefulness.

Do we really want to be told in parentheses where to clap in a praise chorus?

Do we really need numbers and x's to tell us how long we are to stay on the same few words of our lost adoration? It's time to quit making God seem dull because our insipid thanksgivings are. Donald McCullough writes that our worship "has been replaced by the yawn of familiarity. The consuming fire has been domesticated into a candle flame, adding a bit of religious atmosphere, perhaps, but no heat, no blinding light, no power for purification."[13]

We have sadly arrived at such decadent praise that God seems old hat and boring. Goethe's *Prometheus* was one who, having discovered his own creative nature, no longer was impressed with God. "Here I sit," said Prometheus to God, "shaping man after my image, a race that is like me, to suffer, to weep, to rejoice and be glad, and like myself to have no regard for you."

Postmodern humanity seems sadly liberated from all need for the dying Christ. Humankind has saved itself by purchasing its redemption at Auschwitz, Mai Lai, the Killing Fields, Bosnia, Stalingrad. The horror of all this cultural inhumanity provides a humanist theology in which man has become his own savior. Too many cultural and secular heroes die as martyrs celebrating their own glory and never acknowledging their need for Christ or his transcendence. The resulting weakness is an anthropocentric humanism that speaks of human goodwill, brotherhood, and right-thinking. These stories are noble, but never empowered by eternal mysteries. Therefore, they can inspire no real praise.

The twentieth century has been dubbed the American Century. It is generally reported to have been the "Yankee Triumph" of those noble men and women who pursued a new world dream. Over and over it seems that a humanist applause is offered to those who built America. America was built largely by people of faith, but it's the people who are extolled. God is rarely mentioned.

In some ways, contemporary evangelical worship forms exist as ill-at-ease narratives written in a premodern world. But after the romping march of technology, Western culture became less dependent on books to provide distraction, entertainment, and information. Television is here! The manner in which we ingest information has changed. We will never again be content merely to learn something. Now all we learn must come to us gilded with interest. After 1950 the epitome of this interest—whether for learning or leisure—would have to be expressed in the word "entertainment."

Neil Postman's insightful book *Amusing Ourselves to Death*, points out that the information age could be defined as the entertainment age. This generation, more than all that preceded it, demands that the information it accepts must come in an entertaining way. Even if the information is substantive or desperately important, it will not be accepted unless it entertains those it instructs. There is hardly a praise team or drama club that does not now feel this demand placed upon the church by the entertainment industry.

But since the information age is also the entertainment age, the church has often abandoned her servant-calling to welcome new troops of chancel actors. The chief goal of the church in the past may have been to praise, but in these recent days it seems to be called merely to keep attention. The church enters the queue with the rest of the pitchmen, having traded her glorious doxologies for "There's no business like show business. . . ."

We seem to believe we have to do this. It's fundamental to our user-friendly methodology. Everyone knows that glitz is how you attract new members. Smiling and softball are sometimes the main recruiting agents for the suburban church.

There is a better way. Instead of trying to program our way to success, why not let the seeking suburbanites catch us seeking inner substance. Instead of trying to smile or laugh them into the kingdom, why don't we let these secular seekers walk in and catch us at the act of real worship? Let them see that rare and hard-to-forget phenomenon of believers honestly, joyously praising God. As they experience this wonderful mystery, they might want to come back for the sheer glory of seeing it again.

> Praise is our gift to the Almighty. For all he has given us, gratitude is the only gift we can give back. His sacrifice was the cross, our sacrifice is the sacrifice of praise.

Does praise seem too small a reason to have been born? I remember a certain convert who asked me what Christians were going to be doing in what seemed to him to be the long and boring work of living forever. When I told him we were going to spend eternity glorifying God, I could see he was disappointed with the business of heaven. But I knew in my heart that praise seemed eternally boring to him because he had never really learned to do it.

There is a substance to rapture—to find it is wonder—to dwell in the near light of God is joy unspeakable and full of glory. Praise is our gift to the Almighty. For all he has given us, gratitude is the only gift we can give back. His sacrifice was the cross, our sacrifice is the sacrifice of praise.

Our praise should begin each day and end each day. We should fall asleep at night in the warm euphoria that says God is great and greatly to be praised. Ancient Celts had a hymn of praise for the pillow and rune of praise for the sunrise. As they lay down for their evening rest, they faced the great Trinity, whom they called the *Three of my love*. Then they praised him on the mattress of the coming night.

I am lying down to-night as beseems
In the fellowship of Christ, Son of the Virgin golden,
In the fellowship of the gracious Father of glory,
In the fellowship of the Spirit of powerful aid.

I am lying down to-night with God,
And God to-night will lie down with me,
I will not lie down to-night with sin, nor shall
Sin or sin's shadow lie down with me.

I am lying down to-night with the Holy Spirit,
And the Holy Spirit this night will lie down with me,
I will lie down this night with the Three of my love,
And the Three of my love will lie down with me.[14]

Conclusion

Perhaps one final thing needs to be said: The praise of the faithful not only celebrates Jesus but it also celebrates his agenda with the world. We are not only praising Jesus but all that he wants to make of any who would call him Lord. Thérèse of Lisieux wrote,

> *I should like to enlighten souls. I should like to wander through this world, and raising your glorious cross in pagan lands. But it would not be enough to have only one field of mission work. I should not be satisfied until I had preached the Gospel in every quarter of the globe even in the remotest islands.*[15]

Praise will always be the buoyant evidence that the church is telling the truth—a rapturous truth that cannot be done without.

Our praise says, "I have seen my crucified Lord. My inwardness has met with Easter triumph." Who could ever keep silent when they have stood inside the tomb and known its glorious emptiness? Who would not testify in joy, "Pardon me! I must break forth with song before the rocks grow tongues."

Petitioning is stating what we have at heart,
naming the desire we express in prayer and supplication.
In the Lord's Prayer there are seven petitions
besides prayer proper.[1]

—MARTIN LUTHER

Dear Brothers,
You should never doubt your prayer, thinking that it might
have been in vain, for I tell you truly that before you have
uttered the words, the prayer is recorded already in heaven.[2]

—BERNARD OF CLAIRVAUX

The Retreat Master, in one of his conferences,
told us a long story of a man who had
once come to Gethsemane,
and who had not been able to make up his mind
to become a monk,
and had fought and prayed about it for days.
Finally, went the story, he had made the Stations of the Cross,
and at the final station had prayed fervently
to be allowed the grace of dying in the order.

"You know," said the Retreat Master,
"They say that no petition you ask at the fourteenth
station is ever refused."
In any case, the man finished his prayer,
went back to his room, and in an hour or so collapsed,
and they had just time to receive his request
for admission to the order when he died.
He lies buried in the monks' cemetery
in the oblate's habit.[3]

—THOMAS MERTON

Build a prayer circle;
no, be a prayer circle.
Close the circumference of your
fellowship with God around your own
enduring testimony.

Imagine a circle traced on the ground, and in its
center a tree sprouting with a shoot grafted into its
side. The tree finds its nourishment in the soil within
the expanse of the circle, but uprooted from the soil it
would die fruitless. So think of the soul as a tree
made for love and living only by love. Indeed without
this divine love, which is true and perfect charity,
death would be her fruit instead of life. The circle in
which this tree's root, the soul's love, must grow is
true knowledge of herself, knowledge that is joined to
me, who like the circle have neither beginning nor
end. You can go round and round within the circle,
finding neither end nor beginning, yet never leaving
the circle. This knowledge of yourself and of me
within yourself, is grounded in the soil of true
humility, which is as great as the expanse of the
circle. . . . But if your knowledge of yourself were
isolated from me there would be no full circle at all.
Instead, there would be a beginning in self-
knowledge, but apart from me it would end in
confusion.[4]

—CATHERINE OF SIENA

CHAPTER SEVEN

Centering: Avoiding Sterile Fascination With God

Centering is the act of focus in our relationship with God. It is desperately important work. Richard Lovelace wrote, "Many have so light an apprehension of God's holiness and of the extent and guilt of their sin that consciously they see little need for justification."[5]

I believe this deplorable state can only be reversed as Christians begin to see that this is the church's number-one work. It is from this divine conversation that the church secures both the knowledge of her assignment and the power to accomplish it. But even more, this conversation is the only evidence that the church has not gone into business for herself by following some separate agenda from God's.

Prayer is a discipline that begins with the willful act of centering. Centering is the life-consuming art of approaching God where he is to be found—in the center of our souls. When the church sees the glory of her calling, Pentecost inhabits every day. Each moment will birth some trumpet in our moral wilderness. The old hymn will be the new one: "Jesus shall reign where'er the sun does its successive journeys run; His kingdom spread from shore to shore till moons shall wax and wane no more."[6]

"Centering" is a word that walks around the more faddish church clichés when people are speaking of the deeper life. Still, the pursuit of the deeper life with all its attendant clichés is sometimes a way to busy ourselves and thus avoid our need to minister. There is little use of learning to use the "buzzwords" of the inner life movement while we ignore the pain and hurt in the "outer world" around us. Conversely, to only minister and never crave God's presence is to do "the best we can" with our completely powerless lives.

When we really pray, Emilie Griffin says, we approach the dividing line between worlds:

> There is a moment between intending to pray and actually praying that is as dark and silent as any moment in our lives. It is the split second between thinking about prayer and really praying. For some of us, this split second may last for decades. It seems, then, that the greatest obstacle to prayer is the simple matter of beginning, the simple exertion of the will, the starting, the acting, the doing.[7]

Starting to pray, we undoubtedly confess the noise and haste that prevent prayer. Where we volunteer for silence, and put our personal agendas to sleep, God comes to us, and his coming instructs our lives. Indeed, his coming becomes our life.

For a good many evangelicals, the deeper life movement began in the '70s. Those Christians became so fascinated with God they had no time for serving him. There is no human merit in worship, however ardent. Worshipers must lay aside their hallelujahs and put on the apron of service. It is ever a temptation to want to see Jesus transfigured for the mere joy of building tabernacles, settling down on the mount, and becoming useless ascetics.

How honest Shakespeare was when he counseled us in *Two Gentlemen of Verona*, "He does not love who does not show his love." What human husband would be worth his salt if all he did was buy valentines? Real love must declare itself. It must turn from its romantic fits and practice its valentines.

When my son was a boy, I used to say to him, "Son, take out the trash!" And he did! That's how we show our love and respect—by being obedient. But suppose at my command, he had replied, "Oh, Dad, you are so beautiful and resplendent, I want to just sit here and contemplate your wisdom and power."

"But son," I might insist, "rehearsing my attributes are of little real use, if you will not obey me. Take out the trash!"

"But Father, the trash? No, rather let me consider your nobility—you are the ground from which I sprung. When I think of how you conceived me, I consider my own immaturity and I desire to praise you all the more."

"Son, take out the trash."

The illustration has gone on long enough to speak of the danger of lifting our hands in adoration when we ought to be using them to minister. We must first obey, then we can praise. God is never honored by our sterile fascination with him. The whole idea of centering is not to talk about the inner life but actually to move into it. Centering is more than conversation fodder for our next Bible study. It is a serious call—an ardent methodology—for moving into a profound relationship. It is the serious pursuit of God.

I see three distinct dangers in the pursuit of God. The first danger is that the pursuit of holiness breeds its own inner addiction. Since we have already examined this pitfall, there remains little to say except this: Always look for evidences that you are loving the wrong things. If you love the quiet retreat that you create in order to meet God, you may not love God at all but only the pointless discipline of quietness. If you love the literature of the saints more than you desire to emulate their holiness, you are too much the captive of your reading and not the servant of your Lord. If you seem to talk a lot about prayer but pray very little, you are seeking only a godly mystique and not God himself.

> The whole idea of centering is not to talk about the inner life but actually to move into it.

The worst thing about all of this is that you will appear even to yourself to pursue God while in reality you will have abandoned him. The lesson of Matthew 25 is that we can call Jesus "Lord" and never minister unto the "least of these his children." Remember the Judge's final condemnation to those on the left:

> *Depart from me, ye cursed, into everlasting fire, prepared for the*
> *devil and his angels: For I was an hungered, and ye gave me no*
> *meat: I was thirsty, and ye gave me no drink: I was a stranger, and*
> *ye took me not in: naked, and ye clothed me not: sick, and in*
> *prison, and ye visited me not.*
> —MATTHEW 25:41–43 KJV

I've always wondered if some of those who are going off into everlasting fire were not part of deeper life groups who busied themselves with the empty rhetoric of holiness, fascinated with God while sitting on their hands.

The second danger is that the pursuit of holiness can breed an otherworldly aloofness. The key fault in such a mystique is that ordinary, here-and-now people will see themselves as the spiritually elite. The "hypergodly" make ordinary sinners hyper-nervous. Saints may be safely read about, but living with them is sometimes edgy work. The spiritually needy would rather die in their need than risk being around these lofty ones whose "holy" lifestyles seem to condemn all else.

The third danger is that the pursuit of holiness can lure us into the Sweet Little Jesus Syndrome. I've never much cared for those paintings of Jesus where his halo is over-large or his thorn-crowned bleeding heart is painted on the outside of his toga. This Christ of gooey pietism is sometimes a cul-de-sac in the deeper life moment. Yet here is where many a lover of God has wound up. There is a valid romance in the gospel, but we want to be sure that our centering disciplines do not dump us into some religious sugar bin.

Jesus is the sinless Son of God, but he did not come to be a pet for our personal piety. He came on a rugged, double-fisted agenda to save humankind. He should always be adored within the context of his saving mission. Further, he should always be celebrated within the framework of his calling on our lives. If we start adoring him romantically and with no ministry content, he will lose the office of his saving work and become an idol for the sweet and shallow and superstitious.

Prayer: the path to the center

Praying is the art of focusing on God and allowing our focus to conduct us into his presence. Our private prayers need not be intelligible. In fact, when we are lost in prayer the likelihood is that we will be overcome by an urgent wordlessness. The Spirit "helps us in our weakness. We do not know what we ought to pray for, but the Spirit himself intercedes for us with groans that words cannot express" (Romans 8:26). The more earnestly we pray, the more our prayers transcend mere words. In fact, St. Anthony of the Desert wrote, "It is not a perfect prayer if one is conscious of oneself or understands one's prayer."[8]

So how then do we begin this agony of relationship we call prayer? We center! But what is centering? Centering is a function of our wanting to get in touch with God, and prayer is the avenue of this art. First of all, prayer invents the self.

"Self" is a word when merely spoken in the presence of other Christians rings immodest. Why? Because "self" is that original four-letter word that had Adam grasping after the sticky sweet forbidden fruit. Even before Adam fell before the towering "self" of evil, Satan was an archangel saying, "I will raise my throne above the stars."

But in the beginning self was the soul—the *nephesh*; DNA individualism before its time. God made Adam and breathed into him the breath of life and Adam became a living being. There at man's first fashioning, he was a unique, "un-Xerox-able" self. In Eden "self" was a noble word that said God created perfectly and individually. Adam and Eve were strident, unlike, yet both were strongly like their Maker. Each of them was a breath of never-has-been and never-will-be-ever-again. They were selves, souls, *nepheshim*—powerfully free never to be controlled—always their own.

Then they ate, and decayed as half-eaten fruit does. In the eating, the illicit "self" remained unique but it became grasping, serving its appetite, eating what it would. In this one act, temperance became a glutton. Love died. Hoarding scorned the insufficiency of merely having and became a craven materialist.

Humility is the fastest way to the center of the self. Clement of Rome wrote to the Corinthians in the first century, "My brothers, do let us have a little humility; let us forget our self assertion and braggadocio and stupid quarreling, and do what the Bible tells us instead."[9] The Bible is the charter of our self-abandonment.

But our own self-abandonment is most easily accomplished when we see what Jesus did with his. Bernard of Clairvaux confessed, "My Jesus, when I see you so humiliated before me, how can I wish to be esteemed and honored at all?"[10] Alphonsus Liguori wrote, "My beloved Jesus, I kiss the cords that bind thee, for they have freed me from those eternal chains that I deserved."[11] Humility may be such a simple feat as kissing the cords of Christ. For they hold such glory that they must have staggered heaven when the flog fell on the flesh of Christ. No wonder Alphonsus wept, "God, taken and bound! What could the angels have said at seeing their King with his hands bound?"[12] Surely in the humility of Christ we can find the way to the center of our own souls and fall down before the humble Savior and weep till we are humble ourselves.

By the time Jesus came into the world, the word "self" had to be reckoned with and put in its place. Self had to be denied, said Jesus. "Crucified," said Paul. Why? Because the self served only self. The ego thrives best in soil so shallow it can give no root to the purposes of God.

Centering is the merger of two "selves"—ours and his. Centering is union with Christ. It is not a union that eradicates either self but one that heightens both. The sacred individuality of each is made greater in this union. We are never more ourselves and God is never more God than when we enter into union with Christ.

> Centering is union with Christ. It is not a union that eradicates either self but one that heightens both.

Scripture never encourages us to *negate* ourselves (become nonexistent). Scripture teaches us to *deny* ourselves, to abdicate our passions and get rid of those things that claim our lives with petty self-interest. Prayer is a dialogue of lovers. But if we negate ourselves to the point that we are not there, God cannot talk to us at all. Centering is the abandonment of the grasping aspects of selfhood. Catherine of Siena heard God say to her, "You are the one who is not, and I am He who is!"[13] But Catherine knew that it was only her own individuality that made any conversation with God possible.

All of our lives we cry out to be in constant communion with God. But is it really possible to pray without ceasing as the apostle advocates (1 Thessalonians 5:17)? Yes. Of course, the trick is to make your way into the cell of your inward self and be content to live there.[14] This may be one of the great distinguishing marks between Christian meditation and Eastern systems. In yogic systems, one is always trying to stamp out the self. But in Christian meditation, we recognize the self as the basis of our being in God. We should not magnify it too much, but we should thrill that in being human we are permitted this wonderful definition of our significance. We exist. We cannot cease to be. After all, God has wondrous things to say to us.

Thus self-denial, not self-negation, is the path to obedience. Gregory the Great is worth hearing when he says, "To renounce what one has is a minor thing; to renounce what one is, that is asking a lot."[15] To what degree would God ask us not to be what we are? He would never ask us to stop being. He does ask us to stop being self-serving, stop being an addict to any of our passions, stop being shallow in our adoration, but never to stop being.

He wants no self to cease, only to cease being selfish. He can best communicate this to us when we are silent and in "the center" of our relationship with him. We are not the center of our centering, he is. We do not invite the holy God to come to our small center of being. We move into him. Sitting in the middle of God we are more than we would be anywhere on the periphery of our own spirituality.

It is at the center that we know who we are and who is the source of our worth. Inwardness is the fount of our relationship with Christ. Inwardness means that all we hold dear we carry within us. William Law wrote of this treasure:

> The pearl of eternity is the church or temple of God within you,
> the consecrated place of divine worship, where alone you can
> worship God in spirit and in truth. When once you are well
> grounded in this inward worship, you will have learned to
> live unto God above time and place. For every day will be
> Sunday to you, and wherever you go, you will have a priest,
> a church, and an altar along with you.[16]

The God who is within us remains contingent with the God who is beyond us.

One further word must be made clear: God is omnipresent throughout the universe. He is cosmic and vast. We could never get to his center in any geographical sense. He who has no boundaries has no virtual center. I would not ever want to be guilty of encouraging some other cultic scheme of meditation. I don't even want to be guilty of trying to offer a Christian litany that we might use to arrive at centering. I don't want to offer one more push-pull-click-click scheme for becoming instantly godly.

What I am suggesting is the adoption of a principle that will take our walk with Christ to a new level. Most people spend so little time in prayer that they have never derived any spiritual growth from it. They have lived and always will live on the periphery of God's empowering. They need to move on into that kind of prayer life that actually furnishes them with a dynamic God view. The freedom of the venture can never erase the discipline of it.

Thomas More says there are three passions: love, hate, and prayer.[17] Self to some degree is the result of our passions, and any of these three will create the self. We have all known people who loved till they actually epitomized love. The same is true of hate. Then once in some forever, there is a person who prays so much that it seems his or her very life becomes a prayer. But centering prayers are prayers that surpass our infrequent, intermittent petitions. Centering prayers are never those hurried sky-lobs that we toss upward amid our hassled to-and-fro-ings. Such giddy intercession assumes that God replies to our low-caliber asking by shooting back at us his high-caliber answers. Centering prayers are interested in relationship, not answers. Centering prayer wants God alone—all of God—more of God—only God.

Our salvation is secure in the process of being born again, but our sense of discovery has only barely begun when we are converted. From that point on, the self is every morning waking to some new wonder. The self is ever being created or it is dying.

> Centering prayer wants God alone—all of God—more of God— only God.

The creation of the self occurs gradually throughout life. I haven't much patience with people who believe that God is so trivial that all that he is may be encountered in one single moment of being saved. Rather, his glory must come gradually into our fragile, finite lives or we would die overwhelmed by his immensity.

I know of a certain motivational speaker who says we invent ourselves. It is not far from the truth, but it is not the best truth. We can to some extent invent ourselves in the encounter of good books and great ideas. But such self-invention will not be worth as much as when we move into God.

Then as we center we will discover within ourselves a widening knowledge that God's revelation is being born in us.

Listening to our conversation with God

I suspect that the difference between a person of seasoned prayer and one of smaller prayer experience is the amount of time they spend talking rather than listening. I used to be troubled by Paul's admonition to "pray without ceasing." I now believe this is only possible to those who have had enough significant prayer experience to make the listening prayer the largest part of their praying. Those whose prayers are unending monologues make themselves a giant mouth while making God a small ear. The best prayers are dialogues of rapport. Presence is being "with God." It is neither talking nor listening. It is abiding in the presence of God. Rapport treasures oneness so much it will not make of prayer two modes—one mode of talking and one of listening.

Lovers may sit on a long strand of beach so mesmerized by surf and sky that any speech would trivialize their togetherness, not enhance it. Rapport is conversation too. Silent togetherness is better conversation than chatty concord.

Centering becomes the point of greatest rapport between God and his needy children. This conversation goes on and on, and when neither partner

> Those whose prayers are unending monologues make themselves a giant mouth while making God a small ear.

speaks, both are welded into a powerful listening mode. It is then that our wordless conversation reaches its apex. Then we walk throughout the chores or leisure of our day with a sense of rightness. It is then that our settled prayer life sanctifies the world through which we move. Those who love lingering at the center of their relationship with God live more automatically in union with Christ between their times of centering. St. Anthony said that the best prayer comes when we no longer remember we are praying.[18]

There are many liturgical approaches that attempt to keep this conversation going. I am generally not impressed with prayer litanies. Why are not rosaries or schemes for continual prayer more appealing? Because memorized repetitions at last become a dull place to live. Repetitions can keep the mind from completely shutting down, which is their purpose. But they can also leave the mind numb—not fertile with imagination. Thumb-worn litanies are not the most direct way to move into the vital center.

These memorized prayer devices produce a "formalized silence," but ultimately these artificial schemes for centering may not help much. Thomas Merton reminds us that these contrived silences can cease to "become a form of grace and actually become a part of the problem" that blocks the silence.[19]

The onrush of mystery

At the depths of centered praying lies a hush. Gabby godliness is crushed to silence by majesty. In the majesty of final things there was silence in heaven for half an hour (Revelation 8:1). One of the theologians used the term *mysterium tremendum* (Latin for "overwhelming mystery"). In the Holy of Holies we are forbidden trivial speech because the air is too heavy with unfathomable glory.

Remember how Peter sinned by getting chatty at the transfiguration? The hush of things exalted usually leads the naïve to fill the silence with words. It is because they live such surface lives that deeper things leave them nervous and talkative. We are to be like John that first Easter. Seeing the empty tomb, he was forbidden speech by the awe of majesty. This quiet encounter is the most direct route to the center.

> The hush of things exalted usually leads the naïve to fill the silence with words.

What is the power of this mystery? Proximity to God. What is the final step of proximity? The center. Drawing near to the epicenter of power will cause the prudent to shut up. Only the foolish and shallow will speak. This is good. Why? Because listening is a part of centering. God's omniscience informs us that we all know too little and talk too much. How wise the old proverb that says God gave us two ears and one mouth so we would listen twice as much as we speak.

Prayer at its highest is the meeting of a holy God with his child who hungers for holiness. It is a cleansed child, aching for clean values before the God who fills the hungering disciple in the first place. Prayer is good souls asking for good things—and the best of all good things is Jesus himself.

We have already said that prayer may be the communion of silent concord. It needs no words at all to express the togetherness of God and ourselves. Prayer is dialogue, and God would rather have us be overly chatty in his presence than never to enter his presence at all. What Father would want to exclude a child just because the boy talked a lot? But maturity will teach the prudent child that the Father is all-knowing. Still, while he should never silence the overwhelming flow of his immature conversation, it would be good to work at slowing it down.

This is ever a weakness in our intercession. It comes into the throne room so bent on its own agenda that it would rather recite its requests than listen to see if God really has anything to say. But again, when I watch the practitioners of emotional evangelism on television, it is clear that they are caught up in a kind of rapture I would not deny them. Yet it is mostly emotional extravagance, and a tad athletic.

Herein lies the great paradox of the centered life. Quiet listening is the mode of our entering in, but sometimes life at the center grows overwhelming with the pressure of praise. The *mysterium tremendum* begins to swell to the point of rupture. Its vastness becomes too great for its human container. Then it forbids the believer to sit still, and the quiet that at first ushers the believer into the center of God gives way to praise that bursts into his glorification.

But it is important that we do not glorify the manner of our centering. It is easy to be more proud of the technique than the union we want it to achieve. Some who journal to get to the center of God soon are working harder at having a beautiful journal than they are at focusing on God. Some who use notebooks are prouder of their pencil work than their time with God.

> In our official religious lives, there are structures which block awareness and which substitute gestures as a kind of symbolic front or image. They're like a prescription or recipe you write out: get up a two o'clock in the morning, never write home, never eat meat, never miss choir. . . . Before we can become prophetic, we have to be authentic human beings who can exist outside a structure, who can create their own existence. . . .[20]

Centering must not be conceived of as a glazed trance. At the center we are likely to be touched with the all but unbearable voltage of God's presence. It is so volatile at times it may erupt in uncontainable praise. There is always something potentially kinetic in our walk with God. Like those disciples in Acts 2, we cannot possibly sit quietly navel-gazing. Our inwardness becomes too small to hold his immensity. Like our Pentecostal forefathers in the wake of the visitation of God's glory, we must make a place for the wind and fire. And when the tongues of flame come, our quiet propriety may be shattered by a spontaneous, got-to-get-it-out-in-the-open praise. We are much like the old spiritual that says,

"Sit down, Brother!"
"I can't sit down!"

"Sit down, Brother!"
"I can't sit down!"
"Sit down, Brother!"
"I can't sit down.
I just got to heaven
and I can't sit down!"

Thomas More said we know we are deep in his presence when we notice in ourselves a holy foolishness.[21] If religious cable television seems holy foolishness, maybe we should ask ourselves what is it that a cold, forbidding sanctity has ever done for this world? Give me rather holy foolishness. The church would do better to risk a little wildfire than to go on forever celebrating its icy theologies.

The apprehension of beauty

If God is anything at all he must be beautiful! Consider the splendor of this omnipresent adjective in our hymns: "Something beautiful, something good"; "Beautiful Savior, Ruler of all nations"; "He makes all things beautiful in his time"; "In the beauty of the lilies, Christ was born across the sea."

God should wear the adjective "beautiful."

Pretty may happen, but *beauty* is pretty plus discipline.

We are never born beautiful; we acquire those characteristics as the gift of our discipline. Not everyone can be pretty (the most automatic and useless of virtues), but the discipline of prayer makes all who discipline themselves truly beautiful. Beauty is often the channel of our centering.

I know a cerebral-palsied missionary. "Handsome" has never been his adjective, but "beauty" is his word. To be sure, he would decry the notion. He has been oddly twisted and crippled all his life, but his walk with God owns a glassy smooth stride.

One of my favorite Tolstoyan pieces is *Memoirs of a Lunatic*. In this testimony, Count Tolstoy begins the tale of his pilgrimage into faith by starting with his childhood. His nurse had been telling him at bedtime stories about the Savior, always ending with the crucifixion and then abruptly blowing out the candle and telling him to go to sleep. But young Tolstoy found sleep impossible after her reading. He begged her to stay, relight the candle, and tell him why the evil people crucified Jesus when he had done nothing wrong. Insensitively, Mitinka (the nurse) told him not to ask questions and abruptly shut the door and left him in the dark. But it was in the darkness of his mind where the gloom was the thickest. He confessed as a child to crying and to knocking his head against the wall in his frustration to know all there was to know of Jesus' sacrifice. His madness continued for years. He lived with the insatiable need to know the crucified Christ in the splendor of his own redemption. But all was hidden from him, until years later in a moment of centering insight. There as a young man he received Communion, and at once he found the living Lord of the church. His dull, unanswered questions met the reply of joyous faith. In a moment his life was transformed into a thing of beauty.

Thomas More wrote in *Utopia* that what we cannot turn into good we must make as little bad as we can.[22] I would further add that what we cannot keep from being downright ugly, we in the presence of God must make beautiful. Francis de Sales said that as far as possible we should make our devotion to God attractive.[23] It is perhaps for this reason that we should not carry our holy foolishness too far. Jumping pews may indicate our vitality in Christ but not necessary our sanity. And Paul, in commenting on the use of ecstatic tongues in public, said, "If therefore the whole church be come together into one place, and all speak with tongues, and there come in those that are unlearned, or unbelievers, will they not say that ye are mad?" (1 Corinthians 14:23 KJV).

Catherine of Siena says it best for me: "Am I always, because of my faithlessness, to shut the gates against Divine Providence. . . . Lord, unmake me and break my hardness of heart, that I be not a tool which spoils your work."[24] I want to be free in Christ to feel God, but religious exhibition, like any other kind, mottles the face of God for those who do not believe. We are under obligation to make our devotion to God so attractive that all who see us lost in the wonder of our praise might desire to know the object of our praise.

Letting the arts define ourselves

Once again I am back at the arts and the part they play in centering. The arts as prayer have so often brought me to a point of self-definition. But for the moment let me say that I rarely encounter great religious art without feeling an odd force settle over me. I felt this hush of incomparable prayer when first I saw Grünwald's "Crucifixion." The immensity of Rembrandt's "Dutch Masters" also affected me. The crucifixion scene in *Ben Hur* and Spock's self-sacrifice in *The Wrath of Khan* were equally moving. In short, when the arts cause me to see Jesus, I experience the hush of truth. In this hush I center in on union with Christ.

But let us not forget that this *mysterium tremendum* also exists in Scripture. The first time I heard Hebrews 12 read, it woke my soul only to the bowing of my head and crying, "Jesus is Lord." I felt the same way upon reading Job or Psalm 19 or Isaiah 6. Such Scripture reading holds a kind of vitality that is a conduit to the center.

The hush of mystery probably lies at a level of prayers inaccessible to those whose love of church softball defines them. It is unfortunate that modern churchmanship has lifted the Baal of religious entrepreneurs so high that the lesser god has eclipsed the greater. If the modern church has a flaw, it may be that it has supplanted the high love of all things holy for the mere affection of suburban success. Ordinary religion is often so dull a habit it causes its supporters to bow at low altars with a silence that trembles before majesty.

Art is something—anything—crafted or made. What we make does tell us who we are. *Romeo and Juliet* defines Shakespeare. *Carmen* defines Bizet. First Corinthians 13 defines the apostle Paul.

James says that every good and every perfect gift comes down from the Father above. Are not the arts evidences of such a faithful, giving God? When these artistic gifts reach their zenith, God is glorified by the sheer excellence of those gifts that spell out the individuality and the greatness of the human self. But that which defines us also helps us to center on our union with Christ.

Let me illustrate.

The Three Tenors (Carreras, Domingo, and Pavarotti) have been thrilling audiences around the world for the past decade. The first time I heard them sing was on a cassette tape on the stereo system of my car. I was so struck by the power of their talent, I pulled my car to the side of the road, listened, glorified God, and ultimately wept. Why? Were they singing my favorite old hymn? No! In fact, they were not even singing a religious song. But their unique giftedness was from God, spoke of God, and caused me to glorify God. I had to praise God because none of the three is completely responsible for his talent. God has given each the defining talent that has come to define for the world who he is. In this case, the arts had ushered me into the heavenlies, and praise was my response. From my praise, I found myself propelled to the center. At the center, I sat in listening glory while God magnified himself in my life. The arts are often the door through which pass our best magnificats.

I believe it is impossible to plumb the depths of God without struggling to know the arts and those artists who define his power. So often I have people ask me what I do when the arts descend into themes and expressions that are at best *ungodly* (profane, obscene) and at worst anti-God (blasphemous or idolatrous). It is the conversation that rules the situation. No moral person can sit through a vile film with a family member without becoming embarrassed or humiliated. We may actually have to take our children out of such movies because we feel the values of the film do not approach the lofty morality of the Bible.

So if we take our godly rapport into an unholy artistic expression, we have no choice but to leave. If we do not, the rapport will be broken anyway because God will leave. Any conscious involvement of our lives in an unholy art form breaks the conversation as the prayer without ceasing stops because of our spiritual infidelity.

Further, centering becomes impossible to those who indulge themselves in the illicit. The sex drive, once awakened in an illicit situation, serves only the self. There is a kind of mysticism in sex, and in most ways sex has always been the prominent mysticism of the human race. But when illicit, it is only a mystery that serves the primal appetite; its mysticism is totally selfish in following its drive to fulfillment. No nobility is born in it. Illicit sex not only forbids serving others, it is so much in business for itself it cannot even stop to think of others.

Jesus' counsel to be in the world must mean that we walk through a sinful, fallen culture, giving it hope only because we remain in conversation with God as we walk through it. We are writing our best self-definitions, one centered prayer at a time. Our hunger for the inmost God thrills us and defines us. Such prayers tell us throughout our lives who we are. Such prayers at last leave us undistinguishable from Christ himself.

It is a common matter of observation that,
so far as we can judge here below,
the better is the life of the preacher,
the greater is the fruit he bears,
however undistinguished his life may be,
however small his rhetoric and
however ordinary his instruction.
For it is the warmth that comes from the
living spirit that clings;
whereas the other kind of preacher
will produce very little profit,
however sublime be his style and his instruction.[1]

—JOHN OF THE CROSS

O Friend, do you not have a sense
of the way to the Father?
Then you must press your spirit to bow daily before God,
and wait for breathings to you from his spirit.[2]

—ISAAC PENINGTON

Earth holds a strange power
That ties us to dust,
So that ponderous souls are
Bound to her crust.
But the wind whispers tales
Of a force in the sky,
And those with the courage to scorn dust
Can fly.[3]

—CALVIN MILLER

The Savior rises up from Olivet,
Dissolves in sky and then is gone.
The Spirit comes, but how?
Listen what the wind speaks
to the flame.

Love raged.

And then the trebled Spirit mystery
Was one. Yet love begun in open space
Would swell in joy till one was three—
His factor of infinity in grace.

And never shall his Terra understand
This cosmic riddle born ahead of men;
How Spirit can become a sinewed hand
And then a cosmic Spirit once again.

Never was it one but always three.
Never was it three but always one.
Claiming boldly it would always be—
Yet crying out it never had begun.

Let men embrace the rain. Come, Wind, blow free
And stir the warm, sweet breeze!
Dream, dreamless men!
Our empty youths come filled with prophecy.
Our grunts now Spirit-washed are words again.[4]

—CALVIN MILLER

CHAPTER EIGHT

Mysticism: Keeping in Touch With the Holy Spirit

"Mystical" is that wonderful word we apply to things that have ultimate meaning but elude our understanding. Concerning life in the spirit, the mystical reality is a place where two roads converge. The roads are *mystery* and *passion*. Where mystery and passion meet, we are often bewildered but never bored. At this juncture we sometimes crave God most but understand him least. Here we experience the warm and exotic wonder that tells us we are in the vicinity of God. God will not—no, rather, God cannot declare himself to us. He is too vast; we are too finite. Our brains weigh only three pounds. How in such light and little human organs could the great God ever fully describe himself? The most powerful passion focuses upon things too wonderful to be understood. Such great truths cut across our lives and we feel the weight of glory.

And where is the center of this passion—this elation that gives the mystery its power? The Spirit of God furnishes all authentic vitality—gives life—creates meaning. His symbols are flame and wind. There's nothing that can ignite our living like the blessed Spirit of Acts 2. Fire and tornado are his twin eagles. The spirit swoops into our dull, flat earthbound philosophies as a wind-driven fire that keeps our faith from being dead and our confessions from being lifeless.

When Elizabeth of Hungary became a saint in the thirteenth century, she achieved her own day—November 17—on the sanctoral calendar of the Catholic Church. I am not much given to saint days, but I have long been intrigued by Elizabeth. Born in 1207, she grew to marriage age and fell "madly in love" with Louis IV, the Landgrave of Thuringia. There are many apocryphal tales of her life, but all of them converge on her love affair with Louis IV. She loved him so much that she fell into passionate lust whenever she saw him. Their marriage only increased her ardor. She would hold his hand and weep for the delicious joy of being his wife and lover. When Louis decided to go on a crusade, she was crushed. She begged him not to go off to the crusades, but he went anyway and to her dismay was killed.

Following his death, she raved her way in grief through the castle hallways. Only gradually did the pain of her loneliness begin to be filled with the substance of the Savior. Gradually her human passions turned toward Jesus. The romance she knew with Louis took a spiritual direction. She gave herself to Christ. The glory of God settled on her life. She belonged to Jesus. She gave her resources to the poor, depleting her husband's treasury with her charity to the poor of Hungary.

Her passion for Christ and her addiction to the glory of God brought the mystery of godliness and her uncontainable love together. Wherever these things meet, Jesus walks again upon the earth. Pentecost is reborn. Obedience is the watchword. Worship is the mystique. God waits for those who will love him and who hunger for things too excellent to be understood. In my need of Christ I have gone there all too frequently. It is a *terra cognita*, a knowable land, but its approaches are a bridge of yearning. A togetherness won by longing. But the path of this yearning can end in cul-de-sacs of disappointment. Sometimes even as we hunger for God our longing is swallowed up by our need for it.

> God waits for those who will love him and who hunger for things too excellent to be understood.

The ultimate redeeming hunger is to be changed to the glory of his image—to be conformed to his image. Paul expressed this desire for conformity in many ways, but my favorite appears in 2 Corinthians 3:18 (KJV): "We all, with open face beholding as in a glass the glory of the Lord, are changed into the same image." This is Narcissus in reverse. The poor Greek lad! He looked into a pond, saw himself, and drowned struggling to embrace his own ego. On the other hand, we look into a glass and see Jesus and are given life by our desire to become the Christ in our mirror.

"In other words," the apostle says, "hang a picture of Christ in the gallery of your heart. Determine you will be the living portrait of this inner picture, and your desire will in time make it happen." This is the hunger that makes the mystery usable.

I have no need to understand those mysteries beyond all understanding, only to encounter them. But I am eager to find the place of his coming. I cannot by the soul power of my frail hunger entice his presence. But if I listen and scan the lunarscape of my own spiritual boredom, I can still hear the roar of the wind and see the dancing flames. Then I run headlong to stand in his warm reality and know that all that I have sought—the reality of heaven, the proud chair of God—is indeed real.

What lies behind this drive? The Spirit himself! And I am consumed by my need to find him. Yes, I have drunk of such fire, but it was never enough. I thought it was at the time, when I felt the gales and saw the flame. But wherever heaven touches earth, a strange narcosis is born. A desire for Christlikeness is addicting. Having tasted it, we must taste it more and more. Having heard it, we cannot find rest until we hear it again. I am not altogether sure if it is he of whom T. S. Eliot wrote in *The Four Quartets*, but hear his cry for God and ask yourself how long it's been since you have touched such mystery.

> *The dove descending breaks the air*
> *With flame of incandescent terror*
> *Of which the tongues declare*
> *The One discharged of sin and error.*
> *The only hope or else despair*
> *Lies in the choice of pyre or pyre—*
> *To be redeemed from fire by fire.*
>
> *Who then devised the torment? Love.*
> *Love is the unfamiliar Name*
> *Behind the hands that wove*
> *The intolerable shirt of flame.*
> *Which human power cannot remove.*
> *We only live, only suspire*
> *Consumed by either fire or fire.*[5]

Was Eliot too mystical? Not at all. In the mystical is reality of life. When the mystery is gone, so is the church—at least the vitality of the church. I believe we are now in just such an advanced stage of spiritual decline. Unless we figure out how to get mystery back in the church, her vitality will continue to wane. We have how-to'ed as long as we can. We must put the inscrutable wind and fire back in our communion.

Reacquire the fire

It is unfortunate that evangelicals have quit building sanctuaries and began building auditoriums. It seems to makes a statement about our trading mystery for lectureships. We were never good at mystery, smoking incense, towering glass rituals, or veiled entreaties. We have no incense. We have no temples. We have only boxy auditoriums with low ceilings and theater lights. So we have become the plain, pragmatic people. Make no mistake about it, when pragmatism has run its course, there is only death. We must quit making God a practical deity who exists to help us succeed.

A pastor of my acquaintance planned a revival. To contrive the hype he felt necessary, he invited a "flaming" evangelist in to whip up the troops with life and bring a little excitement into his old dead church. One night of the revival, his staid congregation became inflamed with confession and spiritual neediness. The old altar, long dead, was thronged with crying penitents. The joy was overwhelming. But the next night the pastor apologized for allowing the church to go overboard with emotion. The fledgling fire begging a chance to become a real inferno was swallowed up by the extinguisher of staid religious practice. The Spirit never again visited.

What a pity. There is no life in pragmatism, no vitality in business as usual. We must have the Spirit or we are only shallow, small, explainable people. No wonder Karl Rahner said the Christian of the future will either be a mystic or not exist at all.[6]

Once upon a time there was a group of people in Ephesus who believed themselves to be true Christians. Except for the fact that they were premodern, two thousand years out of sync with our day, and lacking one very large Christian publishing and media empire, they seemed in some ways to be rather typically suburban. Seeing them superimposed upon our own day and age, they no doubt Kinko-copied their Sunday bulletin, PowerPointed their worship choruses, and played lots of softball for Jesus.

Acts 19:1-2 does not say exactly how Paul met these believers, but when he met them, he felt compelled to ask, "Have ye received the Holy Spirit since ye believed?" (KJV)

In short, they replied, "No, we have not. In fact, the term 'Holy Spirit' is unfamiliar to us," confessed the confused Ephesians.

The Ephesians are not to be blamed for their confusion. I am much afraid the whole blame must be laid at the feet of Apollos. He was the glib, popular communicator of the day. He no doubt "packed the pews"—a millennium before there were pews—to hear his sermons. He had mastered the homiletic one-liner. It was no doubt hard to hear his sermons, for the applause was frequent. The cheers unhooked the precepts of his standing-room-only speeches.

Still, finding good theology in his sermons was not easy. Finding the Holy Spirit was impossible. In the best moments of church history, the Holy Spirit has dominated and empowered the Christian sermon. But it has never been easy to find him in worship. Apollos wasn't just an anomaly—a one-time person who died, never to reappear. Apollos has lived throughout time in every generation that tried to substitute hype for fire. Jesus is the only authentic alternative to hype. When he is our hunger, we shall see Pentecost—a Pentecost not created by ad campaigns and Christian aerobics. We shall find a church filled with yearning disciples—each of which is a blank page given to God with a plea for his direction.

A church on its knees doesn't win softball games; in fact, it doesn't care much about them. Annie Dillard wrote,

> On the whole, I do not find Christians, outside of the catacombs, sufficiently sensible of conditions. Does anyone have the foggiest idea what sort of power we so blithely invoke? Or, as I suspect, does no one believe a word of it? The churches are children playing on the floor with their chemistry sets, mixing up a batch of TNT to kill a Sunday morning. It is madness to wear ladies straw hats to church; we should all be wearing crash helmets. Ushers should issue life preservers and signal flares; they should lash us to our pews. For the sleeping God may someday wake and take offense, or the waking God may draw us out to where we can never return.[7]

How casually we play with fire. How little we esteem it.

We run between popular pulpits and religious concert halls crying, "Seek! Seek! Is Christ here? Is he there?" How like Diogenes we have become. We thrust our lanterns into the dark, homiletical fissures of postmodernism crying, "We seek the Empowering Spirit, but give us the Spirit of Acts 2, if you don't mind. We like the way he was always doing unexplainable things."

There are other bogus spirits to be sure. There is a *concert-artist spirit*, who knows when to snap his fingers. There is the *politically correct spirit*, who can "him and her" his way through a worship service, never offending any minority or sexual-preference group. There is the *institutional spirit*, who smiles his broad preferences over every particular program. There is the *ecumenical spirit*, who is so tolerant he plays Hearts with the Pharisees and Bridge with the Herodians. This spirit is so tolerant it has convinced many that believing less is better than believing more, that mutual acceptance is better when it is based on small ideas.

So we live in a generation that believes flab is good. It snuggles prickly doctrines into the same padded pews without having our sharper edges inconvenience one another. Flab insulates cold passion till it feels warmer.

Flab is a doctrinal shock absorber; when varying Christologies bump into each other, flab beats bubble-wrap in protecting the sensitive edges of our once-important and individualized heritages.

This spiritual flab is manufactured at several places throughout the kingdom. There is an ever-present tendency to think that if we were smarter in our knowledge of the Bible, and if we consulted with the doctors in the temple, we would get closer to the wind and fire. But, alas, we cannot educate ourselves into spiritual vitality. Catherine of Siena said that it was far better to walk by the counsel of some unschooled person who knew God than to trust in the scholarship of a proud intellectual.[8] We cannot educate away our spiritual apathy.

Sapping the vitality of the Spirit

Another manufacturing center of spiritual flab may be the user-friendly world of church growth. Marva Dawn has urged us to "reach out without dumbing down," but it seems we can reach further, faster when we keep all doctrinal definitions at a minimum. People play at suburban church better if we give them hazy definitions of Christ. We don't trust the Spirit to preserve and advance the church. Indeed, I believe most churches are no longer free to give him full rein. We are afraid that if we really trust him, he will have us behaving like some media evangelists, and the thought of wildfire is so repugnant to us that we avoid fire altogether.

Stepping over the edge of propriety in worship can set people with different worship tastes fighting about how much "hang-loose" is too much. Those who are most proper feel that there is such a thing as too much joy. Such worship takes the "coin" out of our *koinonia*. Its better to pad your propriety with flab than to risk playing around with the high voltage of Pentecostal circuitry.

> We are afraid that if we really trust him, he will have us behaving like some media evangelists, and the thought of wildfire is so repugnant to us that we avoid fire altogether.

On the other hand, you can also lose members if you speak too openly about the deeper life movement. In a Mercedes world you can't talk much about self-denial. The best way to keep Pentecostals and Episcopalians in the same church is to have a long song service and short, happy sermons. Flab, in some cases, is the tie that binds people with widely differing doctrines together.

We are ever reluctant to embrace the mystery of the power of godliness.

We have long emphasized preaching the truth and have usually defined truth as biblical facts that can be ingested and defended. We forget that facts do not produce life, only the mystery of godliness can do that. The key question for vitality is not "Do you have the facts of the faith?" but "Are you in touch with the mystery that empowers?"

A counterfeit Christ?

Spiritually hungry people outside of Christ do not come to the church to be educated. They come seeking the meaning that grows from the mystery that redeems and invigorates. If we will not joyously take up the publication of this mystery we might as well welcome Apollos into our coffee klatch with a jelly roll and send him off to a "funsy" Bible study with a Starbucks benediction. To preach only the "facts" or only the "passion" or only the "fun" is to only preach half a gospel. The other half of the gospel is not preached into people: it is ushered into them by the wind and fire.

My young years were often spent in attending the sermons of Texas evangelists. They were always passionate, but I had a hard time linking their passions to good doctrine. Evangelists' love offerings depended on passion. We wept when they led us in weeping, we laughed when they led us in laughter. They were masters of the human nervous system. Feeling is not all bad. I must confess that far too often these latter days I come and go to church without feeling a thing. I am captive to the mass analgesia, the mass anesthesia, and the mass amnesia. The mass analgesia reminds me that many sermons are nearly painful. The mass anesthesia speaks of their power to drug the vitality of faith. The mass amnesia reminds me that they are eminently forgettable.

I am convinced that most people don't really know how to articulate what they want out of church. In short, they want Jesus, but the Apollos tale in Acts proves the danger of an incomplete Christ. They want his Spirit to permeate their lives, but they don't know him as the wind and fire. The validity of every religious gathering is to be evaluated by Paul's question, "Have you received the Holy Spirit since you believed?"

The Ephesians had been ravaged by glitz but, alas, they confessed, "We have not so much as heard if there is a Holy Spirit." Thus begins the apostle's doctrinal repair work. Properly heralded, wind and fire were to be the methodology of the kingdom. It is odd that the Ephesians had heard of Jesus but not the Holy Spirit. But since the Holy Spirit is one with Jesus, it would appear that they did not have all of Jesus that was to be had. Indeed, they seem to have been surviving on half-a-Jesus.

This docetic Savior always seems to be Jesus. But he hides in the shadows of half-truths and the spiritually naïve minds of immature Christians.

He teaches from good informational outlines, but we need more. We need to embrace the mystery of the Spirit. It's odd that Apollos never noticed he was preaching half-a-gospel. Pentecost had come and gone. There had been tongues of flame and rushing wind. Three thousand people had been converted. The Holy Spirit was moving like a powerful mist of grace across the dry earth. Jesus was on the planet and mystery was his method. Only Apollos didn't know. After all, he had his programs and his calendar was full, and he was popular. Just like today, if you go fast enough and are popular enough, you can go a long way on shallow doctrine driven only by hype. But sooner or later the mystery of things too excellent to understand must come, and we will reject the emptiness of worship services that have no real worship in them.

What do we do when we are too spiritually encrusted to be penetrated by the Spirit? We begin to substitute institutional machinery of one kind or another to make it appear that we have the mystery. These substitutes are a spiritual veneer for decaying altars. What are some of the substitutes we are using to create the aura of life in the Spirit?

Sometimes we set financial or numerical goals. It satisfies the Wall Street managers in the church who want to quantify their spirituality. That way everybody is kept busy and there is no expectation of any baptism in mystery. Soon they will be so numbers oriented that they will be like those two Southern Baptist astronauts who crashed on the moon and immediately set a goal of three in Sunday school.

Maybe we form long-range planning committees. This is an excellent diversion. Get people thinking ten years ahead. If you can keep church members thinking that far away, many of them will be nearly useless in the present.

Maybe we call for a constitutional revision. This is always distracting, and will finally get people so upset that they don't even miss not seeing Jesus at church.

Above all, a technique for living without the mystery is what C. S. Lewis referred to as a lot of hyphenated Christianity. There is the Christ-and-skydiving group, Christ-and-vegetarianism, Christ-and-camping, Christ-and-the-somewhat-deeper-life-group, Christ-and-the-very-very-deep-deeper-life group.

All of those who serve Christ and anything else become aware that serving Christ is somewhat easier than loving Christ. As doing is easier than being, serving is easier than loving. In fact, for a great many believers, serving becomes a substitute for loving. During my many years as a pastor I watched those who began their faith pilgrimage in devotion end it with grudging service. Serving does not make happy Christians, only loving will do that. Serving without love becomes at last a dull habit that gives us a place in the community while it steals our relationship with Christ.

The question may be how do you escape serving wooden religious habits long enough to really begin loving God and enjoying the mystery of godliness? We must find a natural and vibrant way to establish uninterrupted concord with Christ. The answer lies in the mystery of the Holy Spirit. When we learn to "be" instead of "do," the Spirit can begin its work.

This blessed Spirit is our Intercessor. Romans 8:26 says that the Spirit helps us in our weakness: "We do not know what we ought to pray for, but the Spirit himself intercedes for us with groans that words cannot express." He is the all-powerful force at the center of ourselves. Picture him groaning, weeping in the utter serious agony of his desire that our desires never go unnoticed by heaven. Hebrews 7:25 says that Jesus ever lives to make intercession for us. What is the state of this agony of spiritual intercession? The Christ who prays for us from within the cell of our own hearts? Catherine of Siena says, "They receive everlasting life with the fruit of their tears and flaming charity: they cry out and offer tears of fire for you in my presence."[9]

Here are those groanings of the Spirit that cannot be uttered. They are tears of fire that etch the unseeable face of God on our behalf. Are we not redeemed from our daily heartaches by this blessed weeping Spirit? Of course we are.

Conclusion

The one valid question for anyone's church is, "Have you received the Holy Spirit since you believed?" How can we tell that the Holy Spirit is there? Who can describe every aspect of the way he works? When he first came in Acts, his coming seemed to be marked by a kind of madness, everyone babbling in languages they had never learned and acting in some ways as if they were drunk. Perhaps they were; inebriated by the Spirit. "Be not drunk with wine, wherein is excess; but be filled with the Spirit," said the apostle. Heady inebriation this: Spirit intoxication. It is a glorious addiction. If we but take one sip, we pneumaholics must have more of the Pneuma! We may not be wholly doctrinal or crisply theological, but we are alive and the life is in the wind and fire. Wind that blows to disorient our propriety. Fire that burns to ashes our need for printed programs and stiff constitutions. Such worship vitality often comes in what might be called glorious chaos!

When I first arrived in the Philippines at the Baguio Seminary, I was walking across the campus when I was approached by a native Filipino. He was carrying a clear plastic sack inside of which was a copy of my book *The Empowered Leader*. "I bought this book last year," he said, "never knowing we would have a chance to meet."

"Why do you keep it in a sack?" I asked.

"Well," he said, "it's kind of expensive, you know. I love this book and I just don't want it to get dirty. I want to keep it clean."

He looked at my book like it was the *Codex Sinaiticus*. It's hard not to love a man who carries your book around in a plastic bag for fear of getting it dirty.

"I wonder," he said, "if you'd be willing to come and preach to my people? I know they would love to hear you preach."

"Sure," I said. I really didn't know if it was the will of God, but it seemed like the will of God when my new friend was carrying my book around in a plastic sack.

"I thank you very much," he said. "I'm Ifagao," he went on, "and I have to ride the bus eight hours to get here to school."

We set the date. His sister was a Pentecostal pastor too, so I got the president of the seminary to agree to preach in her church too, and we set off on the long drive up into the mountains of Benaue. I had always thought that the students defined the word "poor." But there I got a new definition of poverty. However, among the poor I saw the glorious riches of the gospel for all who are poor. Jesus is a great treasure for the poor. The poor are made rich by his love—and how they love him! Neither the pastor nor any of his people had cars. We sang choruses from huge sheets of newsprint that had been lettered by case markers. I preached on the importance of having a passion for Christ, but the sermon was completely unnecessary. Passion for Christ was the virtue of this very vital church.

The pastor had asked me to extend an invitation, although extend seemed unnecessary. We had hardly begun to sing when it seemed to me that they were all coming forward. I've been a Baptist for a long time. I was used to seeing nobody come forward even after multiple verses of "Just As I Am." It scared me to see so many of them coming. It seemed they were rushing upon me like Philistines from Delilah's bedroom.

The thing that amazed me was the sense of confusion and mayhem. Chaos! Blessed chaos! Everyone hungering all at once for God. All desiring, reaching, weeping for his nearness. Laughing for the pleasure of his visitation. I couldn't remember the last time I gave an invitation and there were so many at the altar I got confused asking them why they had all come.

Pastor Dumia was there helping me try to lead some to Christ, trying to help others with rededication. It was a mess. People were just trying to get to us to pray, and finally I had no idea what was going on. Then to complicate things, there were all these sick people wanting prayer. Pastor Dumia said, "I'll counsel the lost, would you take care of the healing?"

"Please, Pastor," I begged, "I'm a Baptist. I don't do healing. When we

Baptists get sick we take pills. I'm not good at healing."

"Just pray for the sick—that's all you have to do, just pray."

So I did. In thirty or forty minutes the chaos was over, but I will never forget that overwhelming feeling that there were people all over the place and God was doing things in their lives. I have many times blessed this glorious chaos. And now I know what was missing in Ephesus. I know where Apollos fell short. I know the glory of divine mayhem that comes in the visitation of God, and it is not always orderly.

"*Amor non tenet ordinam*"—"Love does not concern itself with order," said St. Columbanus.[10] In fact, if Acts 2 is to be trusted, warm chaos is a better way to measure God's visitation than a printed order of worship. The chaotic fire of Acts 2 is the only fire that ever mattered. And so I crave the holy flame.

Jesus is the only meal for the spiritually hungry. I seek him in the ordinary ways and in things that have too much excellence for me. And when the fire comes and I feel its warmth, then I know the mystery that redeems. Not that I know the dogmas of the faith any better. I still understand so little, but then we are not called to understand everything about God, only to attend him. And I know that when I draw near to God, I am a prisoner of the only reality there is. The reality of the Divine Mystery.

The Informed Life

In the midst of life's gladness,
the betrayal of others and our own infidelity
at times force us by their pain to question
whether there is anything or anyone worthy
of trust or finally true in the world.[1]

—CATHERINE OF SIENA

The *Ecclesia Christi*,
the disciple community
has been torn from the clutches of the world.[2]

—DIETRICH BONHOEFFER

For, truly, if He is with me,
I care not where I go.[3]

—FRANCIS DE SALES

When the light shines in the darkness, does the darkness merely leave or is it changed to light?

O God! We don't know who you are! "The light shines in the darkness" (John 1:5) but we don't see it. Universal light! It is only because of you that we can see anything at all. Sun of the soul! You shine more brightly than the sun in the sky. You rule over everything. All I see is you. Everything else vanishes like a shadow. The one who has never seen you has seen nothing. That person lives a make-believe life, lives a dream.

But I always find you within me. You work through me in all the good I accomplish. How many times I was unable to check my emotions, resist my habits, subdue my pride, follow my reason, or stick to my plan! Without you I am "a reed swayed by the wind" (Matthew 11:7). You give me courage and everything decent which I experience. You have given me a new heart that wants nothing except what you want. I am in your hands. It is enough for me to do what you want me to do. For this purpose I was created.[4]

—FRANÇOIS FÉNELON

CHAPTER NINE

Into the Depths by Finding Our Calling

Booker T. Washington, in *Up From Slavery*, said that every morning of his young life all the slaves were awakened long before daylight by the crow of the rooster. Black as pitch or not, that rooster was their call to hit the floor of their sod shanty and leave for the fields to work. Then came the Emancipation Proclamation. Mr. Lincoln had spoken! The slaves were free! And the first morning afterward, young Booker was awakened by the sound of his mother chasing that rooster around the barnyard with an axe. The Emancipation Proclamation was hard on roosters all across the South. That very day, the Washingtons fried and ate their alarm clock for lunch. Before the Emancipation, their bogus calling was dictated by the endless ritual crow of the rooster. But now their true calling was a wondrous cry of freedom.

I have no way to prove this, but I have the feeling that they live the longest who know why they are alive in the first place. We not only find out who we are when we move into the depths but we also find out what God has for us to do. Then, glory of glories! we discover they are one and the same. What God has for us to do is who we are. It is better to live a decade and know why we are alive than to live a century without any clue.

Perhaps the best thing that happened to Booker T. was that for the first time in his life he had a reason to be alive. Even as a young child he had a vaguely forming sense of why he was in the world. Every earthly father should help his child identify what God means to him and what he means to God. When a child comes to understand what God has for him to do in life, that child will also understand his significance to God. And the first day young Booker T. didn't *have* to get up was the first day he really wanted to get up and get started living for his own reasons. He was set afire by the passion of a calling.

The call of God is a pilgrimage that is forever marked by eating our alarm clocks. I received my call to Christian service in my late teens. For a while afterward I continued working for my brother-in-law each summer. I drove wheat trucks between Pond Creek, Oklahoma, and Presho, South Dakota.

> The call of God is a pilgrimage that is forever marked by eating our alarm clocks.

And all summer long I would get up long before daybreak and grease our Massey-Harris self-propelled combines. I grew to hate the alarm clock for waking me to such misery.

Then in the summer of 1956 a small Baptist church in northern Oklahoma called me to be their pastor. I knew I would never again have to get up early and grease combines. I was certain of my call to preach. In effect, I ate my alarm clock. I did have to get up early for the next forty years in order to preach, but like Booker T., I knew I would be getting up early because I wanted to, not because I had to.

Our call puts a holy centeredness in our living. Time and again I have seen Christians—some who have been in the church for a long time—suddenly come alive. They have finally discovered what God wants for them in life. There falls upon them a new passion for being in the world. Their careers undergo no visible change in most cases, but they are new, nonetheless. They are called. Their alarm clocks at last wake them to joy and purpose every morning.

The call may at various seasons of our lives lead in some new direction. For instance, at age fifty-five I began to notice again a holy discontent when my alarm went off. The joy of my pastoral years eluded me. I no longer found joy in what I was doing. Sunday mornings, which had always been my favorite time of the week, seemed to start too early and required too much stamina. I often felt beat up and dead—inside and out—when the day ended. I would often ask God to "quicken my mortal body" on those dull, demanding mornings.

Then out of the blue—God moved! The president of a large seminary asked me to join the faculty. On November 2, 1991, I woke up at six o'clock, and that morning preached my last sermon as a parish pastor. Once more I felt like I had eaten a drudgerous old alarm clock and started off down a new and exciting path of Christian ministry. I was a professor. I got to be with students! I had a new zeal, a new passion. And the most glorious of all passions is the inner understanding that Jesus has given us a real reason to be in his world.

Still, as Paul pointed out, love is the greatest of the Christian virtues. Love gives validity to our calling. The Christian who is grumpy may be one who is out of touch with what God originally called him or her to do. Richard Baxter wrote,

> *If you love God, you will do everything possible to serve and please him. Love is impatient to do good. It is also quick and active and observant. Faith will encourage you. Hope will set you spinning like the spring in a watch. Reverence for God will rouse you out of your sleepiness. Enthusiasm for spiritual things will set you on fire. The more aware you are of God, the more involved you will be in working for him.*[5]

What is the call?

Jeremiah said of his call that it felt like a fire shut up in his bones (20:9). That fire that kept him going when all else failed. But Jeremiah at Benjamin Gate learned another truth: The holy fire of the call is easily quenchable. Dull churchmanship is a fire extinguisher. Business meetings, deacons meetings, committee meetings, and various assorted congregational criticisms all tend to douse the flame—to quench the fire in our bones.

How wonderful are those churches in which the number of members is identical to the number of ministers. In such a church, laypeople are God-called. Their passion burns. Their inner fire rages. They fry their old alarm clocks and can't wait for sunrise. They have an indestructible spirit. They don't buckle under gossip. They outlast their foes. They survive their critics. They awake to praise God on the mornings of their most foreboding trials.

The call of God is so much more than a divine employment agency. Too often the call is equated with vocation, as if God's call is only valid if it means a job in the ministry. The call is more of a relationship than a vocation. A zeal for God. An ardor for the things of God. Ardor joins the applause of God. The angels cannot help but applaud the kneeling and hungry who are famished for God.

Once in a long ago game, the Green Bay Packers had suffered a lot of injuries and had scored only a few points by the end of the first half. Their coach, Vince Lombardi, overheard their complaining at half time and said, "Men, you can only win the big games when you learn to play with the little hurts of life." I don't know what enables football players to go on playing with the little hurts, but in the Christian life it is the call and only the call.

Fifty percent of those who attend worship services in America enter the church with some kind of a problem. But that's all right, because 50 percent of the time ministers also enter the worship service with some kind of a problem. Yet, of course, they preach anyway, and spiritually healthy laypersons also serve with joy. It is every Christian's call to play through the little hurts.

> The call is more of a relationship than a vocation. A zeal for God. An ardor for the things of God.

But many Christians can't go on playing in pain, or if they do, they do it without much joy. During these seasons they are only the grumbling players. They are blessed of God, cursed of God, caught in the stretch between needing to please God and needing so very much to be healed. Where did they go wrong? Life in Christ suddenly becomes all needles and bruises. The swimming joy of first faith lies beached upon a sour outlook.

At such moments our inner life can seem dead. Beaten by our circumstances, we try to retreat to the depths of God just as we always have. But suddenly even the depths seem like old, shallow, tepid joys. We cry, but God takes no notice of our tears. Weighted by spiritual depression, we find it hard to believe there is a God, and if there is he certainly doesn't seem to be treating us very nicely.

It is hard to remember our calling during these down times.

Jeremiah 20 describes the cyclical condition of every Christian's struggle to remember their calling. He evaluated his calling at the Benjamin Gate. Can you not feel the hurt in Jeremiah's pain? It lures the mind most powerfully! After many years in the ministry, I confess my addiction to the narcotic "foolishness" of clinging to my call while living with pain and criticism.

In exercising my own call as a preacher, I spent a lot of time hanging around Benjamin Gate. I love the neurosis of the place—the utter hate, the fervent love. My needs in those dark times seemed greater than God's supply. My sermons seemed as dead as my joy. I wanted to preach with power, but the fire eluded me. The just-as-I-am conclusions to my sermons always left them just as they were.

Benjamin Gate: what Christian does not know it well? It is a place of waxy faces, comatose after late Saturday nights. Dead from card parties, these spiritually needy souls quarrel their way to church. Sunday morning—the call to worship—the litany of the dead: the pastor reads the light print while those who still have a pulse read the dark. Then comes the sermon. "Here are some general sins," calls the discouraged messenger. "Pick a few and apply them to your neighbors."

Why would any Christian go on with desperate futility clinging to his call? Because the best believers make a covenant with their calling. When they live in covenant with their calling, life flows easily.

In the apocryphal book of Ecclesiasticus, the writer tells us to cherish the trials that taught us to cherish Christ.

> My son, if you aspire to serve the Lord,
>   prepare yourself for an ordeal.
> Be sincere of heart, be steadfast,
>   and do not be alarmed when
>   disaster comes.
> Cling to him and do not leave him,
>   so that you may be honored at the
>   end of your days.
> Whatever happens to you, accept it,
>   and in the uncertainties of your humble
>   state, be patient,
> since gold is tested in the fire,
>   and chosen men in the furnace
>   of humiliation.
>   —ECCLESIASTICUS 21:1–5

My suspicion is that only those who can bless the furnace ever understand the gold.

Francis of Assisi accepted his call and the world came alive for him. He literally blessed the world as he passed through it. Ugolino said that Francis left his companions to go into the world and preach to his little sisters, the birds. And here is what he said:

> My little sisters, remember to praise God because you are in-
> debted to him. You are free to fly wherever you please. He has given
> you beautiful clothes. He provides you with food and teaches you
> how to sing. He saved you with Noah's ark and helped you to be
> fruitful and multiply. Thank him for the air you fly in. Thank him
> for the water you drink from rivers and springs. Thank him for the
> high cliffs and trees where you can build your nests. Thank him that
> you are not required to sow or reap, spin or weave. God gives you
> and your children everything you need. Such things can only mean
> that God loves you very much. Therefore, my little sisters, remember
> to thank and praise God.[6]

It is clear that Francis of Assisi let his call sanctify his world.

How do you feel about your calling? How did Jeremiah feel? Did he lament, "Bad morning, huh, God! Well, it's me, Jeremiah. Remember how I once loved you? Now look at me, God! I'm here at Benjamin Gate, hanging in the stocks with kosher bits of this and that rotting at my feet. Please, help me, I'm dying, God. I preach and weep and weep and preach. Does anybody care? Do you care, God?"

We, like Jeremiah, serve with great authority, but we often whimper and complain between our times of joy. We become all "thus saith the Lord" and "what am I doing down in the dumps when my Myers-Briggs scores are so executive?!"

Some scholars doubt that Jeremiah was capable of such erratic mood swings as occur within the twentieth chapter of his book. Verse 20:13, for instance, is all victory and praise sandwiched in between the suicide notes scribbled on the back of his seminary degree. Jeremiah does seem erratic— could the scholars be right? I think not! The truth is, the only scholars that doubt this tale are those who have never really thrown their hearts over the bar and pursued an unflinching, unwavering commitment to their calling. Those who have see nothing at all unusual about any prophet's mood swings. The crying times and the celebrations of our lives often come close together—so close that we crave a deeper union with Christ even as we doubt that it is possible.

Still, this is the glory of our calling. We keep on serving the call, even when we wonder if our partnership with God has been canceled. As we go on being faithful, we find that the call sooner or later wakes our sleeping adoration to high confidence once again. We are soon back at home in the depths of our union with Christ. Tough times don't last for long, but tough saints go on forever. The calling gets us through the tough times. We serve because we feel called, and then we serve because we don't. It is not as though we fake it till we make it. We *take* it till we make it.

> The crying times and the celebrations of our lives often come close together—so close that we crave a deeper union with Christ even as we doubt that it is possible.

Jeremiah demonstrates that our call helps us stand true even when we cannot sort life into manageable segments. In the prophet's case, the siege machines have moved against the walls of his X-rated culture. His call kept him telling the truth. Our callings keep us honest. But we must be careful lest we begin to substitute little areas of obedience for the big ones. There are times when our orthodoxy can become a substitute for real courage.

Callings are insistent. They keep us on edge, summoning up the courage to do what God wants done.

The Healer

God sometimes heals by breaking. Jeremiah cries out to God, and God, who is his only friend, suddenly is unavailable. The silence of God breaks his spirit so that by his wounds he may mature in ministry.

"All Scripture is God-breathed and is useful for teaching, rebuking, correcting and training in righteousness" (2 Timothy 3:16).

I now know that life flows in one direction. The Katzenjammer Kids were right: *We are too soon old and too late smart.* But what the Katzenjammer Kids didn't say was that you don't get smart just by getting old. You get smart by hurting and healing and evaluating your scars.

Christianity is the tale of a great truth: Christ died for us. Now we are redeemed by his death. But sometimes this God of miracles gets silent. It is usually when we need a great miracle, and the agony is that you usually can't get a real miracle when you really need one. Our service in the church at such times can seem drab, even to ourselves. Any of us would be glad to do his will if he'd just tell us what it is!

So we cry out with a kind of desperate bargaining, "Give us something, God, to tell us you're there. Write anything on our walls, but write it in fire, if you don't mind. Tell us, 'You're serving the wrong call.' Order us, 'Go back to square one and start over.' Say anything, but say something, God! We'll understand. But please don't ignore us."

When God is silent it is usually when we most need him to remind us that we are called. Where is he when the fire in our bones has turned to ashes and we can't find him? Where is he when we cry with Job, "Oh that I knew where I might find him!"? We want to feel positive about God. We want to believe the ad men when they say, "You can do it!"

Julie Andrews in *The Sound of Music* (1965) suggested that the tough times of life can be hurdled by thinking of our favorite things, like "raindrops on roses and whiskers on kittens." She sang so confidently, but the philosophy of the song is shallow. In the same song we are counseled, "When the dog bites, when the bee stings . . ." just to think of our favorite things. Shortly after seeing that musical, I was attacked by a Rottweiler. He tore my leg to shreds, and I had to go to the ER to get put back together. That dog almost killed me, and I never once thought of my favorite things!

Walker Percy asks quite simply, "Where are the Hittites?" He goes on to reason:

Why does no one find it remarkable that in most world cities today there are Jews but not one single Hittite, even though the Hittites had a great flourishing civilization while the Jews nearby were a weak and obscure people?

When one meets a Jew in New York or New Orleans or Paris or Melbourne, it is remarkable that no one considers the event remarkable. But . . . if there are Jews here, why are there not Hittites here?

Show me one Hittite in New York City.[7]

The answer seems clear enough in the biblical record. The Hittites were not less important to God, the Creator, but they found no place in his redeeming plan of the ages.

If we want to be involved with God, we must play with pain—endure the little hurts of the game and maybe survive the big hurts. Playing with the little hurts has been the theme of so many saints of God. All they are may be admired, for all they are is so like Christ. Thomas Arnold wrote of his most beloved sister:

I must conclude with a more delightful subject: my most dear and blessed sister. I never saw a more perfect instance of the spirit of power and of love, and of a sound mind. She had an intense love, almost to the annihilation of selfishness. Hers was a daily martyrdom for twenty years, during which she adhered to her early-formed resolution of never talking about herself. She was thoughtful about the very pins and ribbons of my wife's dress or about the making of a doll's cap for a child. But of herself, save only as regarded her ripening in all goodness, she was wholly thoughtless.[8]

And Elizabeth Barrett Browning, suffering as an invalid for years, could say that her thankfulness to God flowed unstoppable no matter what her hurts were:

I praise Thee while my days go on;
I love Thee while my days go on:
Through dark and dearth, through fire and frost,
With emptied arms and treasure lost,
I thank Thee while my days go on.[9]

The entirety of Jewish history is the long, unbroken tale of great men and women who followed God under great stress—ever playing with the little hurts, and sometimes great hurts—for the sake of their call.

How did these Jews handle their mixture of calling and pain? They triumphed! They hurt, sometimes cried out, but in the end they won! The Jews still remain—beaten, hated, driven into exile, burned, tortured, and wounded, but of the four modern names that have most influenced modern history, three are Jews: Freud, Einstein, and Marx (Darwin was not Jewish). Modern Judaism—which so often sees Isaiah's suffering servant as the nation of Israel, wounded to live out the Abrahamic covenant, blessing all the world—is itself a wounded national soul. Made rich with analyzing and measuring their own bloody heritage, the Jews have changed and gone on changing the world.

So "Where are the Hittites?" is a fair question. It has no clear answer. Perhaps the Hittites are no longer around because they failed to answer God's call. How we must cherish our call, our partnership with God. To lose this, or never to know it, is to lose our identity. To lose our call is never to matter to God. It is to die unused—to go wherever the Hittites went.

But how do we keep from walking the Hittite edges of our own irrelevancy? We are his people, his servants—born to hurt and to cling to our call. Yet we are not just born to cling; we are born to celebrate our calling. And we can go even further than that. We are the God-called who accept our hurt and bless our brokenness. I can look back across all the years of my ministry and see that I was often a broken servant living in the midst of broken servants. But the joint brokenness of those who are called holds glorious counsel. We were always made wise in the binding of each other's wounds. When we cry to be used of God, we find that joy is our best counselor.

Hindsight is 20/20. And now it is clear to me (after sixty-three brief years on the planet) that Jesus and I have won! And what we have not won, we are winning. I couldn't always tell we were winning while I was enmeshed in the conflict. The nearness of the battlefield sometimes obscures the war. But the years I spent clinging to the call lifted me up and I could see at last: We had won!

The wounded Healer

God healed the world once for all on a hilltop through his own incarnate brokenness. Now the world that we have seen can be healed only by our incarnate brokenness. Jeremiah's suffering stirs an old irreconcilable truth: When we get self-important, God often gets quiet. It is not the prevalence of people's words that troubles the prophet. It is the absence of the words of God.

In the absence of pain, the intensity of our devotion is lost. Solzhenitsyn said, "If there are no real writers in the West, this must be the reason: There is no real pain in the West." We are drowning in the cream of utopia. Few real writers? Perhaps few real Christians for the same reason. Jeremiah was caught in the crisis of the war that was destroying his beloved homeland. Like Barth at Safenwil, Thielicke in Stuttgart, or Gilkey in China, Jeremiah lived in times that made him rich with wounds that only God could heal.

What do unwounded servants do? They become arrogant, join country clubs, sell out to middle-class mediocrity, or become fox-hunting Christians. They may even tend toward liberalism, because only the protected have the privilege of making theology a discussion; the endangered cling to it and weep. Liberalism always comes from people with too little need for God.

But we must ask this question, "How do we keep vitality in our faith and calling?" Staying alive in a living faith is a matter of keeping our focus on Christ at the center. Margaret Ebner confessed that her vitality in Christ lay in meditating on a half-dozen key elements of faith.

> *First, how God descended from heaven to earth, entering a woman's womb and living there for nine months.*
> *Second, how Christ had a normal birth and actually lived among us for thirty-three years.*
> *Third, how he was motivated by love and was even willing to die on the cross.*
> *Fourth, how he gave himself to us and continues to give himself sacramentally.*
> *Fifth, how he gives himself daily.*
> *Sixth, how his love is not exclusive.*[10]

Jeremiah lived a wounded life, and wounding kills irrelevance even as Christlike living puts a continuing sense of the call into earnest believers. The old proverb "Sticks and stones may break your bones, but words will never hurt you" simply is not true. Words *do* hurt. Words ultimately wound us with eternal scars. Words can tear divine purpose from our vision and leave us only small reasons for living. Words also test the mettle of our call. Great Christians are married to that call. They are joined to what God wants to do with their lives.

The call is as a fire shut up in our bones. The fire is a Bunsen burner set under a beaker of volatile joy, and joy is infallible proof of the presence of God. It is why Jesus said, "My burden is light" (Matthew 11:30). It is why when our burdens are destructive we still sing not of our triumphs but our need. "I'm dying of this conflict, God . . . I cry out; I need thee. Oh, I need thee. Every hour I need thee."

Conclusion

The trials that keep us kneeling before our lifelong assignments are never haphazard. All the sufferings that are thrust upon us can serve to bring us to maturity. Paul Billheimer said that we should treasure the pain that sculpts us into the image of Christ:

> *My child, I have a message for you today: let Me whisper it in your ear, that it may gild with glory any storm clouds that may arise, and smooth the rough places upon which you may have to tread. It is short, only five words, but let them sink into your inmost soul; use them as a pillow upon which to rest your weary head: "This thing is from me."*[11]

In these apocalyptic times the fire of God's intention awakes the joy that we have been chosen as instruments for his purposes. We are the living crucibles that hold the fire of God.

Paul the apostle never rises higher than he does in 2 Corinthians 12:7–10:

> *And lest I should be exalted above measure through the abundance of the revelations, there was given to me a thorn in the flesh, the messenger of Satan to buffet me, lest I should be exalted above measure. For this thing I besought the Lord thrice, that it might depart from me. And he said unto me, My grace is sufficient for thee: for my strength is made perfect in weakness. Most gladly therefore will I rather glory in my infirmities, that the power of Christ may rest upon me. Therefore I take pleasure in infirmities, in reproaches, in necessities, in persecutions, in distresses for Christ's sake: for when I am weak, then am I strong.* (KJV)

Therefore, since we are made strong by our areas of need, we must treasure our wounds and celebrate our hurts.

William Tyndale also understood the relation of pain and grace as he connected on this passage: "Beloved, think it not strange concerning the fiery trial which is to try you, as though some strange thing happened to you: But rejoice, inasmuch as ye are partakers of Christ's sufferings; that, when his glory shall be revealed, ye may be glad also with exceeding joy. If ye be reproached for the name of Christ, happy are ye; for the spirit of glory and of God resteth upon you: on their part he is evil spoken of, but on your part he is glorified" (1 Peter 4:12–14).

> *Christ is never strong in us until we are weak. As our strength diminishes, the strength of Christ grows in us. When we are entirely emptied of our own strength, then we are full of Christ's strength. As much as we retain of our own, we lack of Christ's.*[12]

Hurt is the essential ingredient of ultimate Christlikeness.

Come fellow crucibles, welcome the fire inside you, treasure the flame of God's intention burning at the center of your souls. May the lessons of Jeremiah 20 never forsake us. May it be said of us that we are Christians who didn't always understand ourselves and sometimes didn't even like ourselves, but in our bones raged the fire unquenchable that at last consumed both our words and ourselves.

Oskar Schindler knew why he was in the world. In the last haunting moments of the film *Schindler's List*, the war is over and he laments the fact that he still owns a gold Nazi lapel pin. He rips it from his coat and cries sadly, "With this bit of gold I could have ransomed two more Jewish lives!" What are two more saved when six million have been lost? Well, to Oskar Schindler, two are everything! No . . . one is everything!

He had not quite spent everything on his calling! He stared at a bit of untraded gold in his hand and wept! Itzhak Stern touches the weeper and gives him a little piece of paper upon which is written a Jewish proverb: "He who saves one life, saves the world in time!"

Do you know why you are in the world?

Have you identified the fire in your bones?

Have you wept with the prophet, yet woke every morning to the agony and ecstasy of your call?

Have you camped out in 2 Corinthians 12, thanking God for your thorns and begging him to give you your passport to meaningful living? When that passport arrives, you will open it to discover your photo appears under that of Christ's. Your calling will be certain. And as you pass every portal of your life thereafter, the immigration officer will smile and stamp your document "Ambassador for Christ."

Morality did not begin by one man saying to another, "I will not hit you if you do not hit me"; there is no trace of such a transaction. There *is* a trace of both men having said, "We must not hit each other in the holy place." They gained their morality by guarding their religion.[1]

—G. K. CHESTERTON

Do you realize what happened at your conversion? God came into your heart and made it his temple. In Solomon's day God dwelt in a temple made of stone: today he dwells in a temple composed of living believers. When we really see that God has made our hearts his dwelling-place, what a deep reverence will come over our lives![2]

—WATCHMAN NEE

Jesus always looks not on what a man has been or is, but on what he is going to be. And that is right. The artist looks not on what a stone has been or is, but on what he is going to bring out of it—the living figure. A group of radiant Christians have as their motto, "My adventure is God."[3]

—E. STANLEY JONES

Character: what is it?
What we are on the inside?
What our mother thinks we are?
What we are in the dark?
No, only this: What we will be
when the finished work of Christ
is added to our unyielding desire
to live for his pleasure.

It was His hands I noticed first. Big, tough,
And weathered, hammer-gripping, sweating fists,
Quite used to driving nails into the rough
And bronze, blue bruised where once the iron missed.
A hand's a thing of beauty, in the eye
Of those whose vision trained can pierce the skin
To see the steel of sturdy bones laid white
And fragile tendons, filament and thin.
I understand the riddle of the hand,
How leathered calluses breed tougher skin,
Hides tiny porcelain machines within.
Yet love defies my wit to understand
How hands that swung the crushing iron grow frail,
And beckon to each palm a killing nail.[4]

—CALVIN MILLER

CHAPTER TEN

The Discipline That Ends in Godly Character

Friends possess a nobility we seldom notice until the crises of life teach us why it was we loved them in the first place. I have a great African-American friend, and it rarely occurred to either of us that we were "ebony and ivory," so to speak. Then the day came when the Los Angeles ghettos were suddenly afire with race riots. Color differences seemed instantly more self-proclaiming. During those incendiary days, my friend was jogging through our suburban area when a car of whites drove by. They rolled down the window, called him obscene names, and spat directly into his face.

Hot shame washed over him. He burned in anger and wept as he wiped the spittle off his face and continued on down the road. He thought of the cross and of Christ. He suddenly realized that he wasn't the first person ever to feel the degradation of someone else's spittle drying on his face. Jesus was a servant; he too knew humiliation. My friend thrived because he remembered the counsel of his Savior: "No servant is greater than his Lord." Time dries old spittle and hot shame. True servants in every age are prone to crucifixion. All who follow Christ must sooner or later learn the hard lessons of dying to self. Once they have, they can breathe prayers of forgiveness from their own cross.

Life in Christ is a warm organism supported by the strong skeleton of self-sacrifice. We must never forget this, because sacrifice that insists on "time off" from its own requirements is little more than indulgence with a small religious habit. Lent is not forty days of forgoing strawberries. Lent is a lifetime of self-denial—character-producing self-denial.

Self-denial begets character and character servanthood. But just giving up "stuff" we enjoy will not bring us to a sterling humanity. We must wait on human need to find that. Character comes gradually in the process of allowing God to make us servants. But oh, the pain that lies in the pathway! Hurt is the unwelcome forge on which God hammers out our Christlikeness. We beg God to cover the hammer with felt. But the iron blows fall and the anvil tears. Some have actually had to die to serve Christ. And sometimes it is the very people we are called to serve who hold in their ungrateful lives the pain that breaks our spirits and crushes us beneath alienation and aloneness.

Unfortunately, serving people is the only way by which we can serve God. And serving people means that we are going to get hurt in the process. If we are not careful, the pain involved in our service can cause us ultimately to despise those we once felt called to love. Charlie Brown is right: We all love humanity, it's people we can't stand! We all want to serve God, but it can be terribly degrading to have to serve people to do it.

> All who follow Christ must sooner or later learn the hard lessons of dying to self. Once they have, they can breathe prayers of forgiveness from their own cross.

Jesus, according to Philippians 2, humbled himself and became a man. Now we must humble ourselves to become servants and people of character. The crucifixion can be a very nasty end to anyone who wants to be a servant. Why? Consider the methodology of servanthood: We must turn our cheek and walk two miles for everyone who forces us to walk one! Serving our antagonists and blessing our persecutors can be the terrible tedium that fashions us in his image.

But how do we become people of character? The character of a servant, according to St. Paul, must be a matter of yieldedness in four areas: the head, the heart, the knee, and the tongue.

The Head of the Servant (Humility)

The head of a servant bows in humility.

Pride is the steel dagger in the heart of humility. No wonder Richard Baxter wrote,

> *Beware of a proud and haughty spirit. This sin puts a great barrier between an individual and God. You will have a hard time*

being aware of God as long as you are filled with pride. If it gets angels cast out of heaven, it will certainly keep your heart out of heaven. It was the downfall of Adam and Eve. It increases our separation from God and expels us from paradise.[5]

Pride sucks the vitality out of our character. Bernard of Clairvaux wisely taught that there are four Christian virtues. The first is humility. The second is humility. The third is humility. And the fourth is humility. Bernard also taught that most of us would like to gain humility without humiliation. Alas, it is not possible. Our arrogance is the least lovely of all our personal qualities. Ego is the barrier that stands between God and his dreams for our lives.

As servants we are to be priests. A priest is soil—intermediary soil, a small patch of ground on which both God and the needy stand to meet. Our work is priestly and it is glorious. Like Jesus, our great High Priest, we too wear the vestments of our mediation of grace. We make his incarnation possible once more. We are the willing amen of Walt Whitman. We must likewise cry to our needy world, "If you want us, look beneath the soles of your boots." Our humility may be easily seen in our love of helping others. Our service is our office. If the King of heaven can wash feet, our calling is clear.

How can we escape the need to be what others would like us to be? Christ, the servant-priest, bowed his head and became nothing—rather, he *made* himself nothing. He declared himself to be free. We usually focus on the word "nothing" in this truth. I suggest we focus on the word "made." To "make" ourselves means that we do not let others make us. Emily Dickinson cried:

> *I'm nobody! Who are you?*
> *Are you nobody, too?*
> . . . .
> *How dreary to be somebody!*
> *How public, like a frog*
> *To tell your name the*
> *livelong day*
> *To an admiring bog!*[6]

> The head must bow . . . it must take off the heavy crown of gaudy narcissism. It must bow as the servant asks, "What can I do, O Christ . . . for how long . . . where?"

The head must bow . . . it must take off the heavy crown of gaudy narcissism. It must bow as the servant asks, "What can I do, O Christ . . . for how long . . . where?"

Richard Baxter would agree with Emily Dickinson:

> *Are you puffed up with pride? Do you welcome the praise of others? Do you seek the highest honors? Do you become angry when your word or will is crossed? Can you not serve God in a low place as well as a high place? Do you enjoy celebrity? Are you unaware of the deceitfulness and wickedness of your heart? Are you more ready to defend your innocence than to confess your faults? If these things describe your heart, you are a proud person. It is not likely you will have any familiarity with God. You too much make yourself a god. You are your own idol. How could you possibly have your heart in heaven? You might speak a few proper words, but your heart does not understand what you are saying.*[7]

The Heart of the Servant (Obedience)

As the head of a servant yields, the heart of a servant obeys. The heart bows on the inside, making it possible for the body to genuflect on the outside. The heart of a servant is committed to integrity and mercy. In fact, the heart of character is mercy. William Tyndale wrote,

> *To be merciful is to have compassion, to feel another's sickness, to mourn with those who are in grief, to suffer with someone in trouble, to help in any way we can, and to comfort with loving words. To be merciful is lovingly to forgive someone who has offended you when they admit their behavior and ask you for mercy. To be merciful is to be patient with sinners, praying that God will ultimately convert them. To be merciful is to see the best in everything, to look through the fingers at many things and not make a grievous sin of every small trifle.*[8]

Jesus knew who he was and committed himself to mercy and to his Father's will with great integrity. Isaiah pictured him as one not to be swayed from his Father's will.

> *I gave My back to those who struck Me,*
> *And My cheeks to those who plucked out the beard;*
> *I did not hide My face from shame and spitting.*
> *For the Lord God will help Me;*
> *Therefore I will not be disgraced;*
> *Therefore I have set My face like a flint,*

And I know that I will not be ashamed.
—Isaiah 50:6–7 NKJV

Integrity in obedience is the lesson of the cross. Jesus could have lied his way out of his dilemma. He could have said, "No, Pilate, I am not God's Son—crucify someone else." But he clung to the truth, even when they poured on the pressure. Pilate might have said, "Why this waste? Why didn't you simply join the ministerial alliance, or go on a speaking tour, or get a film series, or write a book on how to be happy? Bend a little, Jesus! Relax! Give up your cross and take a break from all this."

Obedience is a bending of the will. "Keep your hearts clear of evil thoughts," wrote Cardinal Henry Edward Manning, "for as evil choices estrange the will from His will, so evil thoughts cloud the soul and hide Him from us. Whatever sets us in opposition to Him makes our will an intolerable torment. So long as we will one thing and He another, we go on piercing ourselves through and through with a perpetual wound, and His will advances, moving on in sanctity and majesty, crushing ours into the dust."[9] We must fill the empty, dark fissures of our convoluted hearts with surrender and light.

Obedience is not the major work of the disciple; it is the only work. But how are we to accomplish this yielding of our proud hearts? Fénelon spoke of that organization in our lives that precedes yieldedness:

> *Organize your time so that you can find a period every day for resting, meditation, and prayer. This will become easy when you truly love him. We never wonder what we will talk about. He is our friend. Our heart is open to him. We must be completely candid with him, holding nothing back. Even if there is nothing we care to say to him, it is a joy just to be in his presence.*[10]

Spirit and flesh have a very close marriage. They live and hurt and die as one. It is a rare person who clings to integrity in the face of severe suffering. Yet Jesus did it. He humbled himself and clung to obedience and died in blood and gore. But best of all, he sacrificed himself to the pleasure of his servanthood. That's what conformed servants do. They obey! Obedience is the source of character.

The Knee of the Servant (Surrender)

The knee of the servant bends (Philippians 2:10). Where the knee bends, character is born. Not that posture alone is the key to power with God, but it is an indicator of how we see the Almighty. I used to have a prayer partner who began praying on his knees and ended up on his face before God. Why did he do this? His adoration was a malady that only found a cure when he physically humbled himself.

Karl Barth said that prayer is "our longing for Him, our incurable God Sickness."[11] It is a narcosis, an addiction that can never be pleased merely with sipping God when life is born in the swigging.

The knee must bend.

When the knees bend, the King comes! Once when I was in Avila, Spain, I walked into the low stone cell where St. Teresa and St. John of the Cross prayed. The natives of Avila say that they became so engrossed in prayer they levitated. Outlandish? Maybe, though who can know if they did? When we read their work and discover the inherent prostration of their prayers, we can only imagine the glories God bestowed upon their adoration. But I am convinced that the key to God is a bent-knee attitude.

Kneeling should not be seen only as a symbol of devotion. It is far more than that. It is the posture of humility that welcomes the empowering of our lives. When our knees straighten up, we know we must walk again into the fields of service. There is much to do. John Masefield wrote,

> To get the whole world out of bed,
> and washed, and dressed, and warmed, and fed,
> to work, and back to bed again,
> believe me, Saul, costs worlds of pain."[12]

Our whole lives come down in ruin when we live as though we had no knees! I know now the form of a servant is a kneeling form. Consider the things that keep our legs straight. First there is self-sufficiency. We need to learn poverty of spirit. Besides praying, begging is also a kneeling posture. Begging is a pitiful way to make a living—but it is always done with the head lower than that of the need supplier. See yourself as poor and you will come to Christ kneeling, and kneeling you will receive. Then you will insert yourself into meaningful Beatitudes: Blessed are *we* who are poor in spirit, for *ours* is the kingdom.

Narcissism also keeps us from kneeling. Most of our narcissism isn't blatant. In fact, most of us work hard to keep from looking self-centered. We know how to duck our heads and try to look sheepish and yielding if only for the sake of keeping our spiritual reputation. But we are somewhat false. In our public prayer life we cry, "Oh, to be nothing, nothing!" But in our inner lives we cry, "I love meself, I love meself, I pick me up and hug meself."

Remember this: Narcissus was beautiful. The gods all agreed. But as we said earlier, he drowned trying to embrace his own reflection. The metaphor should be a mirror for our pride. Preachers, concert artists, church committee persons, talented church soloists: how many in all these categories live lives serving their own bogus godhood? The apostle's remedy for narcissism was to bend the knee to Christ—a higher God than ego for our needy adoration.

The Tongue of the Servant (Confession)

In time every tongue will confess (Philippians 2:11).* Ultimately Jesus will be confessed by all men. It is only a matter of when. I have tried to imagine that moment when every tongue confesses. Atheists, university professors, literary giants, all coming before the towering glass throne in the great finale of history.

Sometimes I see them wide-eyed, staring in disbelief at the towering throne of God. The Almighty clears his throat with thunder and says, "Ahem!"

The agnostic philosopher falls to his knees weeping, "Oh, my God."

The know-it-all physicist at last cries "uncle."

Imagine it: Karl Marx, Frederich Nietszche, Bertrand Russell, Madeleine Murray O'Hair, crying the name "Jesus" at the last gates of foreverness. It is the moment of the dumbfounded "yes," every tongue confessing the name it spent a lifetime doubting.

What do we confess? We confess what one poor woman confessed on her seventy-sixth birthday as she came to faith in Christ: "God, I've very little to give you. All I've got left is my future." But this is salvation. To be redeemed is to start where the future begins and breathe the name "Lord." At this word Christian character is born.

A certain king loved his holy man and court prophet so much he ordered his picture to be painted. When the picture was unveiled, it was the holy man to a tee except for his face. The face was leering, hateful, twisted by grudge, and snarling in vengeance.

The king was so disturbed he was about to take the artist's life, when the holy man stopped the execution order.

"Oh, king," he cried, "spare this artist! He has painted a picture of the man all my life I have tried not to become!" Such a servant understands the word "character."

The tongue of the servant must ever be proclaiming, "Jesus is Lord! Master of all things." Anything less would be like the sound of fingernails across a blackboard, a cell phone in a movie theater, or a catfight in the middle of the night. Shrill, irritating, intrusive, and entirely inappropriate.

---

*The spiritual discipline of confession is such an important part of the Christian life that I have devoted an entire section (part 4) to its discussion. Here I merely want to emphasize the act of declaring Jesus as Lord as a characteristic of a servant.

Instead, let our lips forever be filled with adoration and praise for our majestic Savior.

Character: forged *in extremis*

Character is a by-product of our hunger for a deeper relationship with God. None of the saints ever worked on character development. They never hungered to be holy as though holiness were a virtue to be sought. They were needy men and women who cried out for concord with Jesus. The pursuit of any other virtue was unnecessary.

Character is a word of dignity; it finds its life in discipline and work. Character is the hidden "us," what we are in the dark. Our outer lives are veneered by dress and protocol: the politics of all nasty-niceties, our salad-fork relationships. But our inner lives are to be nourished by the seeping springs of character. You can buy personality cheap, but character is not for sale.

How do we get this character? Both character and holiness are best found where our need for Jesus is extreme. And our needs are most apparent where life dumps trials on us! To be tested in the extreme is to learn spiritual dependency. When our torn souls settle on the impaling stakes, we can define our need. It comes *in extremis*! We cringe when we think of letting other people gain control of our lives. Yet the time when we best develop character is when we are no longer in charge of our circumstances. To be under the heel of someone else's will or to suffer the indignity of crushing circumstances, these incarcerations of body give wings to the spirit.

We have to remember that Jesus was never more his own man than when he was bound, flogged, and crucified. He did not come across to any casual Roman observer as a man who was winning. When you are forced to die naked before your own mother, it can make you seem a loser with none on earth to vouch for your character. But Jesus was winning. And through his long ordeal of human abandonment, he remained in perfect union with his Father.

> You can buy personality cheap, but character is not for sale.

Now, says Paul, he beckons us to self-crucifixion. And why voluntarily raise our own cross and die to self? Because self-crucifixion is not only the stuff of character, it is the essence of union with Christ.

So we are to bless our adversities and make them paving stones to our own Calvary of togetherness with God. We must be crucified with Christ (Galatians 2:20). Oh, how we want to turn from the nails. How we wish that we could avoid the naked humiliation of Golgotha. Not possible. Remember, we seldom arrive at humility without humiliation. So we cannot simply bless our finished and final state of being in Christ. We must first bless the crosses that produce our character.

Solzhenitsyn did not enjoy the contemptible Soviet prison or the myopic Soviet justice system that put him there. Why then did he cry at last, where all the world could hear him, "Prison, I bless you!"? Because in losing control of his circumstances he was given what his secure Soviet overlords could never give him—character. Only when he could no longer say he was in charge of his world could the real Solzhenitsyn come to be!

In Philippians 2, Paul, Timothy, and Epaphroditus were all crying, "Prison, I bless you!" Crushed by low stone ceilings and iron bars, Paul sings his liberationist song of servanthood. Christ-character does not come until we have lost control. While we are in charge, we swagger in our arrogance and grow smug in our weaknesses, which we assume to be strengths. But when we lose control, we see our weaknesses and let God transform them into strengths. Those who are in charge long enough finally use their power to crucify others. But the nail side of the cross is the wisdom side of crucifixion; the nail side of dying is the place where character is born!

Born? Nay, *forged!*

The forge is the anvil where heat and hammer are applied to recalcitrant metal. It is the white-hot, clanging, bruising blows that shape the iron:

> *In this you greatly rejoice, though now for a little while you may have had to suffer grief in all kinds of trials. These have come so that your faith—of greater worth than gold, which perishes even though refined by fire—may be proved genuine and may result in praise, glory and honor when Jesus Christ is revealed.*
> —1 Peter 1:6–7

Character: living beyond ourselves

Christian character understands that it is our failure to crave God that alienates us from the rest of the world. Our failure to draw near to God keeps our entire world at arm's length. Then a haunting loneliness possesses us, and we are often so paralyzed by it we cannot care for the world around us. We hurt because of this remoteness.

This caring work of character must often work while we bear inner hurt, and live while we are healing from the hurt. Mehmet Ali Agca was an unknown Turkish teenager before May 13, 1981, when his name was emblazoned around the world in four-inch headlines as the man who shot the pope. The assassin and his victim met later in Rebibbia prison.

Character is like that. It can suffer the wounds of an assassin, then turn in the spirit of Christ to forgive. Character is the pope visiting Ali Agca on Christmas 1983. We know he visited with him for twenty-one minutes, and those near at hand said he spoke with Ali Agca as a "brother." They say he showed him the way to the Father. When a man of great power seeks his enemy, and they sit together and talk of God, character is the issue. This virtue is not forged in a congenial atmosphere of discussion but in the high, thin air of all that threatens our survival.

Character is also found by losing oneself in a cause much larger than ourselves. I used to wonder how Mahatma Gandhi could stand around in a loincloth at a British State function when everyone else was dressed in tuxedoes. Now, I know that his was not a nakedness he assumed to embarrass tuxedo-wearers. Rather, it was a way of identifying with the national dress of the poor of his homeland. Once when Gandhi walked into Buckingham Palace to take tea with the king, he was questioned about the appropriateness of his dress. Gandhi replied, "The king was wearing enough for both of us!"[13]

Wearing only a loincloth, he changed the destiny of India. He was caught up in a cause that, near-naked, would change the world. Christ changed the world in his own naked crucifixion, and said to his followers,

> "And why do you worry about clothes? See how the lilies of the field grow. They do not labor or spin. Yet I tell you that not even Solomon in all his splendor was dressed like one of these. . . . Do not worry, saying, 'What shall we eat?' or 'What shall we drink?' or 'What shall we wear?' . . . But seek first his kingdom and his righteousness, and all these things will be given to you as well."
> —Matthew 6:28–33

Our cause is the kingdom! Our way of service is the matrix of character. One of the great needs in Christianity is to regain the sense of this burning cause. What Paul and other martyrs died for, we live for.

Consider a simple woman—a pastor's wife—whom I had not seen for ten years. She died a quiet death eclipsed by the loud political folderol of Watergate. She had a debilitating cancer that destroyed her by its creeping weakness until her vigorous spirit was swallowed up in a sallow-eyed quietness too weak even to whimper—then she was gone.

I last saw her two weeks before she died. She was weak but her smile was robust. She was not strong enough to live long, and she knew she was dying!

"How are you doing, Nellie?" I asked.

"Fine. I taught Sunday school to four-year-olds yesterday," she chirped.

"But how? You're so weak. You should be in bed," I said.

"Well," she said, "I had to do it! There was no one else! Their regular Sunday school teacher was down with a cold." She seemed not to notice any irony in what she was saying. Character begins its life where ego dies—literally dies—and never notices its passing.

Jesus alone imparts such character. He calls us to it, ordains us in it, and equips us for it.

He died! Death is enough to make a man
And tell us how he did with all his dreams.
He who whimpers or dies mute is he who can
Reveal to us that courage rarely screams.
I've heard it said that those who saw his death
Could hear His breathing seven meters past
The shadow of His cross. His labored breath,
Did not one hateful malediction cast.
Can character alone say He was God?
I think not. Others have been hated too.
Contempt will rarely give its love a nod.
We alone decide which truths are true.
Still, where character bleeds over wood,
God marks the fine and designates the good.[14]

Disease is a loss of balance in part or in all of the organism. It may begin in the spirit and in bodily disintegration. It may start from physical causes and react upon the psyche. But always it is a loss of balance in one's basic being.[1]

—DAVID SEABURY

And here at last we find
Strict diagnosis of our malady,
Which is, in short, that man is heaven-starved—
Men are born thirsting for infinity.[2]

—E. STANLEY JONES

The greatest negative in the universe is the cross, for with it God wiped out everything that was not of himself: the greatest positive in the universe is the Resurrection, for through it God brought into being all he will have in the new sphere.[3]

—WATCHMAN NEE

Know thyself, said Socrates, and you will know the world. Had Socrates known Jesus, he would have seen there is a first step. Know God, said Jesus, or you will never really know yourself.

Love yourself, not out of personal conceit but because God is the object of your love. Another person should not be angry with you if you love that individual as God's child.

Jesus said, "Love the Lord your God with all your heart and with all your soul and with all your mind" (Matthew 22:37). This means that every thought you have, your entire life and understanding, should be focused on God. When he says "with all your heart, soul, and mind," he does not leave any part of you free to love anything else.

If something other than God seems lovable to you, channel it into that river of divine love.

If you truly love your neighbor, let your behavior toward that person be based on a total love of God. Then, when you love your neighbor as yourself, you put both loves into that stream of the love of God, the way creeks feed rivers. All of them lead into the larger body of water and none diminish it.

Love others for the sake of God. Love God for his own sake.[4]

—AUGUSTINE

CHAPTER ELEVEN

Arriving at Self-Understanding

In most every age, being rich and having meaning are generally conceived to be the same thing. But Jesus made it clear that if we have the whole world and lose our souls, we don't count for much. A certain rich man once requested being buried upright behind the steering wheel of his solid gold Cadillac. The funeral connoted wealth, but in reality was a statement of disinheritance. One bystander was heard to remark as the car and its embalmed driver settled into an oversized grave, "Now that's really living!" It is common in these days of the rich and famous to state *who we are* in terms of *what we have*. It is a foolish notion that Jesus died to correct.

In our upside-down world, people who have very little sometimes find wonderful reasons to be happy, while people who have much are miserable. Our skewed philosophy leads us to lament with the words of a once popular song: "Ask the rich man, he'll confess, money can't buy happiness. Ask the poor man, he don't doubt that he'd rather be miserable with than without." Like Tevye in *Fiddler on the Roof*, the poor man cries out to God, asking if it would ruin some wide and divine plan if he were a wealthy man. Solomon was across the gamut from Tevye—he could buy the fiddler on the roof. He was a rich man who had too much of everything. From his abundance came boredom. From his boredom issued despondency, and from his despondency came the book of Ecclesiastes.

The book of Ecclesiastes was written by a man who reflected long and sometimes negatively about the meaning of life. In a day like ours, when good times and wealth look continually beautiful on television, we need

Ecclesiastes. It is the laboratory where the rich may study depression and boredom. Our films and novels glorify riches, power, and indulgence. Sex is the acceptable obsession of those who have everything (Solomon had a thousand wives), and power, as Henry Kissinger so delicately put it, is the ultimate aphrodisiac. Power and its abuse have rarely done the world much good. Still, most people would rather run a show than be a part of someone else's. Milton's Satan testified that it is better to rule in hell than serve in heaven.

Apparently it never occurred to Solomon that indulgence and sacrificial service represent a fork in the same road—one leads to power and the other to sacrifice. But no one chooses point-blank between power and sacrifice. The choice of self-denial is made first. We either choose to deny ourselves and live in relationship with Christ or we pursue some realm of personal influence.

The altar of this decision is the greatest shrine of our lives. When choosing which road we shall travel we are also picking a traveling companion. Jesus beckons us down one road and Satan down the other. Jesus is poorly dressed and is standing next to his own cross while beckoning toward a second cross that he clearly means for us to carry. Satan on the other road is in a sequined jacket holding bank bags and nodding to us with a "come hither" look. Christ aims to make us useful, Satan to make us a star.

We choose. Most travel the Tempter's turnpike. But those who journey with Jesus traverse a road less traveled. Christ reminds his companions that the rich and famous on the popular road are gradually descending into the final abyss of ego and death. Their reward is at best a nice casket and a more expensive gravestone than the martyrs can afford. But the nice road goes nowhere.

We who choose Christ find the destiny is only somewhat better than the journey. We walk with him. We talk. He listens. We hurt. He touches us with healing. We puzzle over life's riddles, and he gives us answers. When there are no answers, he agrees to wait with us till we reach that land where all question marks are banned by instant understanding.

As the journey ends, Jesus is in two places, and a blessed paradox is ours. The same Christ who was always our traveling companion is now our host, extending his arms to welcome us home. At last we can see clearly that a certain destiny was always better than the gilded casket.

A Meaningless Pursuit

But what of the travelers on the wide road? There sex is the holiest mysticism that the rich and famous—and temporal—can know. The body beautiful is the ultimate value on that road. Ego is the small Baal of the surface generation, who choose in favor of themselves. Their values are all chalk and plaster. On that road, Mr. Dow and Mr. Jones direct the traffic. Life is generally conceived to exist at the corner of Wall Street and Sunset Boulevard. There Calvin Klein has an obsession and Victoria a secret.

What would King Solomon have looked like in our day? I believe he would have tried the Wall Street approach, riding a bull market down the wide avenue of financial success. He would have tried moral abandon and Internet sex. He would have tried the drug scene, that long trip punctuated by hallucinations and hangovers.

He surely would have tried sports cars, and gurus, and yoga, and karate, and Tae-Bo, and golf, and Smirnoff, and Canada Dry. He would have experimented with mountain-climbing, and scuba diving, and skydiving, and pearl diving, and Las Vegas, and Disneyland. He would have tried art theaters, celebrity fund-raising, super-cammed Ferraris, Swedish movie actresses, yacht racing, Sun Valley, the Tournament of Roses, parties at Martha's Vineyard, speculating on off-shore oil sites around Santa Barbara, skinny-dipping, sensitivity sessions, and discussing Eric Fromm with his psychoanalyst. But alas, nothing would ever really be any fun for him. The wanton can never get enough e's into their "Wheees" to convince themselves they are truly having a good time.

> # Life is generally conceived to exist at the corner of Wall Street and Sunset Boulevard. There Calvin Klein has an obsession and Victoria a secret.

While most of us do not have the means to live a life of such frivolity, we have succumbed to the notion that this lifestyle represents the good life. Most of the wide-road culture is committed to making everything as beautiful as it can be. But most of the search for meaning ends up empty. The biography of each is two verses from the book of Ecclesiastes: "What a heavy burden God has laid on men! I have seen all the things that are done under the sun; all of them are meaningless, a chasing after the wind" (Ecclesiastes 1:13–14).

What an agonizing cry! Is it true that all of life's pursuits are meaningless? Becket said, "Eat and defecate, the dish and the pot, this is the extremity of man." And Cherea says in *Caligula*: "Here is what frightens me. To lose one's life is a little thing, and I will have the courage when necessary. But to see the sense of this life dissipated, to see our reason for existence disappear, that is what is intolerable. A man cannot live without meaning."

What we need is to sit a spell with God. If there is an answer to meaninglessness it lies in this closet of the heart. Whittier understood this:

> *And so I find it well to come*
> *For deeper rest to this still room,*
> *For here the habit of the soul*
> *Feels less the outer world's control . . .*
> *And from the silence multiplied*
> *By these still forms on either side,*
> *The world that time and sense have known*
> *Falls off and leaves us God alone.*[5]

Oh, how much is lost when we grasp at life's goodies and refuse to unfold our hands to receive what he will give us! Frederick Buechner wrote, "Go where your best prayers take you, unclench the fists of your spirit and take it easy. Breathe deep of the glad air and live one day at a time. Know that you are precious."[6]

Christians evangelize the world because we believe we have the answer to the question "What is the meaning of life?" Solomon was a man who said on nearly every page of his book, "I have encountered God, and I still have doubts about all the things that are supposed to pour meaning into my life." Most suicide notes throb with the questions that lie at the center of Ecclesiastes.

Meaning and malcontentment

The negativity of Solomon's search is completed in the Gospels. Jesus said that truth is freedom (John 8:32). Yet many are imprisoned in a world where truth is hard to come by and where they themselves are shackled to damning, materialistic falsehoods. See if you recognize yourself in Solomon's words: "There was a man all alone; he had neither son nor brother. There was no end to his toil, yet his eyes were not content with his wealth. 'For whom am I toiling,' he asked, 'and why am I depriving myself of enjoyment?' This too is meaningless—a miserable business!" (Ecclesiastes 4:8).

Years ago a movie called *The Love Bug* was released. It was the story of a very animated Volkswagen with the unlikely name of Herbie. In one scene, Herbie is parked at a '50s-style drive-in theater. In an attempt to foster the hero and heroine's romance, Herbie refuses to open his doors or windows and let them out. The trapped heroine begins pounding on the window and shouting to a couple of hippies in the next car, "Help, I'm a prisoner!"

The hairy hippie waves at her, crams a huge hamburger through his mouthful of mottled green teeth, and replies nonchalantly, "We all prisoners, chicky-baby!"

Lofty philosophy for a not-so-lofty movie.

Jesus said unless we accept him as the redeeming truth, we will remain prisoners forever without hope. In America we have almost made a hell of our prosperity. We have more than we can spend—more than we need. But our plenty is not freedom. It is an imprisonment of substance. We are serving lies and are prisoners of falsehoods. How do prisoners of peacelessness ever find contentment? By winning on Wall Street? By getting enough money to move from one shining ghetto to the next? Of course not! If we ever know contentment, we will find it in the wellspring of only one truth: God is in Christ reconciling the world to himself.

> We have more than we can spend—more than we need. But our plenty is not freedom. It is an imprisonment of substance. We are serving lies and are prisoners of falsehoods.

Lorenzo Scupoli understood that just as serving Christ brings joy, self-serving brings peacelessness. As self is the god of unhappiness, self-denial is the balm. Scupoli says we need a healthy distrust of our need to serve the self:

> There are four things we need to do if we would gain this spiritually healthy distrust of ourselves.
>
> Meditate upon our own weakness. *Admit that we cannot accomplish the smallest good without God's help.*
>
> Beg God for what he alone can give. *Acknowledge that we don't have it and that we can't go somewhere and get it. Let's fall down at the feet of our Lord and plead with him to grant our request.*
>
> Gradually discard the illusions of our own mind, *our tendency to sin, and begin to see the overwhelming, yet hidden, obstacles that surround us.*
>
> As often as we commit a fault, we must take inventory of our weaknesses. *God permits us to fall only in order to help us gain deeper insight into ourselves.*
>
> God permits us to sin more or less grievously in proportion to

our pride. Every time we commit a fault, we should earnestly ask God to enlighten us. Ask him to help you see yourself as you are in his sight.

Presume no more on your own strength. *Otherwise, you will stumble again over the same stone.*[7]

Whoever will save his life must give it away, says Christ.

Many years ago my son taught me about saving. He was always a "saver." He had an odd way of phrasing things when he was a boy. He used to capture worms and bugs, put them in jars with perforated lids and say he was "saving" them. I can remember, for instance, when he had a little wooly worm in a jar, and I asked him, "What are you doing with this wooly worm?"

He said, "Dad, I'm saving it."

He did the worm no favor at all. Its beautiful fur gradually fuzzed into a kind of lethal dryness. Caterpillars don't die, they just fade away. Still he was undeterred! He went on trying to "save" things. He saved goldfish until they died.

One day when we were having a family picnic near a stream, he took a milk carton down to the edge of the water and scooped up three tadpoles, whom he called Peter, Paul, and Mary. We took them home. I never knew how he could tell them apart, but he seemed to have each named. He kept them in a jar in his room until the water turned green; but the tadpoles rather liked green water, and they generally did better than most of his pets had done. I asked him from time to time, "Tim, what are you doing?" and he'd say, "Dad, I'm just saving them."

Well, Peter ultimately died. Then Paul died. Mary became the lone survivor of this tadpole trio, and actually achieved froghood. She grew front legs and back legs and lost her tail, but I could tell she wasn't happy. So I said to Tim, "Tim, if you save Mary much longer, she's going to end up like Peter and Paul. If you really want to save Mary, you've got to let her go." He agreed! So we got into the family car and we drove Mary back to her ancestral home at Two Rivers. We took her out of the car, walked down to the river, and opened up her little imprisoning box and let her hop out as we sang a few bars of "Born Free."

Human beings by nature want to hug life and hold on to it, choke it down, save it and keep it. But Jesus taught there's only one way to know life's meaning: "Fear God and keep his commandments, for this is the whole duty of man" (Ecclesiastes 12:13). We gain happiness by letting go of this life.

Cease the desperate grasping for the promises of the world. Instead, give it all to Jesus. Lay it on the altar of God. Only then can contentment begin to make itself known. Paul wrote, "I have learned to be content whatever the circumstances. I know what it is to be in need, and I know what it is to have plenty. I have learned the secret of being content in any and every situation, whether well fed or hungry, whether living in plenty or in want" (Philippians 4:11–12).

Charting the course to self-understanding

John 21 contains a wonderful passage in which Jesus is alive from the dead once again. The apostles, however, are uneasy and unsure about his unexpected appearances. Jesus seems to them to be forever showing up at unusual places, catching them off guard. Then Jesus absents himself for a while. After some days of "no show," they are back on board their boat fishing when, presto! Jesus shows up on the fog-bound shores of the Sea of Galilee, silhouetted against the early gray of morning. He calls out to them, "Children, have you any meat?"

"No!" they cry.

"Cast down your nets on the other side!" shouts Jesus.

They do. And they drag in such a haul of fish that the nets almost break.

Peter, sensing it is the Lord (he is naked aboard ship), throws his fisher's coat about him and casts himself into the sea, quickly swimming to shore. Once ashore, Jesus already has a campfire blazing. Nothing much! In our day it may have been a camp pot of coffee brewing over an open fire. After the others bring the boat in . . .

> Simon Peter climbed aboard and dragged the net ashore. It was full of large fish, 153, but even with so many the net was not torn. . . . When they had finished eating, Jesus said to Simon Peter, "Simon son of John, do you truly love me more than these?" "Yes, Lord," he said, "you know that I love you." Jesus said, "Feed my lambs."
> —John 21:11–15

Within this story can be found a number of common reasons for our struggle to find meaning to our Christianity. Let these discoveries help you begin to chart your course to self-understanding.

We Have Never Made a Decision About How Much We Love Jesus Christ

One of the first reasons Christians remain unhappy in the church and in Christ is that they never make a decision about how much they love

Jesus. In John 21:11, Simon Peter counts fish. It was, after all, his career, his business! Jesus had called him to be a disciple-maker, a fisher of men, but now he's back in the other kind of fishing business again. Jesus wants to challenge him with the supreme question, "Have you ever made a decision, Simon, about how much you love me?" So in verse 15, Jesus asks him, "How much do you love me? More than these?" as he points to the catch of 153 fish.

When Barb and I were first married, we moved to Kansas City, where I was to continue my seminary studies. She had never really seen me as a student, at least not in "her" house. Late one night I was reading Augustine, and she came to me, slipped her arm around me over the back of the chair and said, "Do you love me?"

"Yeah," I said. "Sure, I love you," never missing a paragraph of Augustine.

Now, it's hard for a woman to go from that wonderful euphoria and buoyancy of a honeymoon to nearly being ignored. So she leaned a little farther over the chair and said a second time, like Jesus said to Simon at Galilee, "Do you really love me?"

And I said, "Sure, I love you." Again, I went right on reading.

And then she asked me a third time.

"Sure, I love you," I repeated, getting a little exasperated. "Your mother loves you, the world loves you, and I love you . . . and I'm busy."

It's the only time in our more than forty years of marriage that I've heard her swear, and her profanity that night was the single word *"Toad!"*

I hadn't yet learned to prioritize. When people ask you questions of worship and love, and certainly when Jesus asks you, the world must stop while you answer them.

We Are Seeking a Relationship Without Responsibility

A second cause of Christian unhappiness is that we often seek a relationship without responsibility. Jesus Christ didn't save us to lollygag in his love for the rest of our lives. He has a lost world out there that needs saving.

When I was a pastor, I hated it most when I called on some church member who had to be "wet-nursed" for the week because his or her "little" feelings had gotten hurt. I always wanted to say to them, "Look, while you're here fondling your pettiness, others are struggling with hell itself." Christ wants us to understand our responsibility. If we love him, there's significant work to be done!

If we are unhappy in Jesus, it could be because we have forgotten that God didn't call us merely to enjoy him but to serve him. When we are busy helping other people, it's amazing how unimportant our own little griev-ances can look. There are so many people who walk through the church doors with great hurts. Even when we are among the hurting, we can arrive at personal peace faster by trying to give understanding to others than by seeking it for ourselves.

We Have Failed to Commit Ourselves

The third source of unhappiness is when we say, "I don't want to com-mit myself." In the John 21 passage we referred to earlier, Jesus is using all the big words ("Simon, do you *love* me?") and Simon is answering him using little words ("Yes, Lord, I *like* you."). "Like" is the recipe for poor commitment.

Simon's big failure was to say "Lord" so fast he didn't really mean it. Our failure to say "Lord" clearly and surely brings misery. Ian Thomas said,

> This is a tragedy of Christendom today, as it was the tragedy of God's people Israel then, for forty years in the wilderness. A peo-ple who lived in self-imposed poverty! Every day they spent in the desert was a day they could have spent in Canaan—for God had given them the land! They would not believe, however, that the God who brought them out was the God who could bring them in![8]

We Have Refused to Live by the Will of Another

The fourth reason for Christian unhappiness is the blatant confes-sion, "I just don't want to live by somebody else's will." We rarely ever say this out loud, but that's what we mean. Jesus says to Simon in John 21:18, "I tell you the truth, when you were younger you dressed yourself and went where you wanted; but when you are old you will stretch out your hands, and someone else will dress you and lead you where you do not want to go." It was a less than bright promise that Peter would live to see old age.

The will of God can lead us into some kinds of commitment that we may not want to make. And it's hard to abandon what we want in favor of what God wants! Ian Thomas says we can do anything through Christ, but the key is to allow Christ to work his will through our lives.

> I may say to a glove, "Glove, pick up this Bible," and yet, some-how, the glove cannot do it. It's got a thumb and fingers, the shape and form of a hand, and yet it is unable to do the thing I command

171

it to do. . . . As soon, however, as my hand comes into that glove, the glove becomes as strong as my hand. Everything possible to my hand becomes possible to that glove.[9]

God wants us to yield to his infilling power. Our refusal to yield results in stubbornness, which is powerless.

We Are Too Concerned About What God Is Doing in Someone Else's Life

When Peter gets the bad news of how he is going to die (as a martyr), he is naturally concerned about what kind of deal the rest of the apostles are going to get, so he turns and sees John and asks, "Lord, what about him?"

Jesus answers, "If I want him to remain alive until I return, what is that to you? You must follow me" (John 21:20–22).

If we are going to be truly happy, we need to quit comparing our lot in life with the good deals that someone else is getting. When we dwell on God's seeming unfairness, bitterness begins to grow. So Christ says, "Stop it! Quit comparing yourself with brilliant and talented people. Follow me."

Conclusion

George MacDonald listed what he called three grand essentials—three things without which no meaningful life can be lived: someone to love, something to do, and something to hope for. The world can only be saved as we become that glove into which Jesus Christ inserts the divine hand. With that kind of power working in our lives, what is the limit? There is none! What is joy? It is Christ.

Ecclesiastes points out that we are flawed. So what? There is joy in understanding that God has repaired our flawed natures. Now we who were once of no use to God are mended. Past our healed brokenness we are actually being used. "A soldier asked Abba Mius, one of the Desert Fathers, if God accepted repentance. After the old man had taught him many things, he said, 'Tell me, my dear (friend), if your cloak is torn, do you throw it away?' He replied, 'No, I mend it and use it again.' The old man said to him, 'If you are so careful about your cloak, will not God be equally careful of his creatures?' "[10]

We were torn and now
we are mended,
useless and now used.

172

We were once cast-off
commodities
and now we are
the spendable
currency of God.
Hallelujah!

The Confessional Life

Let us strive to enter by the narrow gate. Just as the trees, if they have not stood before the winter's storms cannot bear fruit, so it is with us; this present age is a storm and it is only through many trials and temptations that we can obtain an inheritance in the kingdom of heaven."[1]

—AMMA THEODORA

Great endeavors and hard struggles await those who are converted, but afterwards inexpressible joy. If you want to light a fire, you are troubled at first by smoke, and your eyes water. But in the end you achieve your aim. Now it is written: "Our God is a consuming fire." So we must light the divine fire in us with tears and struggle.[2]

—AMMA SYNCLETICA

I need Thee, O I need Thee,
Every hour I need Thee!
O bless me now, my Savior,
I come to Thee.[3]

—ANNA S. HAWKS

How shall I approach, thee, O my God?
Come clean, my child.
Scrub yourself up with honesty.
Wash your inconsistencies
with confession.
Then our togetherness will bless me
and I will call you my child.
And our union will grant you
access to my throne.

O Lord, I know not what to ask of Thee. Thou alone knowest what are my true needs. Thou lovest me more than I myself know how to love. Help me to see my real needs which are concealed from me. I dare not ask either a cross or a consolation. I can only wait on Thee. My heart is open to Thee. Visit and help me, for Thy great mercy's sake. Strike me and heal me, cast me down and raise me up. I worship in silence Thy holy will and Thine inscrutable ways. I offer myself as a sacrifice to Thee. I put all my trust in Thee. I have no other desire than to fulfill Thy will. Teach me how to pray. Pray Thou Thyself in me. Amen.[4]

—PHILARET OF MOSCOW

CHAPTER TWELVE

Confession and the Glory of Our Neediness

The inner lie is "I'm OK." The outer lie is "You're OK." The cultural tomfoolery is that everybody's OK. There are two ways to deal with our sin. The first is to look at it and say, "I'm OK." The second is to say, "Well, to be entirely honest about it, I'm not OK, but that's OK because Christ is more than OK, in fact, he's all-sufficient."

Beginning in the middle of the twentieth century the idea of sin began to disappear. Karl Menninger lamented its passing in his outstanding book *Whatever Became of Sin?* He protested the rise of I'm OK—You're OK psychology. He went so far as to say that to speak of our OK-ness in the face of human depravity was like speaking of a bluebird on a dung heap. People who continually congratulate themselves on their own OK-ness are not good candidates for grace. Need is the best incentive to entice us to the all-sufficient Christ. "The martyred archbishop of El Salvador, Oscar Romero, once said that only the poor can celebrate Christmas, those who 'know they need someone to come on their behalf.' "[5] Those who know they are spiritually hungry are swift to find the bread of God. And when they see the cross, they are fast to say, "I'm sorry. Come, Holy Spirit, for my emptiness must have your fullness now."

Could it be that this is why Bonaventure cried at Christmas, "And now my soul embrace the manger; press your lips on the Christ child's feet in a devout kiss; follow in your mind the shepherd's adoration; contemplate with wonder the assisting host of angels. . . ."[6] It is clear to me that our need has been met by the condescending God, who loved us enough to despise the pearl city, preferring straw and stables. And we, the poor of spirit, could not help but mark his coming.

Confession is the key to a right relationship with God. In a tenth-century
poem, Eve confesses her sin and the
cost of it all: "I am Eve; great Adam's
wife; it is I that outraged Jesus of old;
it is I that stole heaven from my Children; by rights it is I that should have

> Confession is the key to a right relationship with God.

gone upon The Tree."[7] With the psalmist Eve understands that her sin is not against Adam alone. It is against God.

In the same tenth-century poem, Judas, the damned, laments, "Woe is me that I forsook my King." While Judas is damned forever in this apocryphal tale, he also understands that his sin is against God.

We are sinners. Sin cost Jesus his life. Sin is real. Sin is serious, and sin is a barrier between ourselves and God. But sin need not cause us to live with guilt or self-condemnation. Confession is God's answer to guilt. Psalm 51 comes with a superscription that reads, "A psalm of David. When the prophet Nathan came to him after David had committed adultery with Bathsheba." Or, to put it honestly, "A Psalm of David, after he had been caught."

There are two times that one may confess a sin: before and after getting caught! If you confess it before you are caught, it's called "confession." If after, "owning up." If you wait till after you get caught, you will find that the pain of "owning up" is harder than you could ever have imagined. And the heaviness burdens the confession. David confessed, and healing fol-lowed his honesty. "For I know my transgressions, and my sin is always before me" (Psalm 51:3). There is born in all of us a strong need to confess our sin. Neediness is not only the state of the unrepentant heart, it is its glory. Confession is the way back to our lost relationship with God.

At the screen of the confessional booth, the confessor says to the priest, "Bless me, Father, for I have sinned. . . . It has been _____ days since my last confession." This referralism sets communicants free from the "priest-hood of the priest" to put in effect "the priesthood of the believer." Still, Protestants and evangelicals are generally less punctual about confession. Could it be we don't take our sins too seriously?

When anyone says to me, "I haven't confessed my sins in a long time," I know it's not because they have less sin than other people. The real prob-lem is that they are self-excusing and have not conceived—or maybe they just don't care—that their sin is in the way of their relationship with God. Every healthy Christian hungers to confess because they take their rela-tionship with God seriously.

In terms of prayer, there may actually be only one sin. It is not the sin of wearying God, *fatigare deos*, with our confessions, but the sin of not longing after God. "If God does not tire, still we may tire of longing," writes Annie Dillard.[8]

And does God hear and forgive the longing lover? Of course. But unconfessed sin always remains our greatest roadblock to grace. St. Nicholas Cabasilas wrote,

> *Of the many things which impede our salvation the greatest of all is that when we commit any transgression we do not at once turn back to God and ask forgiveness. Because we feel shame and fear we think that the way back to God is difficult, and that He is angry and ill-tempered towards us, and that there is need of great preparation if we wish to approach Him. But the loving-kindness of God utterly banishes this thought from the soul. What can prevent anyone who clearly knows how kind He is and that, as it is said, "while you are yet speaking He will say, 'Here I am.'"*[9]

Love means having to say I'm sorry

Husbands and wives must know how to say "I'm sorry" in the day-to-day context of the marriage relationship. Why then would any believer confess to Jesus once and then feel that he or she need never do it again? George Bernard Shaw said of marriage that "people in love are under the influence of the most violent, the most insane, the most transient of passions. They are required," he said, "to testify in court that they will remain in this excited, abnormal, exalted condition till death do them part." New Christians make the same mistake. Many Christians seem to feel it is up to them to keep alive the first joys of their salvation. Not so. The love we bear God is not left to our keeping. There is a wonderful intoxication in grace, but we are not called upon to sustain that elation throughout the whole of our relationship with Christ.

Just as no couple can forever live in that wonderful euphoria of the first months of marriage, Christians cannot maintain the high elation they felt when first they knew the Lord. If you have peace in either relationship, you have to learn the laws of undulation in that relationship. All fervor—even saving fervor—waxes and wanes. The first law of relationship says, "You must live openly before God." First John 1:9 says, "If we confess our sins, he is faithful and just and will forgive us our sins and purify us from all unrighteousness." To acknowledge our sin is to strengthen our God-relationship.

David's sin—so freely confessed in Psalm 51—does not take God by surprise. God is fully aware of all that David has done. But even though God knows all that David has done, he still needs to hear David being open about his sin. Repentance is not just getting God to look at our sin; it's our willingness to stand together with God while we both look at our sins. Does God know that we've sinned? Of course!

What does God really want? "If we confess our sins, he is faithful . . . and will forgive us our sins" seems at first glance to suggest God wants us to confess every last sin. But I don't think God really wants a blow-by-blow description of all our sins. So we need never be neurotic at the end of the day if we can't remember all our sins. Instead of a well-kept ledger of our iniquities, God desires from each of us a penitent attitude of heart. As we confess continually, we grow in our relationship with him.

That demonic relative Uncle Screwtape advised Wormwood that the quickest way to defeat his client was to withhold from him the law of undulation: "Let him assume that the first ardor of his conversion might have been expected to last forever, and that his present dryness is an equally permanent condition. Having once got this misconception well fixed in his head, you can then proceed in various ways."[10] Trying to convince ourselves that the elation conversion is permanent is the sweet path of defeat.

The barrier of unconfessed sin

The carrying of unconfessed need sponsors a kind of neediness that St. Silouan called affliction. It is a crippled state of heart that knows no other healing than what God offers.

> The best thing of all is to surrender to God's will, and bear affliction with confidence in God. The Lord seeing our affliction will never give us too much to bear. If we seem to ourselves to be greatly afflicted, it means that we have not surrendered to the will of God.[11]

But how does this kind of neediness affect us? Let us examine the importance of confession in this way. Suppose you catch a friend of yours in the very act of adultery. As you turn into your driveway, you look into the window of the house next door. There you see your friend embracing the wife of the man who lives on the other side of you. Just as you see him, he glances out the window and sees you. The illicit relationship is discovered by both parties at once. But suppose he forgets your discovery of his sin and never brings it up again. What chance does your friendship have? All great relationships are built on openness. This openness, this acknowledgment, this confession becomes our bridge to the Father. Only this can assuage spiritual neediness.

The great canon of St. Andrew of Crete calls out,

From the depths of Hell
I cried with all my heart to our merciful God,
And he heard me.
And he raised up my life from corruption.[12]

Our confession always meets his forgiveness.

Among our evangelism methodologies, we often learn that faith in Christ is a bridge . . . a two-pier suspension bridge. One pier is in this world, the other pier is in God's world. One pier is fixed in our sinful, messy lives, the other is firmly planted in God's mercy. We're able to meet God in the very center of this wonderful bridge of relationship. But if we don't trust the piers, we won't walk out on the bridge, and then no relationship is possible at all.

One must live so that he and the Father can be one:

Nothing between my soul and my Savior
So that his blessed face may be seen.
Nothing preventing the least of his favor,
I'll triumph at last with nothing between.

Confession opens us up to God. "Against you, you only, have I sinned and done what is evil in your sight" (Psalm 51:4a), says the psalmist. What can David mean by such a phrase? Hasn't he murdered a man to take his wife? Hasn't he slept with Bathsheba and conceived a child in an illicit relationship? Hasn't he lied to the prophet of God? Hasn't he worn the phony, plastic face of self-righteousness at every point of natural diplomacy? Has he not, in effect, considered Uriah's wife and said to the prophet of God, "I did not have sex with that woman"? Having offended nearly everybody he possibly can, how can he now say, "God, against you only have I sinned"? Because he knows that sin against all others has its greatest consequence not on earth but in the epicenter of heaven.

Seeing our sin and its consequences

The great liberation of life is to see that our transgressions are not only in terms of the people we have wronged but also in terms of the living God! Neediness is good if it draws us to God. The orthodox funeral service testifies:

I am the image of Thine ineffable glory,
though I bear the brands of transgressions.

Pity Thy creature, O Master,
and purify me by thy loving kindness.
Grant me the homeland of my heart's desire,
Making me again a citizen of paradise.[13]

Our needy confession ends our separation from our lover and lands us again in his presence.

When we are unreasonable with our mates, it's a sin against God, not just against our mates. When we're unreasonable or abusive with our children, it is a sin against God. Don't write off your social sins as little mistakes in human relationships. Sin against any whom God loves holds a dagger to the heart of the Almighty.

> What happens when we refuse to confess our sins against God? We cut ourselves off from God. Our neediness no longer draws us, but becomes a formidable barrier to our union with him.

What happens when we refuse to confess our sins against God? We cut ourselves off from God. Our neediness no longer draws us, but becomes a formidable barrier to our union with him. We begin to pack up strong emotional luggage for a trip to neurosis. That luggage eventually gets too heavy to carry around.

Cecil Osborne wrote,

> I recall a woman who made life miserable for her church for nearly ten years. She was a self-described "Bible-believing, born-again, all-out-for-the-Lord, dedicated worker in the Lord's vineyard"; which might have been all right except that she kept up a ten-year barrage of criticism of her church, its officers, teachers, and the minister. She boasted that she spent two to four hours a day on the telephone stirring interest in her crusade. She wore a grim smile, quoted Scripture by the ream, and directed a Bible class for women in a downtown building. She had ulcers, colitis, migraine headaches and sundry other assorted illnesses. Peace came to her church only when she moved away.
>
> She was a bitter, vindictive, quarrelsome individual who made life miserable for many people, including herself. Like most fanatics she was convinced of the righteousness of her crusade. Her intense zeal, bolstered with Scripture quotations and pious phrases, initially won her a following until her devotees discovered the bitterness and

hate behind her facade of piety.[14]

Polonius says to Laertes in the great play *Hamlet,* "To your own self be true." Don't carry around any inner lies. Get it out. Confess it to God! God wants each of us to desire truth inwardly.

Healing and inner integrity

John White says that one of his children was born with club feet. He also says he could not face that truth. He looked into the crib and almost instantly noticed but refused to admit the truth that the child had club feet. He was a medical doctor, but said, "I was so reluctant to see the truth. My wife, who is not a doctor, looked at our child and could tell instantly something was wrong with the baby's feet. Finally, I agreed, for there was no chance at all for that child to get well until I had truth in my inward parts."

Because sin is hidden inside our troubled hearts, we can pretend that it's less serious or even nonexistent. We clothe ourselves with pretense and soft-soap our acquaintances with congenial lies. It is both natural and foolish to want to think about ourselves in the best possible way. Still, when we approach God in open acknowledgment, good wholesome truth is born inside us. Honesty and joy come in together. "Restore to me the joy of your salvation and grant me a willing spirit, to sustain me" (Psalm 51:12). Then openness and acknowledgment with God grows. Our need is introduced to God's supply by our confession. There are several Greek words in the New Testament for forgiveness. The first one of those words talks about being released from debt. In the Lord's Prayer, Jesus used the word *aphiemi,* "to forgive as we are forgiven." In forgiveness we are released from a debt. It's that kind of word Dwight L. Moody used when he said, "When I received Christ, God wrote 'Paid in full' across the ledgers of heaven with the blood of Jesus Christ." We who are forgiven are released from a great debt.

There's another word, *apoluo,* which says, "Don't watchdog anybody else's sin." Don't inspect anybody else's morality and guilt in the attempt to feel better about yours. If you want to have real joy, you can't gain it by comparing yourself with those whom you believe sin more than you do. Trying to congratulate yourself into grace is unavailing. Glory in his Cross, exalt his saving work, and come clean.

Begin with a contrite heart

We were at the symphony one night, and as the orchestra exited at intermission, my wife said to me, "Wasn't the music wonderful?"

"Yeah, that was really good. But you know, it's a shame the oboist doesn't like the cellist better."

"Well," she said, "how do you know that?"

"Further," I went on, "the concertmaster doesn't care for the conductor."

"Really," she said. "How can you tell?"

"And the harpist thinks the percussionist plays too loudly."

"How can you possibly know?" she continued to probe.

"Well, I really don't know. I just know in most orchestras there is enough jealousy and intrigue to blow the harmony to bits."

"But," she said, "when they make beautiful music, we forget their attitudes."

"Exactly."

Be released from the bondage of your criticisms. Joy comes when we can say, "My sin is so great I dare not castigate you for yours. Besides, I take into account your maturity level."

We once had a person who lived in our home who was absolutely unreasonable. She woke us up all night long. If she had to have a glass of water, she woke us up. If she had to go to the bathroom, she woke us up! Anything she needed, she woke us up. But it was easy to forgive her. She was our daughter and she was only six months old. We loved her—we treasured our relationship with her so very much that her demanding lifestyle was a point of joy in our relationship. All we had to do was consider her maturity level.

There is an old fable about a thin little baker named Fouke, who had a wife named Hilda, who was open to almost everyone. She was a great counselor. But one day Fouke came home from work early and found Hilda in bed with another man. She became the center of gossip for their little community. Fouke tried to forgive her in his heart, but he said, "I couldn't forgive her. My forgiveness stalled itself."

God at length sent a black angel. Every time Fouke looked at his wife with hate and bitterness, this black angel put a pebble in his heart, one at a time! The weight of those pebbles gathered and grew and became a ponderous burden, breaking him open and bending and bowing his spirit.

Then, in his mercy, God sent a white angel. The old man was bent by bitterness. But the white angel said, "You can yet see a new way. Each time you look at your wife as a person who needs you, I will take a pebble from your heart."

Pebble by pebble, he began to see his wife as God saw her. Not always did he see her as the village prostitute; he began to see her as a special person who needed his love. That's what joy really is.

"The sacrifices of God are a broken spirit," says David, "a broken and contrite heart, O God, you will not despise" (Psalm 51:17). God is touched by genuine penitence. When you find someone whose heart is breaking, what do you do? You want to reach out and love that person. But when you find someone who's proud and arrogant, you have much less desire to reach out to him or her. Arrogance is made approachable by brokenness. It is at such a point of neediness that our salvation begins. Joyce Landorf wrote these words in her twenty-fifth year, greatly in need of God's renewal:

> I stopped in front of the mirror and then gasped in disbelief. I'd never seen the woman before me. She was old, sick, neurotic. She couldn't have been more than twenty-five, but her rebellion had shriveled her face up into ugliness; it sagged with the dried, leathery look of the aged. The lines around her eyes were hard-set in anger, the pinched look about her mouth twitched with nervous worry, her voice level had been preset to "whine" because of the "poor-little-old-me" attitude, and her exaggerated makeup and way-out hairdo added a sad-comic-clown feeling, making the whole face hard, yet pathetic. Worst of all, however, was the vacant nothingness in her eyes.
>
> Standing there before the mirror that day and seeing myself, I could only say, Is that woman me?[15]

Confession is a clean mirror, where we stare at ourselves and remember how far we have fallen. When we come to that place out of brokenness and openness, we discover again the love of God. Then our need is filled. We have cried out. He is all-sufficient, and that all-sufficiency meets us at our greatest point of need—the need to be forgiven.

Conclusion

His grace is greater than our sin. His blessing overfills the abyss of our longings. We have cried out our need only to find our need no longer exists. In its place are riches provided directly and abundantly from the store-house of the forgiveness we so reluctantly approached. Truly we have understood, "My God shall supply all your need according to his riches in glory by Christ Jesus" (Philippians 4:19 KJV).

But let us not speak of confession as though it is painful work. It is the sweetest of all possible ends to self-will. Confession puts a new immediacy into our union with Christ. It overwhelms us with an otherworldly joy.

Confession is hard work sometimes, but it is pain well spent. Its currency purchases an abiding elation. The pain of cancer surgery is forgotten when the doctor says, "We got it all!" A mother considers her labor pain well worth it when her living child wails outside her body.

And when our neediness brings us weeping to the Cross, we bless our tears and celebrate our joy. Our poverty of spirit is exchanged for immeasurable abundance by his grace. Our best confession ends in anthems, celebrating our new cleanness. For God, who in our sin seemed distant and cold, at the words "I'm sorry," draws near.

I was myself so entangled and constrained
by the very many errors of my former life
that I could not believe it possible for me
to escape from them. . . .
But when the stain of my earlier life had been washed away
by the help of the water of birth (baptism) . . .
and the second birth had restored me
so as to make me a new man . . .
what before had seemed difficult was now easy.[1]

—CYPRIAN

The blood is for atonement and has to do first with our
standing before God. We need forgiveness for the sins we have
committed, lest we come under judgment; and they are
forgiven, not because God overlooks what we have done but
because he sees the blood.[2]

—WATCHMAN NEE

Thy work alone, O Christ,
Can ease this weight of sin.
Thy blood alone, O Lamb of God,
Can give me peace within.[3]

—RAY ORTLUND JR.

I am clean for I have confessed.
I shall be clean till I sin . . .
Then I shall confess
and be clean again.
Confession is the window of grace.
We confess and the sunlight
of wholeness streams in through
the streaked glass of our compromises,
cleansing as it comes.

Almightie God, the father of oure Lorde Jesus Christ, whiche desireth not the death of a synner, but rather that he maye turne from his wickednes & lyve: & hath geven power & commanndement to hys ministers, to declare and pronounce to his people beinge penitente, the absolucion and remission of theyr synnes: he pardoneth and absolveth all them which truly repent, and unfeynedly beleve his holy gospell—wherefore we beeseche him to graunte us true repentaunce and his holye spirite, that those thinges may please him, which we doe at this present, & that the rest of oure lyfe hereafter, maye be pure & holye: so that at the laste we maye come to hys eternall ioye, through Jesus Christ our Lorde. Amen.

Take and eate this, in remembraunce that Christe died for thee, and feede on him in thy hearte by faythe, wyth thankesgevinge.

Drinke thys in remembraunce that Christes bloude was shed for thee, & be thankeful.[4]

—BOOK OF COMMON PRAYER
(1552)

CHAPTER THIRTEEN

Confession and Guilt-Free Discipleship

At certain times in our lives we are like children terrified by a midnight thunderstorm. Our terror is a dark divorce—a separation between confidence and need. But fear holds yet another curse. What we fear also imparts to us a kind of guilt. Why? Because we have been told so often by our cliché-driven church friends that no real Christian would ever be afraid. But we are. And knowing we shouldn't be leaves us feeling guilty. We are like a child caught with his hand in the cookie jar from which our parents have told us—almost as though it were in the Bible—"Thou shalt not eat, and the moment thou dost, thou shalt surely be chastised." Fear and guilt so often come and go together in our lives.

One of the four basic human emotions is fear. When we are haunted by it, we must realize that much of the Bible was given so that we would not have to live chained to this demon: "Even though I walk through the valley of the shadow of death," said the psalmist, "I will fear no evil, for you are with me; your rod and your staff, they comfort me" (23:4). Psalm 91 counsels us to hide ourselves under the shadow of the Almighty, and in doing so to make God the fortress of our security. Martin Luther, on reading these verses, wrote, "A mighty fortress is our God, a bulwark never failing."

How right Luther was. We don't have to go through life intimidated by fear. The indwelling Christ becomes our security, or as Psalm 23 says, our staff, our rod, our constant companion, our great shepherd! Our fears should dissolve in his nearness. Our continual confession is the key to his abiding presence. Hildegard of Bingen writes, "Those who are sinful find that their friendships are fragile and easily broken; loneliness is their lot. But their loneliness need not be permanent. Repentance restores friendship; the sinner who repents is rewarded with the pleasures of companionship."[5] His presence is our fortress.

Often, however, in spite of the fortress of God, we act superficially and with swelling bravado. "Bravado" is the art of telling ourselves we are not afraid when we really are scared to death. We are more a trembling fortress than a mighty one! This passage teaches us that courage is not the absence of terror. Courage is the ability to face our fears without blinking.

Three kinds of fear

There are different kinds of fear. First, there is *the instant, sudden, or surprise sort of fear*. "Surely he will save you from the fowler's snare" (Psalm 91:3a). The psalm calls our attention to the fowler that springs up without warning and closes around a poor bird. So in life, we encounter those surprise fears for which we don't have enough time to plot an answer. Life turns on a dime. The grass-covered lid gives way and we are plunged at once into the pit. We are walking down a familiar street, the same street we've walked for years. We turn a corner—the same corner we've turned many times—and the universe falls away, and our world is destroyed. Life sometimes surprises us with such devastating circumstances that we can never go back to living the way we once did.

It's the shattering agony of the Humpty-Dumpty syndrome. We couldn't have suspected it. It happens without warning, and on a beautiful day when we thought we could see forever, we lie fragmented and broken. We are powerless to put the pieces of our lives back together ever again.

But there's a second fear: *the ongoing fear of the grind*. All kinds of things make us afraid in life. Sometimes our greatest fears lie in terms of the hassles of life. Can we cope?

I've heard some say, "True Christians never suffer from burnout." Do not believe it! Are Christians safe from the sudden crush of compounded calamities? Of course not! Sometimes situations come at us so fast we are paralyzed before them. Of course we can burn out, overwhelmed by lilliputian terrors that swarm over us like insects and threaten to overwhelm us.

But burnout is not our final state. Confession can pull us of out of this dark void by making God our partner before the terrors of life. In fact, confession is our only armor against the overwhelming evils of the demonic world. Abraham, the disciple of Abba Agathon, questioned Abba Poemen, saying, "How do the demons fight against me?" Abba Poemen said to him, "The demons fight against you? They do not fight against us at all as long as we are doing our own will. For our own wills become the demons, and it is these which attack us in order that we may fulfill them. But if you want to see who the demons really fight against, it is against Moses and those who are like him."[6] The Desert Fathers considered confession a real weapon in our warfare against the burnout demons that congest our days.

Confession keeps us in touch with Christ. Confession allows us to walk with the Shepherd, our wonderful, sun-crowned King. Catch the real metaphor in Psalm 23. In the dark valley, the sheep move in close to his legs, touching him as they traverse those narrow chasms of darkness and doubt. They see in the shepherd's hand a crook and

> Confession allows us to walk with the Shepherd, our wonderful, sun-crowned King.

a rod. With the crook he touches them gently to guide them and lead them. With the rod he says to them, "There is nothing short of my own life that can threaten your life. I care for you. I love you. Trust me!" God does not set any fear at liberty to have its way with us.

The third fear is *a kind of terror. Fear of the unknown. Fear of stepping out.* The psalmist says, like an eagle God stretches his wings over us and cares for us: "He will cover you with his feathers, and under his wings you will find refuge" (91:4). Only the word really isn't feathers, it's pinions— the large first bones in the eagle's wings that spread the feathers over the nestlings so nothing can hurt them.

God often operates in our lives just as we do with our own children. He often pushes us into some unknown place to make us trust and grow. The mother eagle must sometimes seem heartless. Upon some proper moment of maturity, she shoves her eaglets toward what they fear most: the edge of the nest.

But is the eagle really heartless? She knows that the natural fears of her little ones would leave them stuck, quivering forever in the dead sticks of their high nest. If they never faced their fears, they would finally become fat old eagles who never knew the joy of thunderheads or the thrill of magenta sunsets. So her little ones must learn that the fall they so fear is but an illusion to be tamed. To be changed to flight, their cowardice only has to be overcome. Flight is the wings they give to terror. Are the eaglets' fears real? Yes. But they don't have to face them alone. Against such fear, the mother eagle spreads her pinions. Winter is coming. Ice will soon fall upon the aerie. But by then these little ones will know no fear. The parent has spread the wingspan of her devotion between their fragile lives and the storm.

In a similar way, the Good Shepherd says to us, "I give you freedom from fear. You will not be afraid of the terror by night." Never afraid? No!

We have an intercessor! The Holy Spirit is in constant prayer for our security. "True and unerring attentiveness means that the intellect keeps watch over the heart while it prays. It should always be on patrol within the heart, and from within—from the depths of the heart—it should offer up its prayers to God."[7] No heart need fear while the Spirit remains at his unceasing prayer.

Confession is the birth canal of courage.

Have you ever known the terror by night? Have you ever been afraid of the dark? You're too big now, aren't you? But there was a day when you were afraid of the dark. Demons lurked in the flowers of the wallpaper. You were afraid to turn out the light, and then again, afraid to turn it on too suddenly lest you catch the very fiends hovering over you.

As a child, I feared the terror of the night. I hated the dark. And I would have such terrible nightmares that I made a promise to myself. If ever I had children, I would never let them go through a single night terribly afraid. In a similar way, God does not want any of us to have such fear: "My truth will be your shield," he says. "My truth will be your fortress. I have a staff; I have a rod. Don't trust anything but my rod and my staff." So trust we must.

When the storms gather against us, we must trust: "Do not be afraid of those trials that God may see fit to send upon you. It is with the wind and storm of tribulation that God separates the true wheat from the chaff."[8]

We must enjoin our trials: "Make friends with your trials, as though you were always to live together, and you will see that when you cease to take thought for your own deliverance, God will take thought for you."[9]

We must cry, "Blessed is any weight, however overwhelming, which God has been so good as to fasten with His own hand upon our shoulders."[10]

We must testify that we are blessed by the very terrors of our lives: "Learn to be as the angel who could descend among the miseries of Bethesda without losing his heavenly purity or his perfect happiness. Gain healing from troubled waters. Make up your mind to the prospect of sustaining a certain measure of pain and trouble in your passage through life."[11]

"Trouble and perplexity drive us to prayer, and prayer drives away trouble and perplexity."[12]

"God takes a thousand times more pains with us than the artist with his picture. By many touches of sorrow and by many colors of circumstances He would bring man into the form that is the highest and noblest in His sight."[13]

A good shepherd gives himself for the life of his sheep. I remember a dear person in my first little parish who was not a member of our church.

She had been sick all her life and she decided to go to Lourdes to be cured. I questioned her wisdom: "What can God do in France that he can't do in Cass County?" I asked. I watched her leave. She was still wearing her favorite crucifix as she set off to receive healing in France. She came back to our little town in a few weeks, still a very sick person. Around her neck still hung the crucifix. She said to me, "I learned one great thing in France: never trust a crucifix, only the crucified one." What she was really doing was answering me with her confession. And her confession was healing her fears.

Confession creates no power within us, but it does clear out the clutter of self-preoccupation. Then God's power can fill the cleansed emptiness with courage. Confession causes us to remember we have a heavenly Father that longs to see us be victorious. One of God's long-ago saints, Minucius Felix, wrote,

> What a beautiful sight it is for God when a Christian wrestles with pain; when he takes up the fight against threats, capital punishment, and torture; when smiling he mocks at the clatter of the tools of death and the horror of the executioner; when he defends and upholds his liberty in the face of kings and princes, obeying God alone to whom he belongs; when triumphantly and victoriously he challenges the very one who has passed sentence on him! For he is a victor who has reached the goal of his aspirations.[14]

This is the way to live without fear. It is to rest under the shadow of the Almighty and to walk under the protection of his rod and staff. How far? He will walk with you forever. In my wife's grandfather I clearly saw that the gift of the Good Shepherd was his faithfulness. Some years ago when Grandpa was sick in an Oklahoma hospital, his condition had so deteriorated that it appeared he would not live. He was ninety-six years old, and because his condition was so very grave, the family was assembled to attend him at his passing. Grandpa had walked with the Shepherd for many years, and in trusting the Shepherd, had discovered him to be trustworthy.

Grandpa said to me, "It sure will be good to see Edith again." She had gone to be with Christ thirty years ahead of Grandpa. This rural patriarch had two great loves: his family and his church. Now, as his family gathered around his bed, we thanked God for the church—at his insistence. Then we all held Grandpa's hands and prayed around the circle, commending him to God.

I was the last to pray, and as soon as I said amen, Grandpa asked to close with his own prayer. He blessed each one in his family and church. For a very sick man it was a very long prayer. As he continued, he waxed eloquent, and began praying so loud his voice reverberated down the hallway of the hospital. In fact, his prayer was so athletic and exuberant that when he finished, I whispered to my wife, "We've been called here under false pretenses. There's no way Grandpa is going to die today." He actually lived for six more years, dying at 102! But the thing I will never forget was his demeanor in the face of death. He had zero fears! He had faced the valley of the shadow of death without despair. It was the greatest of all possible gifts he could give to his family.

In the valley of the shadow, the rod and the staff do comfort. We are all to be covered with the pinions of his wings. We are each defended by his shield and buckler. We cannot suffer any wound too terminal to bar us from confidence. Neither the dragon nor the arsenal of hell can make us afraid.

Consider this business of being covered with the wings of a loving God as an eagle covers her chicks. Conrad Willard tells a sad story of when he was a boy. He looked out across the barnyard one day to see an old mother hen strutting across the clearing, clucking proudly. Her little chicks trailed close behind her.

Conrad's brother challenged him, "I'll bet you can't hit that old hen with your air rifle."

"It was a brand new air rifle," said Conrad, "and I had been shooting at anything that stood still or moved. I knew I could do it. I cocked the BB into the chamber and aimed the small rifle at the old mother hen. I pulled the trigger and hit her in the neck.

"Her head fell slowly sideways. I watched her in fascination and double fear. The fear of an old hen in total disorientation about what life was and what it could mean: what sudden calamity had fallen from the sky? Then I saw the fear of her little ones, doing all they knew: running to their mother. Even as she was dying, in an effort to protect them, she spread her wings as far as she could. And in her final moments, those little chicks ran under her wings to receive the last bit of warmth she could give them."

Now I understand the beauty of the Savior's commitment: "I will cover you with my wings. Your freedom is my shield. You are delivered from fear! Your trust is my integrity! Come and receive." But what is the first step in appropriating this security? Confession. We call Jesus "Lord," and all of life becomes manageable—all our fears are paper in the presence of his power.

Sin produces guilt

Some are able to conquer fear only to be rendered ineffectual by guilt. They erect a barrier of guilt by refusing to accept God's forgiveness. We must confess our sin to Christ. Then we must let Jesus forgive us. Then we must trust his forgiveness. To carry around sin that Jesus has already forgiven is a refusal to trust in the completeness of all he died to afford us. Guilt blesses us only when it enables us to say "I'm sorry" to God or to our mates or to our families. But too much guilt, carried overlong, becomes a killer of the human spirit.

When we first come to God and confess our sins, God wants to take the bad stuff out of our lives and leave the good stuff in. But often we prevent him by holding on to the bad stuff. It is then that guilt hurts! Eventually it destroys.

The Holy Spirit's incessant intercession is our keeper. He prays continually that guilt will not conquer us. Isaac the Syrian wrote,

> Therefore it is said that when the Holy Spirit comes to live in a man, he never ceases to pray, for then the Holy Spirit himself constantly prays in him (Romans 8:26). Then prayer never stops in a man's soul, whether he is asleep or awake. In eating or drinking, sleeping or doing something, even in deep sleep his heart sends forth without effort the incense and sighs of prayer. Then prayer never leaves him, but at every hour, even if externally silent, it continues secretly to act within.[15]

To live the confessional life is to live free of this guilt. It is our wish. But more than that it is the desire of the Spirit's unceasing intercession.

But how does guilt begin? Subtly, I think. All kinds of things may suggest guilt in our lives. Let us say we have been on a diet for three weeks. Then someone in the office brings in a box of donuts. We can smell them even as they come in the door! At first we may try to ignore the temptation by keeping our door closed and reading the Bible. But the odor wafts in under the door and, zombielike, we are lured from our work. The "evil" confection draws us to look and to contemplate. Just look, that's all! Then we survey the fried pastry, the sweet glazing. Even as we walk away from them, they call out, "Eat me! Eat me! Eat me!" Soon it's all over! Indulgence begins! Lost and miserable, we abandon three weeks of dieting, crying, "Why? Why? Why?"

> To carry around sin that Jesus has already forgiven is a refusal to trust in the completeness of all he died to afford us.

Then we enter a new kind of misery. Having eaten the forbidden sweet, we feel we must pay for our sin. How odd that a simple donut could pin us to the mat of grief, forcing us to cry "uncle" to our old sin nature. Surely our hellish weakness begs us do some kind of penance. We feel guilty for our loss of self-control. Guilt grown large as King Kong keeps us working at trying to pay for our own sins.

S. I. Milliken says, "The Hans Eysenck study points out that of the emotionally disturbed people who go for psychoanalysis, 6 percent improve within a year. Of those who go for psychotherapy, 64 percent improve within a year, and of those who go for no treatment at all, 72 percent improve within a year."[16] Milliken implies you're better off staying home! I'm a firm believer in getting professional help when it's needed. Still, I believe the place to turn when we feel pain in our sin is to God.

But guilt often builds into our system a false notion that God likes us better when we feel bad. Somehow if we see ourselves as nothing we are more humble before God. Charles Swindoll says,

> If God had wanted you to be a worm, He could have very easily made you one! He's very good at worms, you know. There's an infinite variety of the wriggly creatures. When Watts wrote of worms, he was merely using a word picture. Many others, however, have framed it as a model to follow, calling it humility. This 'worm theology' creates enormous problems. It wears many faces—all sad. It crawls out from between the mattress and the springs in the morning, telling itself, "I'm nothing. I'm a worm. Woe, woe. I can't do anything and even if I appear to be doing something, it's not really me. Woe! I must annihilate self-respect . . . crucify all motivation and ambition. If any good accidentally leaks out, I must quickly hide it or categorically deny I had anything to do with it. How could I accomplish anything of value? I mean, who am I? I'm a worm. Good for nothing except crawling very slowly, drowning in mud puddles, or getting stepped on. Woe, woe, woe."[17]

In the evangelical church, people are forever putting themselves down. And this becomes a negative pathology of spirit that God never intended. Such guilt has made the church a theological center for low self-esteem.

Guilt itself is the most damaging of all sins. When guilt begins to dominate our lives, we are crushed in our self-image and our certitude and pretty soon we are languishing in the fever of all that we have done that is wrong and we see nothing good at all about ourselves. The guilt we harbor is literally killing not only our rapport with God but also our rapport with ourselves.

Are Christians never to feel guilty? Is guilt ever good? Yes, when it has the effect of bringing us to God, but it can also have the effect of obscuring God. Guilt is most worthless when we become so self-preoccupied that we can't see anything but our own selfish needs.

Many Christians are not prone to forgive themselves. They sometimes deal with this by winking at the whole concept of sin. But those who really desire to live in God's presence desire to have the mark of holiness in their lives. The less they have of that holiness, however, the more they recriminate themselves with guilt.

Does guilt hurt?

David committed adultery with Bathsheba. He missed the mark. He failed in his aim at living the straight life. He also failed to make holiness a goal in his life. But with sin in his life, guilt also took hold. David was caught in a web of self-destruction that led to so many lies it makes Watergate look like a Sunday school party. He committed adultery, false witness, racial discrimination, and murder. God finally brought judgment upon the king. But guilt also descended on him—born in the realization that he had been observed by God in his sin.

In C. S. Lewis's *The Great Divorce*, one of the new Ghosts protests,

> *"You!" gasped the Ghost. "You have the face to tell me I wasn't a decent chap?"*
>
> *"Of course. Must I go into all that? I will tell you one thing to begin with. Murdering old Jack wasn't the worst thing I did. That was the work of a moment and I was half mad when I did it. But I murdered you in my heart, deliberately, for years. I used to lie awake at nights thinking what I'd do to you if ever I got the chance. That is why I have been sent to you now: to ask your forgiveness and to be your servant as long as you need one, and longer if it pleases you. I was the worst. But all the men who worked under you felt the same. You made it hard for us, you know. And you made it hard for your wife too and for your children."*
>
> *"You mind your own business, young man," said the Ghost. "None of your lip, see? Because I'm not taking any impudence from you about my private affairs."*
>
> *"There are no private affairs," said the other.*[18]

No private affairs between you and God. Guilt occurs when the holy God and the naked man are under the process of seeing things exactly as they are. That is a moment that can be either healthy or unhealthy, depending upon what we do with the sin that is discovered.

We are too often like Adam after his sin. Our guilt causes us to be repugnant both to God and to ourselves, and so we hear God calling in the cool of the day, "Where are you, Adam?" Guilt stalks us as much as the holiness of God. We feel naked. We hide ourselves. Thus it was with David. "I'm naked," he cried to God, "and I know it. Wash me with hyssop and I shall be clean, wash me and I shall be whiter than snow."

There are two stories of dealing with sin that occurred around the time of the crucifixion of Christ. One is Peter's denial. He managed to open up and look at his sin and confess it and forget it. Not Judas Iscariot—Judas carried his guilt until it finally broke his bones in an act of self-destruction. Such guilt always produces the Judas syndrome; it always destroys. Sometimes it destroys in suicide and sometimes it destroys in defeated living, negativism, or mental breakdown. But the Judas syndrome is always destructive and it separates us from a loving God.

I have known so many who carry guilt because they simply cannot accept the forgiveness of God. How many times has someone said, "I've asked the Lord to forgive me this sin again and again—I've asked him 10,000 times." Well, God forgives on the first request, so the last 9,999 times are unnecessary, and they are always indicative of a man or woman who wants God to forgive what they are unwilling to forgive themselves. God's forgiveness is complete. How complete is yours?

Justin wrote that Christ is the authority over all that menaces us. If guilt is our menace why not just surrender it to his authority? "You can see that the crucified Christ possesses the hidden power of God: every demon—in fact, all and every power and authority on earth—trembles before him."[19]

A while ago I talked with a woman who had been in a mental hospital for some time. In subsequent visits, I could tell that the reason she was still under psychiatric care was that she never had come clean with her doctor and, for all of his degrees, he had never managed to get it out of her. Finally, in desperation she said, "Here's my problem." I could scarcely believe the confession that followed. I felt uncomfortable just hearing it. Sobbing in her anguish, she came out with the whole thing. I could tell it was tearing her apart.

"Do you mean," I said, "you've spent these thousands of dollars in a mental hospital and you've never told these things, which were the cause of your condition, to your doctor?"

"I was ashamed to say them out loud!" she said.

Well, she found healing, because she was able to look at what she was and say, with God looking on, "God, be merciful to me, a sinner."

Conclusion

None of us likes to have the light turned on in a messy room. Here we understand what David meant when he said, "Hide your face from my sins" (Psalm 51:9). Yet the secret sin must be judged. In Romans 2:16, Paul says there is coming a day when God will judge men's secrets. In Mark 4:22, Jesus says, "Whatever is hidden is meant to be disclosed." And in Ecclesiastes 12:14, the writer of that book tells us, "For God will bring every deed into judgment, including every hidden thing."

Romans 8:1 says, "There is now no condemnation for those who are in Christ Jesus." The condemnation comes when we carry things in our hearts and our lives that God has already forgiven. The number-one sin many Christians may need to confess is the sin of carrying guilt. When we carry guilt for confessed sin, we are saying that the cross was too small to cover our sin.

In *Pilgrim's Progress*, Christian comes to the cross. He's carrying such a heavy burden of sin on his back that he can't get rid of it. He falls down before the cross and his burden of sin rolls away and he is free. But he hasn't gone very far when he begins to pick up again the things that God has already forgiven him. If you want to live free, don't take back what God takes off. Christian's tragic error is customary. Resolve before God never to carry more than you have to.

You may remember the old parable of the man who got on a bus carrying a big bag. He stood, hanging onto a ceiling strap, staggering under his burden, when someone tapped him on the shoulder and said, "Look, you don't have to carry that. Put it down and let the bus carry it." Confession recognizes the "bus." Confession causes us to lay down our burdens and stand free.

Keep silence, all created things,
And wait your Maker's nod;
My soul stands trembling while she sings
The honors of her God.[1]

—RAY ORTLUND JR.

"Be not anxious," are his words. "Consider the lilies . . . how they grow." He is directing our attention to the new law of life in us. Oh, for a new appreciation of the life that is ours![2]

—WATCHMAN NEE

The kiss of eternal life, and the warm embrace of God's Word, are so sweet, and bring such pleasure, that you can never become bored with them; you always want more.[3]

—HILDEGARD OF BINGEN

*How shall I ever become a major
player in the kingdom of God?
Confess your sin. Admit your betrayals.
Then shall your significance to God
be magnified in his esteem
while it never occurs to you at all.*

You never enjoy the world aright, till the Sea itself
floweth in your veins, till you are clothed with the
heavens, and crowned with the stars: and perceive
yourself to be the sole heir of the whole world, and
more than so, because men are in it who are every
one sole heirs as well as you. Till you can sing and
rejoice and delight in God, as misers do in gold, and
Kings in scepters, you never enjoy the world.

The world is a mirror of infinite beauty, yet no
man sees it. It is a Temple of Majesty, yet no man
regards it. It is a region of Light and Peace, did not
men disquiet it. It is the Paradise of God. It is more
to man since he is fallen than it was before. It is the
place of Angels and the Gate of Heaven. When Jacob
waked out of his dream, he said, "God is here, and I
wist it not. How dreadful is this place! This is none
other than the House of God and the Gate of
Heaven."[4]

—**Thomas Traherne**

CHAPTER FOURTEEN

Confessional Principles for Personal Growth

Depression is a gloomy mindset that from time to time smudges our moods. At one time or another it afflicts us all. The waves of depression crash upon the shores of our lives in ever-increasing surges. Loneliness and depression have become the common tag-team litany of the workaday world. But shall we wallow in our spiritual depression, feeling morose? Evangelist Billy Sunday put it another way: "To see some people you would think that the essential of orthodox Christianity is to have a face so long you could eat oatmeal out of the end of a gas pipe."[5] But is it hopeless? No, Christ is always the key to winning over our dour moods. The issue of our wholeness lies in making Christ the Lord over all our circumstances.

Roberta Bondi writes, "There is a whole generation of schizophrenic Christians who have two personalities, one for God and the church and another for the everyday world of science and common sense."[6] Trying to submit ourselves to such a split personality can leave us vulnerable. Unless we integrate the Christ of Sunday and the everyday Jesus we shall never arrive at wholeness.

Further, Jesus must be allowed free rein throughout the world of all our relationships. It is this realm of our existence that gives us the most trouble. It is other people who most often plunge us into gloom. Yet the people who leave us discouraged are loved as much by God as we are. Only our submission to Christ can enable us to love all those around us. And only as we love others can we set ourselves free of those grudges that depress and immobilize us.

There are four primary ways that we deal with the people around us. First, we idolize them. I once drove through Tupelo, Mississippi, where a big signboard announced this town was the birthplace of Elvis Presley. The extent to which our culture goes in its idolatry of famous entertainers is bewildering. The life of Elvis Presley demonstrates

> Unless we integrate the Christ of Sunday and the everyday Jesus we shall never arrive at wholeness.

that pedestals are fragile and precipitous places where egos shatter in their fall back to the commonplace. The second thing we can do to people is to demonize them. If for any reason we don't like someone, we can put that person in a negative light, placing upon him or her an awful bearing with our disparaging words. Third, we often utilize other people. When we use someone who is a soft touch to get things done for us, that person's life becomes a vessel we exploit for our own interests. But the fourth and best thing that we can do for others is to humanize them. We can, with Christ's help, make our enemies real, live human beings. Let us consider some confessional principles that help us escape spiritual depression.

Circumstances must never be allowed to control our emotions

This is the first confessional principle: "I will not let my current circumstances control my mood." Paul said in Philippians, "I have learned, in whatsoever state I am, therewith to be content" (4:11 KJV). The apostle is really saying, "I am in charge of my want-to's. I will not join the dark side of my personality, even when others are doing it."

Wherever we go, the circumstances that surround us tend to color our mood. But let us take for our mentors those triumphant souls who are able, wherever they find themselves, to say, "Christ is Lord over all my circumstances. This current moment of misery will not steal my joy."

In *The Unsinkable Molly Brown*, Meredith Wilson has Molly Brown standing in the prow of a crowded lifeboat as the *Titanic* is sinking behind her into a lonely sea. When everyone else in the lifeboat is wailing and crying, she erupts with that one legendary line: "I ain't down yet." To live on top of our circumstances and not be discouraged is to bear the mark of a Christian. François Fénelon observed, "Discouragement is not the fruit of humility, but of pride."[7] Those who are easily depressed are usually those who were confident they could handle anything, until the gaseous bubble of their confidence was pricked by their failure. Their pride had set them up for the fall.

Christ is the grand overcomer. By receiving Jesus into our lives, we erect the inner bracing that enables us to withstand the pressure of all our outer circumstances. Welcoming Christ into our lives, we gain the power to control life and not be crushed by it. Yet to withstand the crush of life, we must always be submitted to his inner lordship. The yielded life becomes the strong life.

It is an odd paradox that says we must bow our neck to the yoke of Christ if ever we would live free. His yoke is easy and his burden is light (Matthew 11:30). We must yield our unshaped futures to the hand of our creative potter. We must be like an archer's shaft, submitting our rigid form to the power of the bow, if we would know the thrill of purposeful flight to God's intended targets. We must mortify our own motives if we would come to know the thrill of a better will. We must crucify the big "me" if ever the great "he" is to live manifestly within us.

Further, we must free ourselves of the pride that causes us to claim more than we really possess. Ugolino says that Francis of Assisi and his companions found joy in the renunciation that bypasses all depression: each of them took "holy poverty" to be his bride. As a result, all depression was eliminated.

> We must crucify the big "me" if ever the great "he" is to live manifestly within us.

"For this is that celestial virtue by which all earthly and transitory things are trodden underfoot and every barrier is removed that might hinder the soul from freely uniting itself to the eternal God. This is that virtue which enables the soul, while yet on earth, to converse in heaven with the angels."[8]

I once planted a church. Another young pastor had moved to our town at the same time and was employed by his denomination to start a church across town. Churches are hard to plant. The soil where they would grow is hard. The rains of nourishing refreshment come too infrequently. It is difficult to gather a stable, formative core group that is willing to serve till the church is strong. People can be hard to motivate. It's sometimes difficult to teach new Christians the kind of commitment it takes to form a cohesive body. New church plants are seedbeds of negativity and depression.

Monday by Monday as I met with this fellow pastor, we had a lot of things to talk about. We found our conversations often turning into joint pity parties. We'd lick each other's wounds and say, "Ain't life awful?" Commiseration is misery on parade, but it does hold a kind of pleasure. So we celebrated each other's sufferings and enjoyed our mutual misery.

Week by week I began to notice that while I could have coffee and leave my dark moods in the coffee shop, his depression lingered with him. It camped in his soul, while I found a way to be free of it. When I found myself coming under the pall of depression, I would make myself go out and knock on doors and lead people toward faith in Christ. Then my depression gave way to joy. It was amazing what making converts did for my ailing spirit.

But my friend knew no therapy for his moods. Depression soon immobilized him. Like a steel curette, it seemed to cut through the very tendons and muscles of his spirit. It left him powerless, and after some fruitless months he became caught up in debilitating weeping. He soon consulted a psychologist, then a psychiatrist. Finally, he got into such rough shape he had to resign his church and leave the ministry altogether.

I was—through Christ—more of a survivor. I do not claim more stable superiority than he had, but I did understand that Jesus did not want me to become powerless under the pall of my depression. I welcomed Jesus as he rose powerful within my anemic intention, till I could say, "I will not, by Christ's power, let my circumstances color my mood." After all, wrote Fénelon, "God never afflicts us except against his own inclination. His fatherly heart is not gladdened at the sight of our misery, but he cuts to the quick, that he may heal the disease in our souls. . . . He afflicts only to amend."[9] How sweet are his amendments. I always found I was healed at the slightest touch of the hem of divine purpose.

Never join the dark side of your moods

Any circumstance that degenerates into a pity party needs one strong Christian who says, "I cannot allow you to feel sorry for yourself or to make me feel sorry for myself. Life was designed by Christ to be an occasion of joy." In every circumstance? *Foxe's Book of Martyrs* might be expected to relate that those dying for Christ died in the doldrums of depression. But they did not! They died singing hymns, even as they were torn to pieces. This confounded their captors. And real joy accompanied them, whatever their circumstance. They had settled upon this second principle of confession: "I will not join the dark side of my personality even when others do."

I am touched by Polycarp's defense of himself before the magistrate as he was about to be burned: "And Polycarp answered, 'Eighty-six years have I served him, and he has never done me any harm. How could I blaspheme my King and Savior?'. . . Polycarp answered him, 'You threaten me with a fire that burns but for an hour and goes out after a short time, for you do not know the fire of the coming judgment and of eternal punishment for the godless. Why do you wait? Bring on whatever you will.' "[10]

Most of our petty martyrdoms seem sacred in their moment. But their cure is only a drop of God's grace. Where I served as pastor, tornadoes were frequent in late spring. One of our staff pastors didn't have a storm cellar in which he could sit out the storms. During severe weather alerts he would call me on the phone and say, "Can we come down to your basement to be safe?" We always said, "Sure, help yourself." They always came. During the twister season they came so frequently that we often left the doors open for them on stormy nights. As often as we could, we met them at the door and asked them if they wanted a soda or some potato chips. Then we would all go down to the basement and sit under the Ping-Pong table, eating chips and waiting out the fury of the winds. It all might have seemed bizarre except that it was so customary. We stayed there munching away at our fears until the danger was past.

This staff pastor had a young son named Todd—a four-year-old—who began to love these parties and so looked forward to stormy nights. He liked the under-the-Ping-Pong-table camaraderie that munched its way through dread. I never saw it like Todd did. One night when it looked like the end of all flesh was at hand, the skies boiled black, and Todd said (I love him for it), "Aren't there any potato chips tonight?" There in the midst of our worst circumstances, the child counseled us, "Celebrate the moment. Never play pity at a pity party. Let's eat!"

Never compare your blessings with others

The habit of comparing our blessings with those around us can never be the key to our joy. In suburban churches all across America, members gather from every state in the union. The years that I was a pastor in Nebraska, I most enjoyed those members who loved the state. Those disciples who could bloom where they were planted said, "God must have brought me here for a wonderful reason. I love it here. I can hardly wait to discover why I am in this place."

But so often those transplanted from other parts of the nation spoke negatively of the state. I wanted to reform all such critics who felt that God was punishing them by locating them in Nebraska. Their negativity never allowed them the chance to be used where they found themselves. When there were so many people in need, their foolish excuses seemed odd and petty: The weather was too cold. The snow was too deep. They were too far from home to see anything of real value in the state.

Can you imagine David Livingstone going to Africa and saying, "I wish God had never sent me to this land. These natives never use deodorant, and it's always hot here. There's malaria and mosquitoes. There are tribal wars and headhunters." In fact, Livingstone saw it quite another way.

Africa was his arena for the activity of God.

God has no sanctified geography that he prefers over another. Anywhere there are people is God's favorite part of the world. Only there can he act.

Comparison only leads to discontentment, and discontentment to sin, and sin to separation from God. And what is it you are comparing anyway? Physical possessions? Picture-perfect children? Not being chosen for a committee chair? Confess your sin of envy and let God begin to show you riches greater than your wildest imaginings.

Every potential enemy is a friend of God

The fourth principle is "I will never allow a potential enemy to become an actual enemy. I will always remember that a potential enemy is a friend of God." The day and the moment we are saved, we are taken over and invaded by the invisible God in the person of Jesus Christ. In all of our personal relationships, we should not become negative but set the loving Christ free in us to love people as God does. "If it be possible, as much as lieth in you," wrote the apostle, "live peaceably with all men. Dearly beloved, avenge not yourselves, but rather give place unto wrath: for it is written, Vengeance is mine; I will repay, saith the Lord. Therefore if thine enemy hunger, feed him; if he thirst, give him drink: for in so doing thou shalt heap coals of fire on his head. Be not overcome of evil, but overcome evil with good" (Romans 12:18–21 KJV). Before you received Christ, you were the offender. Then Jesus, the great forgiver, included you in the kingdom of God. To extend this inclusiveness became God's purpose for your life.

Simon Wiesenthal, the renowned Jew who was imprisoned in a concentration camp in the last world war, tells about working in a makeshift hospital on the Polish border. A young bedridden German soldier confessed to Wiesenthal that his military detachment was ordered to put full cans of gasoline in a house filled with two hundred Jews. Then the house was set afire and the German soldiers became a firing squad ordered to shoot anyone that tried to jump out of the windows. The young soldier recalled,

> *Behind the window of the second floor, I saw a man with a small child in his arms. His clothing was alight. By his side stood a woman, doubtless the mother of the child. With his free hand the man covered the child's eyes—then he jumped into the street. Seconds later the mother followed. We shot . . . Oh, God . . . I shall never forget it—it haunts me.*

The young man paused and then said,

I know that what I have told you is terrible. I have longed to talk about it to a Jew and beg forgiveness from him. I know that what I am asking is almost too much, but without your answer I cannot die in peace.

Wiesenthal tells us what he did: "I stood up and looked in his direction, at his folded hands. At last I made up my mind and without a word I left the room."[11]

There are great issues of forgiveness that require the spending of the soul. But we who are the people of God should live triumphantly with a positive spirit, free of depression. This is not because we have the ability in ourselves; it's because we have the crucified Jesus in us! He managed to forgive the horror of all that was done to him. Now Christ, the enabler, commands us to love our world, perceiving it through a better eye than our own.

Conclusion

We can use these four principles to keep our inner confession a growing and positive one. The key is to remember that Jesus is Lord, and this is the primary positive confession that should define our lives. Humility is our bread, obedience our wine. We gain true humility not by putting ourselves down but by standing next to Christ. Once we see how great is the Savior's love for us, we know our lowly place in the world. Humility thus gained is power and triumph.

When Abba Macarius was returning from the marsh to his cell one day carrying some palm leaves, he met the devil on the road with a scythe. The (devil) struck at him as much as he pleased, but in vain, and he said to him, "What is your power, Macarius, that makes me powerless against you? All that you do, I do, too; you fast, so do I; you keep vigil, and I do not sleep at all; in one thing only do you beat me." Abba Macarius asked what that was. He said, "Your humility. Because of that I can do nothing against you."[12]

Satan is defeated by the absence of pride.

It is a positive focus that gives our confession its joy.

Use all your faculties to appreciate God's creation. Use your soul to understand other souls. Use your body to sympathize with other people's bodily experience. Use your emotions of anger and revenge to understand war. Appreciate goodness through distinguishing it from evil. Appreciate beauty through distinguishing it from ugliness and deformity. Define poverty by contrasting it with wealth. Rejoice in good health by comparing it with sickness. Distinguish the various opposites: length and shortness; hardness and softness; depth and shallowness; light and darkness. Enjoy every moment of life by constantly reminding yourself of the imminence of death. Look forward to paradise by reminding yourself of eternal punishment. You understand so little of what is around you because you do not use what is within you.[13]

Confess Christ and triumph over depression and negativity.

God is the friend of silence . . .
See how nature, the trees, the flowers, the grass
grow in deep silence.
See how the stars, the moon and the sun
move in silence.
The more we receive in our silent prayer,
the more we can give in our active life.[1]

—MOTHER TERESA OF CALCUTTA

I place an offering at thy shrine
From taint and blemish clear,
Simple and pure in its design,
Of all that I hold dear.

—MADAM GUYON

Central's never busy, always on the line
You can talk to heaven almost anytime.

—"THE ROYAL TELEPHONE,"
A COUNTRY HYMN

Is prayer a conversation?
Yes, between lovers.
Is prayer a journey?
Yes, a trek for those who
walk between worlds.

Oh, my Lord, how obvious it is that you are almighty! There is no need to understand the reasons for your commands. So long as we love and obey you, we can be certain that you will direct us on to the right path. And as we tread that path, we will know that it is your power and love that has put us there. It is as if the path which leads to you is narrow and rough, with steep cliffs on either side plunging down into dark valleys. Yet the path on which you have put me is a royal road, broad and smooth. It is safe for anyone who chooses to take it. And your Son holds the hand of all who walk on it. If we become tired or discouraged, we need only look up to see your smiling face in the distance inviting us to share your joy.[2]

—TERESA OF AVILA

CHAPTER FIFTEEN

Dwelling in Foreverness

Charles Kingsley said that on that great day of reckoning when he stood face-to-face with the judge of all the ages he would say,

> *Lord, I am no hero. I have been careless, cowardly, sometimes all but mutinous. Punishment I have deserved, I do not deny it. . . . I have not been good, but I have at least tried to be good. Take the will for the deed, good Lord. Do not strike my unworthy name off the roll call of the noble and victorious army . . . let me, too, be found written in the Book of Life, even though I stand lowest and last upon the list. Amen.*[3]

Fénelon said that "when St. Ambrose was dying, they asked him if he had any fear of the judgments of God. He replied, 'We have a good Master.' Such is the kind of answer which we ourselves must give."[4]

It was true that in the Victorian era people spoke quite openly about death but very guardedly about sex. But that was all at the end of the nineteenth century. Here at the dawn of the twenty-first, we speak very openly about sex and very guardedly about death. It is as though we are ashamed of death. We who control space probes and CT scans cannot avoid dying. We have pushed the limits of death farther away, but we have not been able to erase its inevitability.

The more secular a culture becomes the more we address death as an anomaly to be regretted. In Scripture it seems to be presented as a part of life, and certainly in the New Testament it is presented as a kind of achievement. It is the victorious end of the glorious pilgrimage. It is a changing of residences, the trading of clay for gold, the bartering of protoplasm for spirit, the exchange of temporality for immortality.

The psalmist concludes the Twenty-third Psalm with a burst of hope: "I will dwell in the house of the Lord forever." In some ways, it seems wrong to jam doctrine into beautiful psalms. Still, there are few verses (even in the New Testament) that speak as beautifully about eternal life. We shall never move into the depths of God until we treasure the house of the Lord.

But the treasure and the house to come are secondary to the goal of our finished relationship with Christ. No wonder Tennyson wrote, "And though from out the bourne of time and space the flood may bear me far, I hope to see my pilot face to face when I have crossed the bar." How we anticipate our final union with Jesus. It is more than streets of gold, more than gates of pearl, more than jasper walls and crystal seas. We have sung our finest hope so often: "We shall know him, and redeemed by his side we shall stand. We shall know him by the prints of the nails in his hand."

> We shall never move into the depths of God until we treasure the house of the Lord.

Our anticipation of heaven has only to do with Jesus. I have never yet known any mature and dying person who hungered for the treasures of eternity, only the face-to-face relationship with Christ. How easy it is to distrust those who anticipate heaven without ever mentioning their anticipation of Jesus. A Jesus-less heaven is no heaven at all. If we do not long to see him beyond the grave, we were too little fascinated with him before we faced the grave.

The great thing about knowing Jesus Christ is that while we may not live through the individual chapters of our life securely, we will find the final chapter as secure as God himself. Having received Jesus Christ, there is not the slightest doubt in our mind that one day we will stand in his presence and wait while he finishes us in his own excellence: fashioned into his self-portrait. Having begun his work in us in these uncertain times, he will complete us in a secure future. Carlyle wrote, "Here on earth we are as soldiers fighting in a foreign land . . . behind each one of us lies six thousand years of human effort. Before us is boundless time . . . unconquered continents and El Dorados that we, even we, have to conquer to create. From the bosom of eternity there shines for us eternal guiding stars."[5]

Heaven is our home

How firm are God's eternal promises? We cannot know all the stopovers, but we can know the final address in life. The newspaper some years ago contained an incredible article. A parakeet with the unlikely name of Pootsie escaped in Green Bay, Wisconsin. The small bird miraculously came into the keeping of the Humane Society. When no one else claimed the parakeet, Sue Gleason of Green Bay did. She enjoyed Pootsie immensely. They talked together (the bird knew some words). According to the paper, they took showers together (how they did that is not described). They spent a lot of time together and really got to know each other, but one day the little bird flew over to her shoulder, put its beak up in her ear and whispered, "1500 South Oneida Street, Green Bay." Ms. Gleason was dumbfounded. She looked the address up and found that a seventy-nine-year-old man named John Stroobants lived there. Ms. Gleason called him on the phone and said, "Sir, would you happen to have a parakeet?"

"I use to," he said, "and I've missed him terribly."

"I'll be right over," said Ms. Gleason.

When the old man saw his parakeet, he was delighted. "You know, Pootsie also knows his phone number!" What an informed creature! Pootsie's vocabulary sure beat "Polly wants a cracker." It's an unusual parakeet that is smart enough to know its way home.

In walking with Jesus Christ, you don't have to understand exactly where you are if you have the final address fixed in your mind. Security in Jesus Christ begins with this great passage:

> I will lift up mine eyes unto the hills,
> from whence cometh my help.
> My help cometh from the Lord,
> which made heaven and earth.
> He will not suffer thy foot to be moved.
> —PSALM 121:1–3A KJV

Jesus is the very tread on our Adidas. He will keep your foot from slipping. God marks your name and destiny. Something wonderful begins in our lives that will one day come to consummation in the very presence of God.

The security of heaven

Will we dwell in the house of the Lord forever? Sometimes our security trembles before our own disbelief: Doubt is that rag-toothed demon who nibbles at the edges of God's promises. How do we dare doubt such sturdy promises as Psalm 121? And Psalm 23:6, like a banner, flies far above our doubts.

Still, doubt is ever with us. We learn early to doubt. Some of us teach our children that a sandman comes at night and sprinkles grains of sand in our eyes so we get sleepy. (Sure enough, when they awake in the morning, they have a "sandy" residue in their eyes.) They seem to believe, and we encourage their belief. Unfortunately, they must unlearn these stories later. Somewhere the tooth fairy, the Easter bunny, and he whose belly shakes like a bowl full of jelly must be filed under "fables we earlier believed." In this fable filing we learn to doubt.

I called on a man's home not too long ago and asked him, "Do you go to church much?"

"No, I'm an atheist," he replied.

"Well, what about your wife?" I asked. "Does she go to church?"

"Yeah, she's a Methodist" (as if they were similar denominations).

As I walked away, I could still see him framed in his doorway. I thought of him as "the naked unbeliever." The person who doubts is left cold in the middle of a frigid world of doubt. He has nothing to protect him. Self-confidence must be trumped up. The Christ of Revelation condemns our poor values: "Because thou sayest, I am rich, and increased with goods, and have need of nothing; and knowest not that thou art wretched, and miserable, and poor, and blind, and naked . . ." (Revelation 3:17 KJV). We should clothe ourselves in the security that comes from God alone. God is our keeper. Nothing is more certain in life than the predictability of God's promises. Whatever goes on around us, we can count on him.

Those who know him speak easily of their approaching death and of the ultimate victory that Christ will gain in their lives. Those outside of Christ, however, fear death, but in some cases are equally fearful of learning a new worldview at the last moment of life. I had a friend whom I knew from the first grade until his fifty-third year of life. As I bore witness to God's saving grace, he did receive Christ at the end of his life. But I found a certain reluctance—a kind of embarrassment in him—as he spoke of Jesus. He loved his Lord, there was no doubt in my mind about it. But he had spoken to his family and close friends about only secular matters all his life. It was hard for him to change his entire way of thinking and speak of spiritual values. Those who live earth-oriented lives have a hard time finding a new naturalness in speaking of heaven. It is rare to see lifelong unbelievers change to open, vibrant believers in the shadow of their tombstones. People generally die as they have lived.

Neville Shutte was one of the first writers of a doomsday novel. *On the Beach* deals with a creeping band of radiation—residual from the last great nuclear war—that is slipping ever southward over Australia. There is, in the movie version, a group of Salvationists faithfully extending the gospel to the doomed Aussies. While most of those who hear their sermons want to believe, they do not. The movie ends with all life on earth extinguished and none coming to faith in Christ. Is it too brutal a suggestion? Probably not. Those who live secular lives usually cannot be threatened into vibrant faith. They cannot manage the turn in their volition to embrace the great, redeeming Christ they have so long ignored.

We exist to get ready to meet God. If we are not ready for that eventuality, whatever we have achieved will not mean much.

> We exist to get ready to meet God.

No healthy husband fails to honor and speak nobly of his wife. No healthy child refuses to brag about a godly parent. Surely no lover of Christ would find the name of Jesus slow upon the tongue. To be redeemed is a gift of such treasure that all our lives should be lived in magnifying his office in our lives. One way to magnify Christ is to anticipate our ultimate union with him. "I'm going to heaven when I die," should flow as freely as "I'm going to Orlando Thursday."

The issue of our destiny was secure the moment we came into a genuine relationship with Jesus Christ. Whatever heartaches come in the meantime, we know God neither slumbers nor sleeps. He watches over us and he cares.

Foreverness is our glorious destination

Our life is in Christ, enduring in the heavens. Andraé Crouch sings, "I've got confidence, my God's gonna see me through." George Beverly Shea intones, "I don't know what the future holds, but I know who holds the future." And Fanny Crosby wrote, "Blessed assurance, Jesus is mine. Oh, what a foretaste of glory divine!"

But our foreverness is not a destination we were smart enough to choose and map out. Foreverness for the believer is not so much the end of the journey as a leg of it—an expected lap of life—a confident part of the whole trip. James Martineau said we are poor wayfarers who trudge along the pathway of time, sometimes with hot and bleeding feet. But never do we take a step without a certain confidence. Death is a matter of enrollment in the census of a better kingdom than the small country where we once lived. Martineau testified, "Death, in short, under the Christian aspect, is but God's method of colonization, the transition from this mother country of our race to the fairer and newer world of our immigration."[6]

In 1977 I came face-to-face with foreverness. My sister called me in the middle of night to say two words that could wear no ornamentation: "Mom's dead." There it was—out at once—with no way to make it sound pretty or even decent. Mom's faith for her nine children was the rock at the center of our family. We had never known life without her. Her gracious faith walk made her a paragon of all that was good in a sometimes-corrupt world.

We traveled a great distance to attend her funeral. They were heavy miles in which I tried to balance all that I believed about heaven with the tonnage of my reluctance to have my mother be with Jesus. The children and Barbara and I walked from the limousine to her grave. We listened to the preacher say the words: "We will not all sleep, but we will all be changed—in a flash, in the twinkling of an eye, at the last trumpet. For the trumpet will sound, the dead will be raised imperishable" (1 Corinthians 15:51–52). How long were those steps from the limousine to the ugly hole in the earth. Yet I never learned the doctrine of "ugly holes" from Mom. She was convinced that to be absent from the body was to be present with the Lord. There were no "holes" in her theology of victory. And it would not be long before I would return to all she believed. I grasped my children by the shoulders and hugged them and wept.

She was buried in a graveyard that had been only open fields when she moved to northern Oklahoma, and those fields were not far from the little house where her brood was born. On that October day (she was laid to rest on her seventy-seventh birthday), I thought of Stuart Hamblen's old song:

> *Ain't gonna need this house no longer,*
> *ain't gonna need this house no more.*
> *Ain't got time to fix the shingles,*
> *ain't got time to fix the door.*
> *Ain't got time to fix the ceiling*
> *or to mend the windowpane.*
> *Ain't gonna need this house no longer,*
> *I'm gettin' ready to meet the saints.*

Heaven truly is the heart's deepest longing.

But I was doing one other thing with my children that very hard day. I was getting them ready for the day they would take that long limousine ride to take care of the earthly remains of their own parents. There is a circle of life, even as Disney's *Lion King* suggests. But it's not as bleak as the children's film portrays. Our circle of life doubles back upon a more steely confidence than the Lion King knew. We shall live and reign with Christ forever, with only brief stopovers here and there to place our unenduring bodies in a holding pattern, till we join all the ages in the presence of our King.

When does this great foreverness start? What does the Bible teach about security in Christ? There's not one verse in the entire Bible that teaches we are going to have life after death. The Bible teaches we can have life instead of death. Jesus Christ comes into a life, and at that precise moment eternal life begins. Someday pulse or respiration may cease, but not *us*—we will already have taken the giant step into the pleasure of God! Heaven begins at that moment. Eternity is now.

Foreverness is life with Christ, life in heaven, and heaven is a grand category. It is not a family reunion. It is not a place where we do grand deeds. Heaven is a place for being.

The parallax wheel on a camera is a focusing device that cranks two separate images into one. At the point when they merge, it is ready to take the picture. Consider the spiritual implications of the parallax view. Think of God cranking the focus wheel until two people come into concert, one against the other. The image of Jesus Christ and my own image will be coalesced into one. I will experience what I've been saying is the hunger of life: *union with Jesus Christ.* How ever does God fix the categories? Whatever does heaven look like? Whatever is this great mystery of godliness? We must leave it all to his keeping. The important thing is, we have a chart! We have a destiny!

Emily Dickinson wrote,

I never saw a moor,
I never saw the sea;
Yet know I how the heather looks,
And what a wave must be.

I never spoke with God,
Nor visited in heaven;
Yet certain am I of the spot
As if the chart were given.[7]

For now we are living out a destiny ordained for us. We hear again the psalmist, "I am your shepherd. You will dwell in the house of the Lord forever. The sun will not smite you by day nor the moon by night. The Lord is your keeper; he will preserve your soul."

The night my sister called me to tell me my mother had traded earth for heaven, I was possessed of a deep melancholy. It was a kind of gloom that hung about me and seemed to dare God to come to me with any light. Then the gloom fell back as I thought of two things. The first was a passage from Hebrews that reminded me that those who inherit heaven before us become a part of that great "crowd of witnesses" that oversee the approaching victory we shall know when we inherit heaven. These who have gone before us ever cheer us toward that great union with Christ that envelops death in life, darkness in light. And we shall ever reign with Christ a thousand years.

Still, the victory cannot absolve us of all tears. The second thing that came to me that night my mother entered heaven was that the promise of heaven was the assuaging of grief. God caused me to remember the hymn:

> *Come, ye disconsolate,*
> *where'er ye languish,*
> *Come to the mercy seat,*
> *fervently kneel;*
> *Here bring your wounded hearts,*
> *here tell your anguish:*
> *Earth has no sorrow*
> *that heav'n cannot heal.*[8]

Earth's heartaches are healed by the promises of God. When we are home at last, the homesickness will be over. We shall praise the King who knew how to cut eternal doorways in mere holes cut in sod. Joy belongs to all those who understand that earth is but a rehearsal for heaven. Nothing in life is wasted that remembers this.

On dim evenings, if you squint at sunsets, you can all but see the promise. In our Father's house there really are many mansions—one of them is ours. Alleluia!

We hear Jesus the shepherd say, "My sheep hear my voice, and I know them, and they follow me: And I give unto them eternal life; and they shall never perish, neither shall any man pluck them out of my hand. My Father, which gave them me, is greater than all; and no man is able to pluck them out of my Father's hand. I and my Father are one" (John 10:27–30 KJV).

Alleluia!

Unfurl the sails and let God steer us where he will.[1]

—BEDE

Obedience is meant to make a person supple, free from
attachment to self-will.[2]

—THOMAS MERTON

Hold on to instruction, do not let it go;
guard it well for it is your life.

—PROVERBS 4:13

*Life in Christ is the only life built
from heaven earthward
and from the inside outward.*

Life's not always easy to assemble. Just when you think all the pieces fit, you discover the whole assembly is a bit off. A kind of dread occupies your thoughts. You have the overwhelming feeling that nothing will ever make sense again. " 'Meaningless! Meaningless!' says the Teacher. All things are wearisome, more than one can say. The eye never has enough of seeing, nor the ear its fill of hearing" (Ecclesiastes 1:2, 8).

What puts life back together? Grace!

Grace is the healing generosity of God that touches us so powerfully that nothing is ever quite the same again.

Grace is never to be deserved, yet grace assembles the odd pieces of our lives.[3]

—**CALVIN MILLER**

Into the Depths

I almost missed going to the Great Barrier Reef. Why? I think I was afraid. I am a landlubber. I am no swimmer, and the ocean is wide and deep and treacherous. I was older than most who take that sort of excursion. Beaches are my favorite way of getting close to the ocean, not standing in the middle of it.

But the need to be safe is a dungeon of our own making. Fear is ever the jailer of our souls. We live at last in very small cells of *I-can't-do-this*. To really know God is the special job of the courageous. It is for those martyrs who have earned their own plaster niches in cathedrals. But this is not for us. We are too ordinary—too afraid of people who really want to know the deeper things of God. Those who hunger to know God are not like us. They are otherworldly. They are funny looking. They live in monasteries. They are God-freaks who don't comb their hair. They preach on street corners, and carry Second Coming signs.

We rarely confess these fears out loud, but we spend a lot of our lives keeping them at a distance. Our playing-it-safe is done without fanfare. It is our way of amoeba-like living. We loll about in our environment, bumping into life.

We prefer Gilligan's Island

The ocean is too vast and scary for us so we dump the Great Barrier Reef in favor of Gilligan's Island. I think most Americans liked *Gilligan's Island* because it was fixed sociology. The island was a proscribed world where Gilligan, the Skipper, Mary Ann, Ginger, the Professor, and, of course, a couple of rich plutocrats were making life work as best they could. None of them were going anywhere really. They were just living, and talking about a bigger world. But their conversation never amounted to much and none of them sacrificed themselves in any major way to get off their island prison.

How often the church is like Gilligan's Island. Christians aren't really living on the edge. The church doesn't encourage them to break out of their insular spirituality. In fact, the best way to live comfortably as believers is to accept island living. Never even think about taking up your cross and risking yourself in some genuine spirituality. Keep your nose clean. Do your committee work, read your Sunday school leaflet. Tithe. Attend the deeper life studies. It is enough to study the deeper life—but remember, you could lose your place in the bridge square if you actually began to live it.

Recently a very popular study called "Experiencing God" swept through the church. It is a very beautiful, demanding, and profitable study. But I began to notice that many of those who enrolled in the Experiencing God study course, weren't reading *Experiencing God* and experiencing God. They were only experiencing the book *Experiencing God*

> We huddle in the cleft of the rock to avoid the storms, not to stand on the craggy heights and let them exhilarate us.

and then talking as if they had actually experienced God. It seemed an odd substitution to let the study of it serve as the experience. But it is fashionable these days to talk about how deep we are while we live on a "Gilligan's Island" of church life. Everything goes on as usual. The committee quarrels, the petty resentments of important families, the four-page multifold programs, the budget drives, Mothers Day Out: all these "opportunities for service" are parallel offerings to the Experiencing God study course.

I see the church not as an armory where we plan our conquests of fire, but as bunkers—island bunkers—where the furniture is nice and faith is a discussion. Occasionally we hear the roar of fusillades and we know that out there somewhere is a war. But for the moment the bunker is nice, the island is safe, and our friends are here with us. Indeed, casseroles have become the bland symbol of life without danger. I am struck by the oft-told story of the schoolteacher who asked three little children to bring to school the central symbol of their faith. The next day they all complied. One little boy brought a Star of David. A little girl brought a crucifix; but the little Baptist boy brought a casserole.

So many of these deeper life studies are not always a place to really contemplate a way to get off Gilligan's Island but to show off your latest casserole to those who want to show off their latest casseroles. Churches rarely ever take people to another level of knowing God. They only imprison people in padded pews where praying for each other, bowling, and affirming the sermon is pretty much the work of the kingdom.

Gilligan's Island might more properly be called Cape Fear. We huddle in the cleft of the rock to avoid the storms, not to stand on the craggy heights and let them exhilarate us. I was struck one day by all the hymns that center on faith as a protective refuge: "O Safe to the Rock That Is Higher Than I"; "Haven of Rest"; "I Have Found a Hiding Place"; "Out of my bondage, sorrow, and night, Jesus, I come . . ."; "The Solid Rock"; "Hold the Fort, for I Am Coming"; "Under His Wings I Am Safely Abiding"; "Jesus Is a Rock in a Weary Land"; "Rock of Ages, Cleft for Me"; "A Mighty Fortress Is Our God," to name a few.

Going deep

I will ever be grateful for the Great Barrier Reef. For once in my life I faced my fears as I stood to board the boat, even as I felt a churning in the pit of my stomach. I wanted the adventure but doubted my ability. Oddly, I even thought of sharks. *Jaws!* Could I? Should I? I climbed aboard. Glass-masked young people, like movie stars, stretched their rubber suits around them and looked like glamorous Martians ready for an interplanetary invasion. My son was among them and seemed to fit right in. By comparison, I seemed white and soft and unacquainted with the sea.

But the Great Barrier Reef? Should I?

So often these days I am caught trying to figure out what daring things I still have the courage to do. When I was younger, no roller coaster ever intimidated me, no precipitous hike seemed too dangerous. I once dived off a seventy-foot waterfall. I have hiked the Grand Canyon at night, rafted the Mendenhall River in Alaska and the Rio Grande through the Box at Taos, New Mexico. Now I consider those things I still haven't done and yet want to do. I have recently climbed partway up Ayres Rock in the Outback of Australia, hiked some distance along the Great Wall, taken a helicopter ride over Mount Rushmore, parasailed around the Gulf of Mexico, and ridden "The Rattler" at Astro World.

Jesus' point in the parable of the talents is that the kingdom of God is not for those who want to play it safe (Matthew 25:14–30). One servant received five talents, another two, and still another one. The man who received one was not rebuked because he only had one but because he was afraid to invest it and see what he could do with it. The man who is cast into outer darkness for his failure to try to increase his holdings is candid about why he didn't risk himself: "I was afraid" (Matthew 25:25).

Fear.

I couldn't help but wonder if I might not be able to scuba dive into the depths. I even wondered if the lithe divers before me might not be able to locate a size 42 wetsuit so that I could dive with them.

There are three primary fears that kept me away from such a proposition. First the fear of *I've never done that before*. I believe that most Christians at one time or another wonder what life is like at the depths. But they are frightened away simply in knowing they've never done it before. I have a friend who took his family to a national franchise pizza parlor. These pizza parlors are famous for their children's play areas, which include a tube maze. His very small son wanted to go into the maze and play, but it was dark inside the tubes and he was paralyzed by fear. His daddy sensed his fears and did a wonderful thing. While his son watched from a safe distance, his father crawled into the tubes and emerged smiling and happy. His son, in joyful abandon, went and did likewise.

This, of course, is the meaning of the Incarnation. Jesus became a man to show us that what we fear is altogether possible. He didn't live close to God to show us his special status but to say that everyone can do this. Hebrews 12:2, speaking of Jesus, says, "Let us fix our eyes on Jesus, the author and perfecter of our faith." The word "pioneer," *archegos*, is used here. It means "first goer." Jesus lived the deeper life not to intimidate us with something unmanageable but to mentor for us a wholly accessible lifestyle.

The second fear that intimidates us is *I don't want to wind up some kind of kook*. We all know of religious fanatics who have gone off on some kind of tangent. Their lives are lived beyond the circle of "normal" people. These fanatics may appear odd to those on the inside, but they have one great gift that those on the inside do not: perspective. They—because they are on the outside—can see the whole circle at once.

Jesus in this sense was tangential to official Judaism. Not being a member of the Pharisees and Sadducees may have left him without the academic credentials he needed to be certified as a genuine Rabbi, but it gave him the perspective to see the oddities and inconsistencies of those inside. Most often those who have lived the deeper life were outsiders to popular esteem. Wesley, the Carmelites, Luther, and others were forced out of the circle by those inside. But in the light of history they were not kooks but luminaries. Those who never risk themselves to know the deep never know the triumph of a daring spirituality.

The final fear we have is *I am just not material for the deeper life*. To this I can only say that those who have risked themselves in the depths of God never did it to establish themselves as saints. They never saw themselves as heroes. In fact, they turned from every notion that they were in any sense a religious specialist or icon. They were merely people hungry for God.

But once you have known the depths of Christ, being captain of the church volleyball league seems less important. Those who dared to live the deeper life never meant to orient their preferences around the contemplative life, it's just that once you've been to the Barrier Reef, wading pools hold little interest.

Ezekiel saw the God who ever entices us into richer experience with him. God is always out ahead beckoning us into the deep. Ezekiel wrote,

> As the man went eastward with a measuring line in his hand, he measured off a thousand cubits and then led me through water that was ankle-deep. He measured off another thousand cubits and led me through water that was knee-deep. He measured off another thousand and led me through water that was up to the waist. He measured off another thousand, but now it was a river that I could not cross because the water had risen and was deep enough to swim in—a river that no one could cross. (47:3–5)

But Ezekiel's flood does not threaten us. It is the grand enticement that overwhelms us with joy. It fits us for the anthem of our addiction to all things glorious:

> O the deep, deep love of Jesus,
> vast, unmeasured, boundless, free!
> Rolling as a mighty ocean
> in its fullness over me;
> Underneath me, all around me,
> is the current of thy love;
> Leading onward, leading homeward,
> to my glorious rest above.[4]

Study Questions

Introduction—A Hunger for Inwardness

1. Can you isolate three prayer experiences in which your need for God caused you to linger in his presence to the point where you were lost to all your earthly agendas?
2. Being near to God is the way to be overcome by his majesty. Where did the "awe" of God first meet your willingness to wait in his presence till your whole being was made more alive by his entrance into your life?
3. If mystery is the distance between our smallness and his vastness, how do you think we can best come to know God in all of his greatness?
4. How do each of the spiritual disciplines—prayer, Bible reading, ministry—play a part in moving us into the depths of God?

Chapter One—Breaking the Sensual Thrall

1. What does it mean to be "hungry for God"?
2. What did Thérèse of Lisieux mean when she said, "Love alone attracts me . . . my only guide is self-abandonment"?
3. What did John of the Cross mean when he said, "I have finished all other work except the work of love"?
4. Have you ever lived under the coercion of the "doctrine of quitting"? What in your opinion is this doctrine? How can we break free of it?
5. In what way do WWJD bracelets fall short of God's view of complete sanctification in the Christian's life?
6. Can real Christians ever fall under the power of appetite addiction? If so, how can they ultimately break those addictions?
7. Is it fair to ask—before we indulge in any area of appetite—does God have an opinion on this? If he does, how do we go about discerning it?
8. What did Oswald Chambers mean when he said we lose our visions through "spiritual leakage"?

Chapter Two—Breaking the Thrall of Materialism

1. What does it mean to say misery is *miser-y*?
2. Why did Catherine of Siena say that the destitute are often more materialistic than the wealthy?
3. Does he who has the most toys really win? How can we reconcile this bumper-sticker proverb with the real truth?
4. Why do we insist that the word "grieve"—as found in Ephesians 4:30—is a love word?
5. What do the words "glorify God in your body" mean to you?
6. What did the poet Wordsworth mean when he said, "Soon or late, getting and spending, we lay waste our powers"? How does it relate to the subject matter of this chapter?
7. What does it mean to say, "The heart given to Christ is not a toy-shopper"?

Chapter Three—Breaking the Tyranny of the Urgent

1. Which is the safer question and why? "What wilt thou have me to do in life?" or "What wilt thou have me to do today?"
2. What Scripture verse best describes how you view the gift of time?
3. Can you isolate a specific prayer time that put you in a listening mode rather than a talking mode? Describe how you felt about the experience when it was over.
4. Have you come to the place where you have had to deal firmly with the agenda your church places on you in order that you can devote more of your time to prayer and the inner life? If so, how did you handle it?
5. Contrast "hurry, worry, bury" with "cling, linger, savor."
6. Can you remember a time when your life was characterized by sanctified exhaustion? How did you triumph over the pace and return to a settled walk?
7. What is your spiritual ritual for changing "time zones"? How do you deal with the clock in setting time aside for God?
8. Are there specific steps you take for arriving at holy leisure? How can you be sure that you are not running in and out of the throne room and never seeing God?
9. Do you have a specific form for "praying your praises" to God?
10. Are you able to quickly discern the difference between what the church may want you to do and the actual will of God? What are some signals that help you to see the difference?
11. In terms of inwardness, what does it mean to "lay your watch on the high altar of prayer"?

Chapter Four—Aesthetics: Enjoying the Beauty of God

1. Evaluate the opening paragraphs of this chapter. What does the "poor Methodist woman" mean when she gazes at the grandeur of God and feels complete?
2. Evaluate the statement "Art is a form of praise."
3. Differentiate between the goals of secular and Christian artists.
4. When does an ordinary statue become an idol?
5. What does the phrase *imago dei* mean concerning God's artistry in our lives?
6. In what ways do both art and faith focus on "life"?
7. What does Eugene Peterson mean when he says we tell stories "to locate ourselves in the human condition"?
8. How does the Greek myth of Prometheus relate to the artist's struggle to create?
9. How did God the Master Artist feel as he created humankind, knowing they would betray him with self-will? Why do you think theologians call this idea the "burden of God"?

Chapter Five—Christ: The Desire of the Heart

1. What do the Scriptures really mean when they say, "Delight yourself in the Lord, and he will give you the desires of your heart"?
2. Evaluate the following: "There will be no turbulence in the tide of your trusting."
3. When did the demon of "what if" terrorize you into paralysis? How did you exorcise that demon?
4. Make a list of safeguards that will help you remove selfishness from your prayers of intercession.
5. Habakkuk 3:17–18 is a cry to be faithful in the hard times. Describe one such hard time when God proved himself to be faithful to you.
6. What does it mean to say, "To be spiritually mature is to create a sense of abundance, whether or not we are actually experiencing hard times"?
7. What did Tatian mean when he wrote, "Die to the world by renouncing the madness of its stir and bustle"?
8. What is the one sure way that we can have all that we desire in Christ?

Chapter Six—Expression: The Place of Praise

1. Paraphrase the statement: "Jesus is the epicenter of the only reality that has ever mattered."

2. If thanksgiving is the source of praise, what is the fount of our in-gratitude?

3. What did Ernest Becker mean when he said we try to deny our own temporal nature by worshiping our heroes?

4. What did Dag Hammarskjold mean when he said, "The goal of all worthy emulation is Jesus"?

5. What did Hans Kung mean when he said, "Christian worship is essentially reconciliation"?

6. What is the relationship between spiritual ecstasy and transcendence?

7. How have "how-to" sermons injured the preaching of heaven and hell?

8. Why did Eric Hoffer say that technology was humankind banging on the gates of Eden?

Chapter Seven—Centering: Avoiding Sterile Fascination With God

1. In your own words, define "centering."

2. What does it mean to say that the pursuit of holiness breeds its own inner addiction?

3. What does it mean to say that the pursuit of holiness breeds an other-worldly aloofness spirit?

4. What is the "Sweet Little Jesus Syndrome"?

5. What did Paul mean when he said, "I am crucified with Christ"?

6. What did God mean when he said to Catherine of Siena, "You are the one who is not, and I am He who is"?

7. Distinguish between self-denial and self-negation.

8. What did D. H. Lawrence mean when he said, "There is no end to the birth of God"?

9. What did Paul mean when he said, "Pray without ceasing"? How is this possible?

10. How can silent rapport be conversation with God?

11. Explain this statement: "Real prayer is good souls asking for good things." What do both uses of the word "good" mean?

12. What is the *mysterium tremendum*?

13. How do the arts become a path to the center of our souls? In your opinion, would it be possible for people without Christ to make the arts a form of religious faith? How would they do this? How would you be able to point out such a substitution to those who might be guilty of it?

Chapter Eight—Mysticism: Keeping in Touch With the Holy Spirit

1. Explain the statement: True reality is born where mystery and passion meet.
2. Describe the process of becoming like the portrait of Jesus, which hangs alone in the central gallery of our heart.
3. How can evangelical Christians continue to emphasize their different heritages and doctrinal distinctives while they genuinely hunger for unity in the body of Christ?
4. In a culture that is constantly "dumbing down," what are some ways that believers can keep growing intellectually in their pursuit of the Christian faith?
5. What is the balance between spontaneity and planning, both in personal and public worship?
6. How can each of us as responsible followers of Christ help our fellow Christians to distinguish "hype" from authentic visitations of the Spirit?
7. The Spirit of God is your intercessor. For what weak points in your own discipleship is he constantly praying?
8. What are the symptoms of the divine chaos that marks the coming of the Spirit in public worship? How do we keep the unusual nature of such visitations from being rejected in the church?

Chapter Nine—Into the Depths by Finding Our Calling

1. At what point did you first identify God's call in your life? Are you still walking in that original call? Are you feeling any new directions in that call?
2. Finish this statement in twenty-five words or less: "As far as God is concerned, the main reason I am in the world is to _____

   _____

   _____."
3. Jeremiah defined his call as a "fire shut up in his bones." Obedience to such a call carries intensity. How do we strike a balance between this inner intensity and living a life of peace?
4. List three times in your life when you were forced "to play with the little hurts" while you continued your service to Christ.
5. Do you ever wrangle with your need to be loved by your peers and your need to serve God without compromise? Describe a time in your life

when you had to live through this tension.

6. How do you maintain a sense of your calling while you live through such times?

7. Describe the number-one trial you have had to endure. How did your later evaluation of that trial show you God's purpose for your life?

8. Discuss the Jewish proverb: He who saves one life, saves the world in time. Relate your thoughts to the proverb: If you had been the only person who was lost, Jesus would still have died for you.

Chapter Ten—The Discipline That Ends in Godly Character

1. Character is the gift of servanthood. Isolate one experience in which Christ asked you to perform some difficult act of service, and in that act you found some new issue of character.

2. "We are not likely to gain humility without humiliation," said Bernard of Clairvaux. Can you recall some time of shame or embarrassment when Christ taught you not only an aspect of character but humility itself?

3. How can we come to identify occasions of pride while we take steps to minimize its influence in our attempts to become Christlike?

4. List some practical steps by which we can move from inordinate pride to poverty of spirit.

5. Truth is the pier of character. How much latitude do you allow yourself for "inflating" it into near-truth? How can you take practical steps toward minimizing your need for others to praise you?

6. Why are crosses good places to study character?

7. Do you have trouble saying "I'm sorry" even when it's clear you are wrong? What are some steps you can take to set aside your pride and learn to genuinely seek forgiveness?

Chapter Eleven—Arriving at Self-Understanding

1. What are the evidences that materialism is making some inroads into your life? What is it that you want—that you "have to have"—that keeps you tied to materialism?

2. What allurement does Milton's Satan demonstrate when he says, "It is better to rule in hell than to serve in heaven"?

3. Vanity is emptiness. If it were not for Christ, how much would the dour and hopeless mood of Ecclesiastes be justified?

4. Knowing Christ is being free. How do you equate Jesus, truth, and freedom?

5. Describe the point at which you feel you quit relying on your own

strength and begin to depend on Jesus.

6. Are you ever guilty of comparing the "good deals" God gives others in life with the "rotten deals" he seems to dish out to you? Describe one such "pity party" in your life. How did you eventually get out of the dark mood?

Chapter Twelve—Confession and the Glory of Our Neediness

1. Healing follows honesty. Can you isolate an occasion when honesty came hard, but looking back on it, you can see how God used your confession to heal you?
2. Why if God already knows all your sins is it important for you to confess them to him?
3. Is it possible to lie to ourselves within our spirits? How much harm is done when we do this? How can we get these lies we tell ourselves out into the open?
4. What is the general difference between open dishonesty and the lies we tell ourselves? Which is the hardest error to correct and why?
5. The parable of Fouke included in this chapter describes the result of residual bitterness. How do we keep such bitterness from building up in our lives?
6. In Psalm 51, what does David mean when he says, "The sacrifices of God are a broken spirit"? Is there a difference between a broken spirit and broken will? Would God want to break our will?
7. What does it mean to say, "His grace is greater than our sin"?
8. If God loves a broken and contrite heart, in what way is our hurt over our sin pleasing to God?
9. Our neediness evokes God's abundance. Why?

Chapter Thirteen—Confession and Guilt-Free Discipleship

1. What hymn gives you the most confidence in the face of your fears?
2. What kind of fear is expressed in the image of the fowler's snare (Psalm 91:3)? Can you think of a time when you were captive to this fear?
3. Do you agree or not with the following statement: "True Christians never suffer from burnout." Why or why not?
4. Psalm 91 also speaks of the "terror by night." What is an example from your own life of such a terror?
5. Why do we suggest that confession is the birth canal of courage?
6. What does it mean that we should "make friends with our trials"?
7. How does confession help clear out the clutter of self-preoccupation?
8. Explain the statement, "Guilt, carried overlong, becomes a killer of the

human spirit." Can you think of an example of this actually happening to someone?

9. Does "Restore unto me the joy of thy salvation" indicate that truly born-again people can become captive to dour moods? What is the way back to more radiant discipleship after such low times?

10. Why do you think that evangelical Christians are low indicators of self-esteem?

11. Is guilt ever good? If so, when?

12. In terms of God's forgiveness, what does it mean to say, "There are no private affairs"?

Chapter Fourteen—Confessional Principles for Personal Growth

1. What are some of the things that have caused depression in your life?

2. What is to be the relationship between our circumstances and our moods?

3. What are some steps you can take to keep potential enemies from becoming actual enemies?

4. How does the phrase "Jesus is Lord" serve to teach you triumph over your circumstances?

5. There are four ways we can deal with other people. How might you have dealt with someone in one of these ways in the past? The questions that will guide your thinking are, Who have you idolized? Who have you demonized? Who have you utilized? Who have you humanized?

6. What did Francis of Assisi mean when he said he had taken "holy poverty" as his bride?

7. How do you keep from "rehearsing your woes" when you are in a circle where everyone else is doing it?

Chapter Fifteen—Dwelling in Foreverness

1. Does your anticipation of heaven have mostly to do with Jesus? Why or why not?

2. Explain the metaphor "Doubt is that rag-toothed demon who nibbles at the edges of God's promises."

3. Explain the idea that—spiritually, at least—people usually die as they have lived.

4. In what way should the parallax wheel on a camera be a metaphor of our conformity to Christ?

5. What does the statement "Nothing is more certain in life than the predictability of God's promises" mean to you?

6. What does it mean to say, "One way to magnify Christ is to anticipate our ultimate union with him"?
7. "I will dwell in the house of the Lord forever" is David's testament to destiny. Contrast this idea with Jesus' statement in John 14:2, "In my Father's house are many mansions."

Epilogue: Into the Depths

1. Explain how "I can't do this" can become an insult to the call of God.
2. Differentiate and contrast these three fears:
      —I've never done that before.
      —I don't want to wind up some kind of kook.
      —I'm just not material for the deeper life.
3. Explain Ezekiel 47:3–5 and correlate it with your own willingness to pursue God into the depths of inwardness.

Notes

Introduction

1. Quoted in Anne B. Johnson, *Catherine of Siena* (Huntington, Ind.: Our Sunday Visitor Publishing House, 1987), 162.
2. Author unknown, *The Way of a Pilgrim*, trans. Olga Savin (Boston: Shambhala, 1991), 141.
3. Charles Haddon Spurgeon, *Morning and Evening* (Nashville: Thomas Nelson, 1994), from the November 16 reading.
4. F. B. Meyer, quoted in *Changed by the Master's Touch* (Springdale, Pa.: Whitaker House, 1985), 54–55.
5. Emilie Griffin, *Clinging* (New York: McCracken Press, 1984), 7.

Chapter One

1. Raymond C. Ortlund Jr., *A Passion for God* (Wheaton, Ill., Crossway Books, 1994), 148.
2. Gregory the Great, quoted in Woodene Koenig-Bricker, *365 Saints* (San Francisco: Harper San Francisco, 1995), from the September 3 reading.
3. Frances de Sales, *Thy Will Be Done*, trans. Henry Benedict Mackey (Manchester, N.H.: Sophia Institute Press, 1955) 34–35. (Originally published 1894.)
4. Abraham Maslow, a prominent psychologist, was the first to identify these five basic needs.
5. Mary Ann Fatula, *Catherine of Siena's Way* (Collegeville, Minn.: The Liturgical Press, 1987), 186.
6. Thérèse of Lisieux, *The Story of a Soul*, trans. John Beevers (New York: Doubleday, 1957), 109.
7. Ibid.
8. Frederick Buechner, *Telling Secrets* (San Francisco: Harper San Francisco, 1991), 74–75.

9. Fatula, 190.

10. Oswald Chambers, *My Utmost for His Highest* (Uhrichsville, Ohio: Barbour & Co., Inc., 1963), from the December 7 reading.

11. Dietrich Bonhoeffer, *The Cost of Discipleship*, trans.: R. H. Fuller (New York: Touchstone Books, 1959), 20.

12. Chambers, from the January 24 reading.

13. Ibid., March 11.

14. Emilie Griffin, *Clinging*, 15.

Chapter Two

1. Thomas Merton, *The Seven-Story Mountain* (New York: Harcourt, Brace, and Jovanovich, 1948), 404.

2. F. B. Meyer quoted in *Changed by the Master's Touch*, 55.

3. Oswald Chambers, *My Utmost for His Highest*, from the May 31 reading.

4. Thérèse of Lisieux, *The Story of a Soul*, 148.

5. Kathleen Norris, *Amazing Grace* (New York: Riverhead Books, 1998), 32.

6. Annie Dillard, *Tickets for a Prayer Wheel* (New York: Harper & Row, 1974), 125.

7. LEADERSHIP magazine (Summer 1988): 81.

8. Francis de Sales, *Thy Will Be Done*, 8.

9. François Fénelon, *Talking With God*, 86.

10. Thérèse of Lisieux, 72.

Chapter Three

1. Madeleine Sophie Barat, quoted in Woodene Koenig-Bricker, *365 Saints*, from the August 5 reading.

2. François Fénelon, quoted in Richard Foster, ed., *Devotional Classics* (San Francisco: Harper San Francisco, 1989), 46.

3. Hannah Whitall Smith, quoted in Richard Foster, *A Spiritual Formation Journal* (San Francisco: Harper San Francisco, 1989), unnumbered page.

4. Alvin Toffler, *Future Shock* (New York: Bantam Books, 1970), 15.

5. Thomas Merton, *The Spring of Contemplation* (Notre Dame, Indiana: Ave Maria Press, 1992), 20.

6. William R. White, *Stories for Telling: A Treasury for Christian Storytellers* (Minneapolis: Augsburg Publishing House, 1986), 83–86.

7. François Fénelon, *Talking With God*, 10.

8. E. M. Bounds, *The Possibilities of Prayer* (Grand Rapids, Mich.: Baker Books, 1994), 102.

Chapter Four

1. Richard Wilbur, quoted in Richard Foster, *A Spiritual Formation Journal*, unnumbered pages.
2. Dorothy Gurney, quoted in Woodene Koenig-Bricker, *365 Saints*, from the December 28 reading.
3. Cheryl Forbes, *Imagination* (Sisters, Ore.: Multnomah Press, 1986), 151.
4. Dietrich Bonhoeffer, *The Cost of Discipleship*, 20.
5. From Mary Tileston, ed., *Daily Strength for Daily Needs* (Springdale, Pa.: Whitaker House, 1997), 21.
6. Kathleen Norris, *Amazing Grace*, 199.
7. *Holman Bible Dictionary* (Nashville: Holman Bible Publishers, 1991), 870.
8. Thomas Merton, *The Spring of Contemplation*, 6.
9. Forbes, 151.
10. Eugene Peterson, *Working the Angles* (Grand Rapids, Mich.: William B. Eerdmans Publishing Co., 1987), 19.
11. Isak Dinesen, *Out of Africa* (New York: Vintage Books, a division of Random House, 1985), 42–43.
12. "Devotions Upon Emergent Occasions," *The World Treasury of Religious Quotations*, 92.

Chapter Five

1. Hildegard of Bingen, from *Secrets of God*, selected and trans. Sabina Flanagan (Boston: Shambhala, 1996), 12.
2. Ugolino, from W. Heywood, ed., *The Little Flowers of St. Francis of Assisi* (New York: Vintage Books, 1998), 14.
3. Sayings of the Desert Fathers, "Take Care of the Sick," Andrew Harvey, ed., *Teachings of the Christian Mystics* (Boston: Shambhala, 1998), 42.
4. Guigo I, "Meditations," *Near to the Heart of God*, compiled by Bernard Bangley (Wheaton, Ill.: Harold Shaw Publishers, 1998), from the July 8 reading.
5. St. Patrick, quoted in Esther De Waal, *The Celtic Way of Prayer* (New York: Bantam Doubleday Dell Publishing Group, 1997), 21.
6. "Ignatius of Antioch to the Romans," chapter 4, *Early Christian Writings*, trans. Maxwell Standforth (New York: Penguin Books, 1968), 87.

7. Andrew Murray, *The Ministry of Intercession* (Springdale, Pa.: Whitaker House, 1982), 106.
8. "Ignatius to the Ephesians," chapter 4, *Early Christian Writings*, 64.
9. Justin Martyr, "First Apology 15," Eberhard Arnold, ed., *The Early Christians* (Farmington, Pa.: Plough Publishing House, 1997), 106.
10. St. Bonaventure, quoted in Rawley Myers, *The Saints Show Us Christ* (San Francisco: Ignatius Press, 1996), 127.
11. Ibid., 126.
12. Ibid., 319.
13. Ibid., 104.
14. Tatian, "Address to the Greeks," from *The Early Christians*, 296.
15. "Ignatius to the Ephesians," chapter 7, *Early Christian Writings*, 63.

Chapter Six

1. Thomas Merton, *The Spring of Contemplation*, 170.
2. Hildegard of Bingen, quoted in Richard Foster, *A Spiritual Formation Journal*, unnumbered pages.
3. William P. Mackay, "Revive Us Again," *The Baptist Hymnal* (Nashville: Convention Press, 1975 edition), 263.
4. Carmina Gadelica I, quoted in Esther De Waal, *The Celtic Way of Prayer*, 75.
5. Annie Dillard, *Tickets for a Prayer Wheel*, 123.
6. Ignatius of Antioch, quoted in Rawley Myers, *The Saints Show Us Christ*, 88.
7. Dietrich Bonhoeffer, *The Cost of Discipleship*, 266.
8. Malcolm Muggeridge, *Jesus Rediscovered* (New York: Doubleday, 1969), 10.
9. Francis de Sales, *Thy Will Be Done*, 227–28.
10. Oswald Chambers, *My Utmost for His Highest*, from the May 17 reading.
11. O'Laoghaire, "The Celtic Monk at Prayer," quoted in De Waal, 188.
12. Mary Ann Fatula, *Catherine of Siena's Way*, 113.
13. Donald McCullough, *The Trivialization of God* (Colorado Springs: NavPress, 1995), 13.
14. Carmina Gadelica I, quoted in De Waal, 93.
15. Thérèse of Lisieux, *The Story of a Soul*, 153.

Chapter Seven

1. Martin Luther, quoted in Richard Foster, ed., *Devotional Classics*, 132.
2. Bernard of Clairvaux, ibid.

3. Thomas Merton, *The Spring of Contemplation*, 332.
4. Suzanne Noffke, *Catherine of Siena* (Collegeville, Minn.: The Liturgical Press, 1996), 18.
5. Richard F. Lovelace, *Dynamics of Spiritual Living* (Downers Grove, Ill.: InterVarsity Press, 1970), 101.
6. Isaac Watts, "Jesus Shall Reign," *The Baptist Hymnal*, 587.
7. Emilie Griffin, *Clinging*, 3.
8. St. Anthony, quoted in Kathleen Norris, *Amazing Grace*, 58.
9. "I Clement 13a," *Early Christian Writings*, 28.
10. Bernard of Clairvaux, quoted in *The Saints Show Us Christ*, 287.
11. Alphonsus Liguori, ibid., 293.
12. Ibid., 292.
13. Mary Ann Fatula, *Catherine of Siena's Way*, 79.
14. Ibid.
15. Gregory the Great, quoted in Woodene Koenig-Bricker, *365 Saints*, from the September 3 reading.
16. William Law, from Mary Tileston, ed., *Daily Strength for Daily Needs*, 312.
17. Thomas More, *Meditations* (New York: HarperCollins, 1940), 17.
18. Thomas Merton, *The Spring of Contemplation*, 46.
19. Ibid., 18.
20. Ibid., 109.
21. More, 11.
22. Thomas More, *Utopia* (New York: The Penguin Group, 1976), 33.
23. Francis de Sales, *Thy Will Be Done*, 46.
24. Fatula, 37.

Chapter Eight

1. John of the Cross, *Ascent of Mt. Carmel*, 313.
2. Isaac Penington, quoted in Richard Foster, ed., *Devotional Classics*, 236.
3. Calvin Miller, *Guardians of the Singreale*, opening epigram (San Francisco: Harper San Francisco, 1988), 10.
4. Calvin Miller, *The Song* (Downers Grove, Ill.: InterVarsity Press, 1978), 192.
5. T. S. Eliot, *The Four Quartets* (San Diego: Harvest Books, 1968), 143–44.
6. Mary Ann Fatula, *Catherine of Siena's Way*, 13.
7. Annie Dillard, *Teaching a Stone to Talk* (New York: HarperCollins, 1988), 40–41.
8. Fatula, 69.

9. Ibid., 103.

10. St. Columbanus, quoted in Esther De Waal, *The Celtic Way of Prayer*, 8.

Chapter Nine

1. Mary Ann Fatula, *Catherine of Siena's Way*, 61.

2. Dietrich Bonhoeffer, *The Cost of Discipleship*, 272.

3. Francis de Sales, *Thy Will Be Done*, 228.

4. From François Fénelon, *Meditations and Devotions*, quoted in Bernard Bangley, *Near to the Heart of God* (Wheaton, Ill: Harold Shaw Publishers, 1998), from the November 10 reading.

5. From Richard Baxter, *The Saints' Everlasting Rest*, quoted in Bangley, from the February 5 reading.

6. Ugolino, from *The Little Flowers of St. Francis of Assisi*, quoted from the October 22 reading.

7. Walker Percy, *The Message in the Bottle* (New York: Farrar, Straus & Giroux, 1984), 6.

8. Thomas Arnold, quoted in Mary Tileston, ed., *Daily Strength for Daily Needs*, 230.

9. Elizabeth Barrett Browning, ibid., 133.

10. Margaret Ebner, *Revelations*, quoted in Bangley, from the October 31 reading.

11. Paul E. Billheimer, *Don't Waste Your Sorrows* (Ft. Washington, Pa.: Christian Literature Crusade, 1977), 65.

12. William Tyndale, *Preface to Obedience*, quoted in Bangley, from the September 5 reading.

Chapter Ten

1. G. K. Chesterton, *Orthodoxy* (New York: Image Books, 1959), 68.

2. Watchman Nee, *The Normal Christian Life* (Wheaton, Ill.: Tyndale House Publishers, 1957), 143.

3. E. Stanley Jones, *Abundant Living* (Nashville: Abingdon Festival Books, 1978), 108.

4. Calvin Miller, "The Form of a Servant" (August 3, 1986).

5. From Richard Baxter, *The Saints' Everlasting Rest*, quoted in Bangley, *Near to the Heart of God*, from the November 16 reading.

6. Emily Dickinson, Mabel Loomis Todd and T. W. Higginson, eds. *Favorite Poems*, (New York: Avenel Books, 1978), 155.

7. Baxter, quote in Bangley, from the November 16 reading.

8. From William Tyndale, *Exposition on the Sermon on the Mount*, ibid.,

from the November 23 reading.

9. Cardinal Henry Edward Manning, quoted in Mary Tileston, ed., *Daily Strength for Daily Needs*, 298.

10. From François Fénelon, *Meditations and Devotions*, quoted in Bangley, from the October 30 reading.

11. From Evelyn Underhill, *The Spiritual Life*, quoted in Emilie Griffin, *Clinging*, 86.

12. John Masefield, *The Everlasting Mercy*, quoted in Sherwood E. Wirt, *Jesus Man of Joy* (Eugene, Ore.: Harvest House Publishers, 1999), 113.

13. Mahatma Gandhi, quoted by Larry Collins & Dominique Lapierre in *Freedom at Midnight* (New York: Simon & Schuster, 1975), 70.

14. Calvin Miller, "The Character of a Servant" (August 4, 1986).

Chapter Eleven

1. David Seabury, quoted in E. Stanley Jones, *Abundant Living*, 189.

2. Ibid., 95.

3. Watchman Nee, *The Normal Christian Life*, 88.

4. St. Augustine, quoted in Bangley, *Near to the Heart of God*, from the July 19 reading.

5. John Greenleaf Whittier, "The Meeting," quoted in Harry Farra *The Early Years of the Little Monk* (New York: Paulist Press, 1999), 10.

6. Frederick Buechner, *Telling Secrets*, 92–93.

7. From Lorenzo Scupoli, *The Spiritual Combat*, quoted in Bangley, from the May 15 reading.

8. Major W. Ian Thomas, *The Saving Life of Christ* (Grand Rapids, Mich.: Zondervan Publishing House, 1961), 42.

9. Ibid., 41.

10. *Apoth., Mius* 3:159, quoted in Roberta C. Bondi, *To Love As God Loves* (Philadelphia: Fortress Press, 1987), 51.

Chapter Twelve

1. Amma Theodora, from *Daily Readings in Orthodox Spirituality*, Peter Bouteneff, ed. (Springfield, Ill.: Templegate Publishers, 1996), 42.

2. Amma Syncletica, ibid.

3. Anna S. Hawks, "I Need Thee Every Hour," *The Baptist Hymnal*, 450.

4. Philaret of Moscow, quoted in Bouteneff, 51.

5. Kathleen Norris, *Amazing Grace*, 226.

6. St. Bonaventure, quoted in *The Saints Show Us Christ*, 168.

7. Esther De Waal, *The Celtic Way of Prayer*, 121.

8. Annie Dillard, *Tickets for a Prayer Wheel*, 119.

9. St. Nicholas Cabasilas, quoted in Bouteneff, 25.
10. C. S. Lewis, *The Screwtape Letters* (New York: Macmillan, 1961), 42.
11. St. Silouan the Athonite, Bouteneff, 46.
12. St. Andrew of Crete, ibid., 59.
13. Orthodox funeral service, ibid., 77.
14. Cecil G. Osborne, *The Art of Becoming a Whole Person* (Waco, Tex.: Word Books, 1978), 60–61.
15. Joyce Landorf, *His Stubborn Love*, 64–65.

Chapter Thirteen

1. Cyprian, quoted in Tony Lane, *Exploring Christian Thought* (Nashville: Thomas Nelson Publishers, 1984), 24.
2. Watchman Nee, *The Normal Christian Life*, 17.
3. Raymond C. Ortlund Jr., *A Passion for God*, 68.
4. *Book of Common Prayer (1552)*, quoted in Lane, 156–57.
5. Hildegard of Bingen, *Hildegard in a Nutshell*, Robert Van de Weyer, ed. (London: Hodder & Stoughton, 1997), 66.
6. *Apoth., Poemen* 65:176, quoted in Roberta C. Bondi, *To Love As God Loves*, 68.
7. St. Symeon, quoted in Andrew Harvey, ed., *Teachings of the Christian Mystics* (Boston: Shambhala, 1998), 60.
8. Miguel Molinos, quoted in Tileston, ed., *Daily Strength for Daily Needs*, 347.
9. Francis de Sales, ibid., 321
10. Frederick William Faber, ibid., 342.
11. Cardinal John Henry Newman, ibid., 72.
12. Philip Melanchthon, ibid., 76.
13. John Tauler, ibid., 305.
14. Minucius Felix, quoted in *The Early Christians*, Eberhard Arnold, ed., 127.
15. Isaac the Syrian, quoted in Harvey, 63.
16. S. I. Milliken, quoted in Anthony Campolo Jr., *The Power Delusion* (Wheaton, Ill.: Victor Books, n.d.), 34.
17. Charles R. Swindoll, *Starting Over* (Sisters, Ore.: Multnomah Press, 1983), 51.
18. C. S. Lewis, *The Great Divorce* (New York: Macmillan, 1946), 35.
19. Justin, quoted in Arnold, 148.

Chapter Fourteen

1. Raymond C. Ortlund Jr., *A Passion for God*, 129.
2. Watchman Nee, *The Normal Christian Life*, 193.

3. From *Hildegard in a Nutshell*, Robert Van de Weyer, ed., 29.
4. Thomas Traherne, quoted in Harvey, ed., *Teachings of the Christian Mystics*, 135–36.
5. Billy Sunday, quoted in Sherwood E. Wirt, *Jesus Man of Joy*, 60.
6. Roberta C. Bondi, *To Love As God Loves*, 26.
7. François Fénelon, *Talking With God*, 72.
8. Francis of Assisi, quoted in Heywood, ed., *The Little Flowers of St. Francis of Assisi*, 30.
9. Fénelon, 97–98.
10. Polycarp, quoted in Arnold, ed., *The Early Christians*, 70.
11. Simon Wiesenthal, quoted in Lewis B. Smedes, *Forgive and Forget* (San Francisco: Harper & Row, 1984), 126–27.
12. Bondi, 42.
13. *Hildegard in a Nutshell*, 37.

Chapter Fifteen

1. Mother Teresa, quoted in Richard Foster, *A Spiritual Formation Journal*, unnumbered pages.
2. St. Teresa of Avila, quoted in Calvin Miller, *Images of Heaven* (Wheaton, Ill.: Harold Shaw Publishers, 1996), 98.
3. Charles Kingsley, quoted in Tileston, ed., *Daily Strength for Daily Needs*, 183.
4. François Fénelon, *Talking With God*, 140.
5. Thomas Carlyle, quoted in Tileston, 358.
6. James Martineau, ibid., 212.
7. Emily Dickinson, CXXVII (no title), from Mabel Loomis Todd and T. W. Higginson, eds., *Collected Poems of Emily Dickinson*, 250.
8. Thomas More, no title *The Baptist Hymnal*, 67.

Epilogue

1. Bede, *The Voyage of Brendan*, trans. J. F. Webb, *The Age of Bede* (New York: Penguin Books, 1965), 228.
2. Thomas Merton, *The Spring of Contemplation*, 170.
3. Calvin Miller, *An Owner's Manual for the Unfinished Soul* (Wheaton, Ill.: Harold Shaw Publishers, 1997), 125.
4. Samuel Trevor Francis, "The Deep, Deep Love of Jesus," *The Baptist Hymnal* Copyright, Pickering & Inglis, Ltd., Glasgow. Used by permission, 340.